Designing Education Policy for Sub-Saharan African Countries

Designing Education Policy for Sub-Saharan African Countries

A Comparative Analysis of Global Systems, with Focus on Southern Cameroons

Elizabeth Bifuh-Ambe

SPEARS BOOKS
Denver, Colorado

Spears Books
An Imprint of Spears Media Press LLC
7830 W. Alameda Ave, Suite 103-247
Denver, CO 80226
United States of America

First Published in the United States of America in 2024 by Spears Books
www.spearsbooks.org
info@spearsmedia.com
Information on this title: www.spearsbooks.org/designing-education-policy-for-sub-saharan-african-countries
© 2024 Elizabeth Bifuh-Ambe
All rights reserved.

No part of this publication may be reproduced, distributed, or transmitted in any form or by any means, including photocopying, recording, or other electronic or mechanical methods, without the prior written permission of the publisher, except in the case of brief quotations embodied in critical reviews and certain other noncommercial uses permitted by copyright law. For permission requests, write to the publisher, addressed "Attention: Permissions Coordinator," at the above address.

ISBN: 9781957296388 (Paperback)
ISBN: 9781957296401 (eBook)

Spears Media Press has no responsibility for the persistence or accuracy of urls for external or third-party internet websites referred to in this publication, and does not guarantee that any content on such websites is, or will remain, accurate or appropriate.

Designed and typeset by Spears Media Press LLC
Cover designed by Doh Kambem

Distributed globally by African Books Collective (ABC)
www.africanbookscollective.com

For my late dad who valued education so much, he made sure his children had the best, and my mom who continued his legacy in us.

Contents

Foreword	xvii
Preface	xix
Acknowledgments	xxv
Abbreviations	xxix

PART I: EDUCATION IN SUB-SAHARAN AFRICA — xxxiii

CHAPTER 1 — 1
The Case of Cameroon — 1
  Historical Perspectives — 3
  The Unique Case of Cameroon — 5
  Postcolonial Tensions — 11
  Problems with Southern Cameroons Sub-System of Education — 12
  Lack of Goodwill of Administrative Officials — 14

CHAPTER 2 — 17
Defining Education Policy — 17
  Problems with the Design and Implementation of Education Policy — 19
  Approaches to Policy Design and Implementation — 21
  Top-Down or Managerial Approach — 21
  Weaknesses of Top-Down Approach — 22
  Bottom-Up or Phenomenological Approach — 23
  Weaknesses of Bottom-Up — 23
  The Combined Approach — 24
  Conclusion — 25

CHAPTER 3   27
Teacher Selection, Education, Development and Deployment   27
    The Problem of Teacher Shortages   28
    Education Challenges in Sub-Saharan Africa   31
    Problems with Southern Cameroons Teacher Education   33
    Lack of Adequate Teacher Training Colleges   33
    Low Admission Standards into Teacher Training Colleges   36
    Short Duration of Training   36
    Elimination and Lack of Emphasis on Key Subjects on the Curriculum   37
    Teacher Deployment   39
    Issues with Gender Deployment   39
    Overstaffed Administration   39
    Abuse of Parent Teacher Association (PTA)   41

CHAPTER 4   42
Designing Policy for Teacher Education   42
    The Case of the Teaching Profession in Southern Cameroons   42
    Lessons from Singapore   43
    Problems with Teacher Recruitment and Training in Sub-Saharan Africa   45
    Lessons for SSA from Singapore on Teacher Recruitment and Deployment   46
    Policy Guidelines for Southern Cameroons   48
    Adequate Supply and Effective Deployment   50
    Standards and Benchmarks for Performance   51
    Career Management and Monitoring   54
    Financing   55

CHAPTER 5   57
Early Childhood Development and Education   57
    Lessons from the United States of America   58
    Massachusetts Guidelines for Supportive Early Childhood Environments   61
    The State of Early Childhood Education in Sub-Saharan Africa   63

The Case of Southern Cameroons: Problem Diagnoses	64
Policy Guidelines for Early Childhood Education	65

CHAPTER 6 — 67
Basic Education — 67
  The State of Primary Education in Sub-Saharan Africa — 67
  Sociopolitical Context of Southern Cameroons Primary Education — 68
  Problems with Southern Cameroons Basic Education System — 69
  War and Civil Unrests — 74
  Lessons from Finland — 75
  Assessment of Learning — 89
  Designing Basic Education Policy for Sub-Saharan Africa — 94

CHAPTER 7 — 97
Secondary Education — 97
  The State of Secondary Education in Sub-Saharan Africa — 97
  Teacher Shortage — 100
  Inadequate Resources for Expansion — 101
  Inequitable Distribution of Secondary School Opportunities across Different Communities — 102
  The Need for Science, Technology, Engineering and Mathematics (STEM) Subjects — 102
  Lessons from Some International Education Systems — 105
  Policy Implications for Secondary Education in Sub-Saharan Africa — 107
  The Case of Cameroon: French Cameroun versus British Southern Cameroons Systems — 108
  Challenges in both Systems — 110
  Policy Implications for Southern Cameroons — 110

CHAPTER 8 — 114
Conceptualizations of Curriculum for Policy Design — 114
  Definition of Curriculum — 114

The Dynamic Nature of Curriculum   115
Determinants and Interpretations of Curriculum   116
Educational Philosophies that Influence Curriculum Development   118
African Philosophies of Education   123
Prescriptive and Descriptive Perspectives of Curriculum   125
Prescriptive Perspective Definitions of Curriculum, by Date,
Author and Definition   125
Descriptive Perspective Definitions of Curriculum, by Date,
Author and Definition   126

Part II: Blueprint of Southern Cameroons National Education Policy   129

Chapter 9   130
Mission and Vision of the Consultative Body for Policy Development 130
   SCEB Vision   131
   SCEB Mission   131
   SCEB Core Educational Beliefs   131
   SCEB Strategic Goals and Objectives   132
   SCEB Broad Policy Statements and Implementation Strategies   133
   Access to Education   134
   SCEB Objectives   134
   Quality and Relevance in Education   135

Chapter 10   136
Special Education   136
   Policy Framework   139
   Strategies   139
   General Guidelines   141

Chapter 11   142
Health and Nutrition   142
   Importance of Health and Nutrition Education   142

Goals	143
The State of Health and Nutrition Education in Cameroon and Southern Cameroons	145
Guidelines	146
Strategies	148

CHAPTER 12 — 150
Character Education — 150
  Norms and Standards for Teachers, Learners, and Parents — 150
  Why We Need Character Education — 150
  Policy Goals — 151

CHAPTER 13 — 152
Focus on Gender and Culture — 152
  Eliminating Gender Disparities and Ensuring Gender Equality in Educational Opportunities, with Special Focus on the Girl Child — 152

CHAPTER 14 — 156
Education Planning and Management — 156
  Goals — 156
  General Objectives — 158

CHAPTER 15 — 160
School Admission — 160
  Admission Process — 160
  Determining Admission/Enrollment in Schools — 162
  Required Published Admission Number (rPAN) — 163
  Oversubscription Criteria — 163
  Siblings at the School — 166
  Distance from School — 166
  Catchment Areas — 166
  Feeder Schools — 167
  Social and Medical Needs — 167

Selection by Ability or Aptitude	167
Attendance Policy	167
Education levels	167
Language Policy in Public Schools	169
Grammar Schools	169
Pre-existing or Partially Selective Schools	169
Selection by Aptitude	170
Banding	170
Where the School is Oversubscribed	171
Test for Selection	171
Random Allocation	172
Faith-Based Oversubscription Criteria in Schools with Religious Character	172
Children of Staff at the School	173
Children Eligible for Pupil Premium or Service Premium	173
Maintained Boarding Schools	174
Consultation	174
Determination	175
Composite Prospectuses	176
Applications and Offers	177
Allocating Places	178
Withdrawing an offer or a Place	179
Waiting List	180
Infant Class Size	180
Admission of Children Below Compulsory School Age and Deferred Entry to School	181
Admission of Children out of their Normal Age Group	182
Children of Southern Cameroons' Service Personnel	183
Children from Overseas	183
Coordination	183
Offering a Place	185
Right to Appeal	185
School Closure	185
Suspension and Expulsion from Public Schools	186

Fairness in Resolving Issues	186
Children with Challenging Behavior and Those Who Have Been Excluded Twice	188

CHAPTER 16 — 190
Norms and Standards for Educators — 190
- Scope and Purpose — 191
- Competencies Required for Teachers — 191
- Teaching Methodology — 191

CHAPTER 17 — 193
Norms and Standards for Learners — 193
- Definition of a School — 194
- Definition of a Public School — 194
- Definition of a Private or Parochial School — 195
- Expected Behavior and Attitude — 196

CHAPTER 18 — 201
Assessment and Other Procedures — 201
- Examination — 202
- Plagiarism — 202
- Textbooks and Stationaries — 202
- Coursework and Certificates — 202
- Electronic Devices — 203
- Money and Valuables — 203
- Lost Property — 203
- Identification Cards — 203
- The Local Community — 203
- Leaving School — 204

CHAPTER 19 — 205
Disciplinary Structure and other Expectations — 205
- Stages of Disciplinary Measures — 206

Student, Parent/Caregiver, and Institution Contract ... 207

Chapter 20 — 211
Instructional Time ... 211
- Guidelines to Setting School Hours ... 211
- Provisions for Changing School Session Times ... 212
- Minimum Weekly Teaching Times ... 214
- Implications for Teachers ... 215

Chapter 21 — 216
Education Financing, Resource Mobilization, School Infrastructure and Investment ... 216
- School Infrastructure and Investment ... 217
- Components of the Education Infrastructure ... 218
- Funding Models ... 221

Chapter 22 — 222
Monitoring and Evaluation ... 222
- Policy Strategy ... 222

Appendix ... 225
Glossary ... 230
References ... 237
Index ... 251

List of Figures

Figure 1.1. Map of Sub-Saharan Africa.	3
Figure 1.2. Map of the Ten Administrative Districts, Cameroon.	7
Figure 1.3. Map of British Kamerun, 1916. Map of the Southern part of the trust Territory of British Cameroons.	10
Figure 1.4. Map of Present Southern Cameroons.	11
Figure 1.5. Map of Cameroon, 1972- 1983.	13
Figure 6.1. Back view of Kirstin Koulo Elementary School, Espoo, Finland.	76
Figure 6.2. First grade classroom wall with math skills.	76
Figure 6.3. Author inside the English high school in Finland, 2018.	77
Figure 6.4. First grade teacher, reading an excerpt from this open page.	78
Figure 6.5. Students draw various pictures as response to oral reading of text.	79
Figure 6.6. Students draw various pictures as response to oral reading of text.	79
Figure 6.7. Students draw various pictures as response to oral reading of text.	80
Figure 6.8. Students draw various pictures and write as response to oral reading of text.	80
Figure 6.9. Student drawing of the author.	81
Figure 6.10. First grade students at work in response to oral reading of text. Source: author.	81
Figure 6.11. Finnish Education Model.	82
Figure 6.12. Finnish Distribution of Lessons in Finnish Basic Education.	84
Figure 6.13. Fifth grade students participating in the telephone game.	86
Figure 6.14. English Language Arts seventh-grade quiz on *The Catcher in the Rye*.	90

Figure 6.15. Partial student response of seventh-grade quiz
  on *The Catcher in the Rye*. 91
Figure 6.16. Student's notebook on Catcher in the Rye. 92
Figure 6.17. Observing a ninth-grade class World History lesson. 93
Figure 6.18. Picture on wall of ninth-grade, World History classroom. 93
Figure 6.19. World History classroom at the English School,
  Helsinki, Finland. 94

List of Tables

Table 3.1. Student/Teacher Ratio in Government Schools in
  the Northwest Region. 35
Table 7.1. 2014 Statistics of Government Secondary Schools
  in the Northwest Region of Southern Cameroons. 111
Table 11.1. Characteristics of an Effective Health
  Education Curriculum for Sub-Saharan Africa 145
Table 15.1. Suggested Structure of Southern Cameroons Education 168

Foreword

Felicia Sullivan

In *Designing Education Policy for Sub-Saharan African Countries: A Comparative Analysis of Global Systems, with Focus on Southern Cameroons*, Dr. Elizabeth Bifuh-Ambe embarks on a profound journey into the heart of educational challenges and opportunities in Sub-Saharan Africa, with a unique lens on Southern Cameroons. This work stands out not just for its depth of research and analysis but also for the courage to confront a topic that is as complex as it is critical. By weaving a narrative that stretches from the historical underpinnings of education in Africa to the contemporary struggles and triumphs, this work does more than inform—it inspires action.

What sets this work apart is the meticulous approach to understanding education as a multifaceted system, deeply intertwined with colonial histories, cultural identities, and modern-day challenges of globalization. Dr. Bifuh-Ambe's journey, from a passionate educator in Cameroon to an astute academic, enriches this work and offers an intimate and insightful perspective. The work draws from an expansive survey of global educational systems and the lessons they offer. Through a comparative analysis that spans continents, a central theme throughout this book is an unflinching examination of the remnants of colonial educational policies, and the manner in which they have perpetuated systems of exclusion and of inequality. By illuminating these challenges, Dr. Bifuh-Ambe not only critiques the status quo but also sets the stage for a future where education in

Sub-Saharan Africa is characterized by inclusivity, quality, and the capacity to empower individuals and communities alike. The book underscores the transformative power of education as a conduit for societal change, economic development, and cultural preservation.

Moreover, this important exploration does not merely diagnose problems but also offers a path forward through detailed policy recommendations that are both visionary and practical. From early childhood education to secondary and vocational training, the author proposes a comprehensive overhaul of the educational system by emphasizing creativity, critical thinking, and adaptability. These recommendations are not abstract ideals, but rather actionable strategies informed by an astute understanding of the sociopolitical, economic, and cultural fabric of Sub-Saharan Africa.

As we look toward a future where education is the cornerstone of development and societal well-being, *Designing Education Policy for Sub-Saharan African Countries* serves as both a roadmap and as a beacon of hope. It challenges us to envision an educational system that not only meets the logistical demands of the twenty-first century but also honors the rich cultural heritage and potential of its learners. This book is a testament to the power of education as a force for good, offering a new paradigm for policymakers and educators alike to create more equitable, effective, and inspired educational landscapes.

Preface

> The pen is mightier than the sword.
> —Edward Bulwer-Lytton, 1839

This expression which indicates that the written word is more effective than violence in effecting social or political change, captures my rationale for writing this book: *Designing Education Policy for Sub-Saharan African Countries: A Comparative Analysis of Global Systems, with focus on Southern Cameroons*.

Education is a universal construct, yet, its conceptualization differs from context to context, and among policy makers, educators, politicians, philosophers, and nations. Notwithstanding, the general purpose of education is to transmit knowledge, skills, values, and belief systems from one generation to the other. While education, in and of itself, may not directly account for economic growth, there is a consensus that education is a vital factor necessary to stimulate human and societal development. Unfortunately, in postcolonial settings such as Sub-Saharan Africa, education was misused to become part of the problem of human development. European colonial powers considered education to be an effective tool for the domination of African colonies and a privilege for the "uncivilized" Africans that received it. Western education was often used as a divisive wedge separating those that received the white man's education, and those that had not.

Although many African societies, such as Southern Cameroons, had a rich history of education, culture, and identity that indigenous peoples practiced and taught younger generations, the advent of colonialism witnessed the destruction of indigenous educational practices, and in its place, the British and German missionaries and governments opened up networks of schools that were designed based on structures in the metropole, but limited to basic curricula content, that was much inferior to those of the metropolitan state in the scope of knowledge and resources. Postcolonialist education theorists maintain that education served as an important vehicle through which Western cultural hegemony were promoted, protected, and maintained in Sub-Saharan Africa. While independence may have granted more groups access to education and deepened human resource capital, education policies still remained heavily steeped in Western traditions and were dismissive of indigenous cultural, linguistic, ideological, and philosophical ethos. Postcolonial education did not provide citizens with the agency to contend with global forces such as the spread of information and communication technologies; the inescapable spread of capitalism from western European countries; the economic expansion of Eastern countries like China, Japan, and India; and the migration of Africans into the metropole. This has accounted for the broader political, cultural, economic, and social unrests that can often flare up in parts of Sub-Saharan Africa. For example, in 2018, a violent conflict broke out between La Republique du Cameroun and Southern Cameroons.

The ongoing conflict has been several decades in the making, following a fraught reunification between La Republique du Cameroun and Southern Cameroons in 1961 when the former British Southern Cameroons gained independence by joining the French-speaking Cameroun. The reunification project has been characterized with tensions as a result of the clash of colonial cultures inherited from the British and the French, as well as a sense among the English-speaking minority not only that they were being marginalized by the French majority, but also that an assimilationist agenda was being forced upon them, when the United Nations (UN) failed to implement UN General Assembly Resolution 1608 (xv) of April 21, 1961. The implementation of UN Resolution 1608 would have preserved Southern Cameroons' territorial integrity through the establishment of a Union treaty that would have been in line with the

UN General Assembly resolution 1541(xv) of December 15, 1960. The failure to complete the reunification process left Southern Cameroons at the mercy of France, that decided to annex Southern Cameroons for the exploitation of its natural resources.

French colonial sociopolitical and educational policies toward its colonies, including Cameroun, had been mainly assimilationist and associative. The rationale behind such a policy was to establish the French culture as a tool for the "civilization" of the Africans, and the exertion of economic exploitation, and political domination. From the time of reunification, Southern Cameroonians felt shut out of the educational, legislative, economic, and cultural representation of the country. After five decades of trying to get greater autonomy from La Republique du Cameroun in its educational and socio-political affairs, lawyers and teachers organized peaceful protests. Unfortunately, these protests were met with excessive force and brutality by the French-speaking military of the dictatorial regime in power. Many were killed and many more wounded. Outraged by La Republique du Cameroun government's continual use of force against peaceful protesters, many individuals, both at home and in the diaspora, called for the total separation of Southern Cameroons from La Republique du Cameroun. I was one of those people whose innate quest for social justice for the people of former Southern Cameroons convinced me that I could not sit on the sidelines, while my people were being arrested, maimed, imprisoned, and killed. A concerned group of Southern Cameroonians in the diaspora came together to provide support to the Freedom Fighters in the Motherland. A Southern Cameroons Education Board (SCEB) was formed in 2017, and I was appointed Chair of the Board. At the time, none of us expected that the conflict would still be on-going in its seventh year. Despite the eventual dissolution of the SCEB, my dream of offering something tangible to Southern Cameroonians through my literary abilities and educational background never waned. This book is a culmination of that effort.

As an academic with almost four decades of service, and with experiences that span different countries and continents, I undertook this extensive research project to understand the far-reaching ramifications of effective education policies, or the lack thereof in a people's socioeconomic life. In 2019, I submitted a book proposal to write an education policy that befits a twenty-first-century nation. The publishers requested that I do a comparative analysis with systems that work. Not knowing that this would be quite a formidable task, I accepted their request, and got to work. It has been five years since I started working on this manuscript, that also examines best educational practices in a variety of contexts. In the meantime, I have published two scholarly articles on the subject in two top tier journals: "Educational policy for postcolonial Africa" (Bifuh-Ambe, 2020b); and with a group of other Southern Cameroonian academics "Harnessing the transformational potential of education to meet national and global developmental needs: Re-Thinking theory and practice in education policy of Southern Cameroons" (Bifuh-Ambe, 2020a).

Whether or not a new African nation is born from the ongoing conflict is immaterial. What is important is that education is and will always be important for all societies. For emerging global economies, the need for education that meets twenty-first-century challenges is urgent. This book examines the problems inherent in the current educational systems imposed upon some Sub-Saharan African countries by colonial systems, using the former British Southern Cameroons as a case study. The volume examines effective education policy models and analyzes how inadequate the educational systems in Sub-Saharan Africa are in preparing the citizens for self-governance; a situation that often leads to wars and other civil unrests. The volume discusses barriers experienced by students and teachers at all levels of education involving matters like disabilities, disease, teacher shortages, financial hardships, and cultural practices that exclude some demographics of children from education. The author makes proposals on how these issues can be ameliorated for better academic outcomes, through state funded initiatives and effective curricular programs. The guidelines for designing effective education policy will harness the strength of the citizenry of countries in Sub-Saharan Africa, create links between school and the workforce, bridge the skills and socioeconomic gaps that continue to exist between developing and developed nations, and ensure a more peaceful and just world.

Education policy is a topic of interest globally. This volume would be valuable in a wide variety of institutions and academic disciplines. The book will be a good resource for countries in Sub-Saharan Africa in general, Cameroon and Southern Cameroons in particular. Researchers, university lecturers, professors, and students affiliated with departments of psychology, economics, sociology, sociology of education and human development, schools of education or public policy, as well as international and comparative studies departments, African and postcolonial African studies departments in the social sciences and the fields of Sociology and Sociology of Education, and other interdisciplinary undergraduate and graduate programs that study policy, curriculum theory, or related fields would find the material in this volume useful. Any scholar interested in the impact of colonialism and imperialism in Sub-Saharan Africa will find this volume valuable. Others likely to find this volume interesting include critics, journalists, and historians examining the historical foundations of education in postcolonial Africa. This resource will also be useful to many stakeholders in education, especially those who recognize that the world is a fast-growing global village, and no continent should be left lagging behind in educational attainment. The recommendations for education policy design would be suitable for other 21st-century emerging nations seeking a spot in the global political and economic landscape.

The book is organized in two main Parts: Part I, comprising of eight chapters, is a comparative analysis of various global education systems, examining what makes them effective and contrasting them with ineffective systems, such as that which exists in La Republique du Cameroun and Southern Cameroons. Part II offers a blueprint for education policy for Southern Cameroons. It is broken up into fourteen chapters that correspond with various aspects of education policy design and implementation.

Acknowledgments

> Writing is easy. You just sit in front of your type-writer, open your veins, and bleed.
> —Red Smith (1905–1982), Syndicated Sportswriter.

Red Smith's (1949) tongue in cheek quote aptly captures the sentiments I felt while writing this book. Writing is hard. Writing takes time. Anybody who has ever written anything for publication would attest to that. However, scholarly writing is a different kind of writing due to the complexity of the research involved, the specialized writing process, and the variety of skills and applications that a scholar is expected to master in order to produce work that meets empirical research standards. It has been five years since I first decided that I would contribute to the scholarly literature on education policy in Southern Cameroons. When the publishers asked me to expand the scope of work to the Sub-Saharan region of Africa and do a comparative analysis with global systems that work, I said "Yes," without realizing the amount of research and inordinate amount of time that such a lofty project would take. Resources on education policy for Sub-Saharan Africa are scarce and most of the research work on the topic has been commissioned by the United Nations or other international organs that do not always disseminate results of studies to the public in a timely manner. Visiting sites to get firsthand information for the comparative aspect of the work was expensive, and finding gatekeepers who would help me gain access to schools in foreign countries was not easy.

There were days that I felt that I had bled out, and there was nothing else to give to this project, but my husband, Dr. Augustine Ambe

Tanifum kept encouraging me with words such as: "Why would you give up now, when you have already done so much?" I would sit down again at my desk and start thumping away at my keyboard. During the times when I was completely exhausted, he would start searching the Internet for scarce resources on Sub-Saharan African education policy. Although most of what he would find would be discarded because it did not meet the threshold of empirical research appropriate for this manuscript, his dedication to the completion of the work encouraged me to go on. He came along with me on my field trips, and although he has never worked in a classroom, he tried to make himself comfortable in classroom contexts in Finland and other places; carrying laptops, taking pictures when I was interacting with teachers and students, and facilitating my research as best he could. Augustine has arguably put in as many hours as I have in the writing of this manuscript, doing "secretarial" tasks that I would not have been able to do without external assistance. There are few people I have met in this life who give of their time and efforts so selflessly. I thank the universe for providing me with such a good man as a life partner. "Thank you," Austin. I know no other phrase that can express my gratitude.

I am grateful to Dr. Felicia Sullivan who read parts of this manuscript and drew upon her expertise in public policy and work in Africa to share ideas and theories that improved the content of this book. Finding somebody to read or revise any piece of writing is difficult, mainly because academics are always swamped with a plethora of tasks. Because scholarship is arguably the aspect of the job that takes up most of the time, especially in a research-intensive university like the University of Massachusetts Lowell, we hardly dedicate that time to somebody else's work. When I asked Felicia to revise the manuscript and she said "Yes," I heaved a huge sigh of relief. Although not in academia, her rich and diverse background has added more to the overall quality of the book. It is fitting that she is also the writer of the foreword.

I would like to thank the members of the defunct Southern Cameroons Education Board (SCEB). When a team was put together and I was appointed Chair of the board, most of us worked with the hope that by now, we would be implementing ideas that we were brainstorming about education in an environment that was much different in terms of equality, justice, and autonomy. None of us could have foreseen that for the next seven years, we would still be in what is now popularly known as the "Anglophone crisis." We came from diverse backgrounds, but we had a common motivation: generate educational policies tailored to meet the needs of students in a 21st-century emergent nation—policies that engender innovations and inventions that match and surpass those of the Western nations in which we lived and worked. While I thank the entire board for their various contributions to policy drafts, I would especially like to mention those whose dedication was unmatched, such as Dr. David Njibamum and others who went beyond just contributing ideas to the general policy, to drafting syllabi for various subject areas …syllabi that are still sitting in the proverbial "drawers, gathering dust."

The extensive research conducted in the production of this work, would not have been possible without two research grants from the University of Massachusetts Lowell, one that enabled me visit some schools internationally to collect data from primary sources, and present at conferences where I interacted with scholars in the field of policy.

I would like to thank everybody whose support and encouragement has kept me on this journey in the academic landscape of the United States. This is not an easy profession. It is even harder for a Black woman from Africa, with a distinct sense of self, entering a field with neither role models to show her the ropes nor any powerful White allies to teach her the rules of the game. I have therefore had to work doubly hard in order to be excellent, charting my own path, and facing challenges head-on. Every challenge that I have encountered on this journey has been a worthy learning experience from which I have come out better and stronger.

Finally, while this is an academic and scholarly venture, it was borne out of a political crisis. Unfortunately, politics is inescapable in the world in which we live; for as long as we are humans and social animals, there would be matters to dispute, rights to reclaim, and conflicts to resolve. I would like to thank the heroes of the former British protectorate called Southern Cameroons, who have continued to fight for justice and freedom from an oppressive regime. These heroes date back six decades, to present-day heroes and heroines, too many to be named individually. Many fought through diplomacy and other peaceful means for justice, autonomy, and basic human dignity. In any dictatorship, standing up for justice is a high risk. Some paid the supreme price with their lives, while others died of natural causes without seeing the principles for which they fought, come to fruition. While no one can predict the outcome of the current conflict, academics, historians, and other concerned individuals have a responsibility to record the various ramifications of the failed reunification project between La Republique du Cameroun and Southern Cameroons. This scholarly volume that examines education policy is just one factor in a bigger problem. It is important to document this and other factors for future and present generations, lest we forget. Thanks in advance to all who will pick up this book and read; but above all, many thanks to those who will open their hearts and allow the words from these pages to light a fire … a fire that will inspire them to be a part of the struggle for the second liberation of Africa… liberation from dictatorships, neo-colonialism, imperialism, and their resulting outcomes of ineffective socio-political, educational, and other systems that continue to keep the people in parts of Sub-Saharan Africa and especially Southern Cameroons in bondage.

Abbreviations

AAI	Africa-America Institute
AAC I	All Anglophone Conference
ACC II	All Anglophone Conference
ACHPR	African Commission on Human and People's Rights
ADHD	Attention-Deficit/Hyperactivity Disorder
ASAL	Arid and Semi-Arid Lands
AU	African Union
BOT	Build, Operate, and Transfer (model)
BPI	Buea Peace Initiative
CAF	Common Application Form
CDC	Center for Disease Control and Prevention (United States)
CEF	Cameroon Education Forum
CESA	Continental Education Strategy for Africa
CPD	Continuing Professional Development
CRPD	Convention on the Rights of Persons with Disabilities (United Nations)
DESE	Department of Elementary and Secondary Education (Massachusetts)
DHS	Department of Health Services (United States)
DSHS	Department of Social and Health Service (Washington State, US)
EARC	Education Assessment Resource Centers
ECCD	Early Childhood Care and Development
ECDE	Early Child Development Education
ECE	Early Childhood Education
ECED	Early Childhood Education and Development
EEC	Early Education and Care (Massachusetts, Department of)
EFA	Education for All (Dakar)

EHC	Education, Health, and Care
EMIS	Education Management Information Systems
FAPE	Free Appropriate Public Education
FDSE	Free Day Secondary Education
FPE	Free Primary Education
FSLC	First School Leaving Certificate examination
GBSS	Government Bilingual Secondary School
GCE	General Certificate of Education
GCE "A"	General Certificate of Education, Advanced Level
GCEE	Government Common Entrance Examination
GCE "O"	General Certificate of Education Ordinary Levels (or GCE O/L)
GDP	Gross Domestic Product
GER	Gross Enrollment Rates
GHS	Government High School
GNI	Gross National Income
GR	Gender Ratio
GTTC	Government Teachers' Training Colleges
HHS	Department of Health and Human Services (United States)
HI	Himalayan Institute
HIETTC	Higher Elementary Teacher Training Colleges
HIPC	Highly Indebted Poor Country
HIV/AIDS	Human Immunodeficiency Virus/Acquired Immunodeficiency Syndrome
HRM	Human Resource Management
HTTC	Higher Teachers' Training College
ICT	Information and Communication Technology
IICBA	International Institute for Capacity Building in Africa (UNESCO)
IKS	Indigenous Knowledge Systems
IPAR	Institutes de Pedagogiques Applique a Vocation Rurale
ISCED	International Standard Classification for Education (UNESCO)

IT	Information Technology
LEA	Local Education Authority
MDG	Millennium Development Goals (United Nations)
M&E	Monitoring and Evaluation
MMWR	Morbidity and Mortality Weekly Report
MoE	Ministry of Education
MoES	Ministry of Education Sports
NAEYC	National Association for the Education of Young Children
NEA	National Education Association
NIE	National Institute of Education (Singapore)
OECD	Organization of Economic Cooperation and Development
O/L	Ordinary Levels (General Certificate of Examinations)
PD	Professional Development
PhenoBL	Phenomenon-Based Learning Curriculum (Finland)
PISA	Programme for International Student Assessment
PPP	Public Private Partnerships
PRSP	Poverty Reduction Strategic Plan
PSLE	Primary School Leaving Exam
PTA	Parent Teacher Association
PTR	Pupil-Teacher Ratio
REQV	Relative Education Qualification Values
rPAN	Required Published Admission Number
SBMC	School-Based Management Committee
SCAC	Southern Cameroons Advisory Council
SCAPO	Southern Cameroons Peoples Organization
SCEB	Southern Cameroons Education Board
SCMIS	Southern Cameroons Education Management Information Systems
SCNC	Southern Cameroons National Council
SCPC	Southern Cameroons Peoples Council
SDG	Sustainable Development Goals
SEIA	Secondary Education in Africa (Department of the World Bank)
SEN	Special Education Need

SMC	School Management Committees
SNE	Special Needs Education
SPED	Special Education
SSA	Sub-Saharan Africa(n) Countries
STEAM	Science, Technology, Engineering, Arts, and Math
STEM	Science, Technology, Engineering, and Mathematics
TIMSS	Trends in International Mathematics and Science Study
TSC	Teacher Service Commission
TTC	Teacher Training Colleges
TVET	Technical, Vocational Education and Training
UIS	UNESCO Institute for Statistics
UN	United Nations
UNDP	United Nations Development Programme
UNESCO	United Nations Educational, Scientific, and Cultural Organization
UNICEF	United Nations International Children's Emergency Fund
UNPO	Unrepresented Nations and Peoples Organization
UPE	Universal Primary Education
USE	Universal Secondary Education
WASH	Water, Adequate Sanitation, and Proper Hygiene
WHO	World Health Organization

Part I

Education in Sub-Saharan Africa

"Of all regions, Sub-Saharan Africa has the highest rates of education exclusion. Over one-fifth of children between the ages of about 6 and 11 are out of school.... Without urgent action, the situation will likely get worse as the region faces a rising demand for education due to a still-growing school-age population" (UNESCO, Institute for Statistics (UIS), 2024). Although lack of access to education is widespread in Sub-Saharan Africa (SSA), the case of Cameroon is unique due to its cultural, colonial, geo-political, and linguistic heritage. Cameroon inherited two separate systems of education from two colonial powers: Britain and France. English and French were adopted as the official languages for the over 200 ethnic groups. Uniting two different cultures and academic systems was deemed a symbol of national integration, but fraught with tensions that left the English-speaking minority feeling marginalized. The problems originated from a contested decolonization process, from the late 1950s and early 1960s, and range from political, economic, judiciary, and linguistic. Part I of this book examines the problems inherent within the current educational system imposed upon the English-speaking part of the country (former Southern Cameroons) and shows how unsuitable and inadequate it is to meet the needs of self-governance. Problems with the Southern Cameroons educational sector include the lack of effective education policy, lack of educational resources, and poor personnel and resource management. Part of the solution lies in designing a 21st-century educational policy that meets the personal, academic, and social needs of Southern Cameroonians in a global world economy. A comparative analysis of some of the best education systems of countries such as the United States, Finland, Australia, South Africa, Germany, and Ghana, informs the recommendations of policies that would be more suitable for Southern Cameroons. In Part I, aspects pertaining to attendance policy, age, class size, and teacher-student ratio from Finland are analyzed and compared. Class size and class organization are major issues that directly correlate with higher education quality and outcomes (Glass et al., 1982). Singapore serves as a model for teacher preparation, certification, and development; and Ghana, a democratically emergent African nation that appears to be positioning itself as a viable player on the world stage, provides a model for educational, financial management and accountability systems that are cost effective and sustainable, based on the natural and financial resources available in Africa. Other factors such as school choice, graduation requirements, teacher pay, and best practices in teaching and curricular content are examined and integrated within the analysis. Special emphasis is placed on pre-school, kindergarten, and early childhood systems, which are presently completely neglected in Southern Cameroons, or left largely unregulated by the government. Yet research indicates that the formative years from ages 3–7 years can be the most important years in a child's life, since the foundations of most learning are laid at these early ages.

Chapter 1

The Case of Cameroon

Education is a fundamental human right. Most countries around the world including Sub-Saharan African (SSA) countries have invested heavily in education in an effort to build human capital and effectively compete for jobs and investments on the world stage. Human capital theory posits that investments in education increase the skills and abilities of the workforce, leading to greater productivity and economic growth. Based on the human capital theory, the role of education in enhancing an individual's economic value and productivity cannot therefore be over-emphasized (Becker, 1964).

Despite impressive economic advancements and various educational initiatives, SSA still lags behind other regions in educational success and there appears to be a steady decline in both the quality of education and of access to education. More than 93 million youths of primary and secondary school ages are out of school, and at least 15 million of these children will never set foot in a classroom (United Nations Educational, Scientific, and Cultural Organization (UNESCO), 2016). These statistics occur within an environment faced with overwhelming challenges including: (a) a burgeoning population, (b) mounting fiscal austerity, (c) widespread corruption, (d) violent cultural and ethnic conflicts, (e) unstable political and administrative institutions, and (f) abject poverty and disease such as HIV/AIDS. This perfect storm of factors can be mitigated through education. Education itself is a system within a larger social system, and the interconnections and interdependencies among various components of the education and social systems (schools, teachers, students, policies, societal expectations, and other factors) can pose formidable challenges, because changes in one part of the system will inevitably affect other parts (Banathy, 1992). Policymakers in SSA have the difficult task of identifying, designing, and implementing effective education policies amidst conflicting social and economic conditions that can potentially erode prospects for success. The nature of interacting systems highlights the need for holistic policy approaches that mobilize all sectors of society.

Sub-Saharan Africa is a vast geographical location. The *New World Encyclopedia* (2024) defines this region as the area of the African continent which lies fully or partially south of the Sahara Desert; with the term sub-Saharan corresponding to the standard representation of north above and south below as depicted in Figure 1.1. Sub-Saharan Africa is diverse in many ways: ecologically (extremely harsh arid climates, tropical rain forests, sub-tropical grasslands, and Mediterranean biomes); linguistically, and culturally.

Among the 750 million people in SSA, there are different cultural and ethnic groups, each with its own history, language, and religion. This variability is evident in educational attainments and the political and socioeconomic factors that affect educational outputs in different countries. Therefore, policy discussions cannot be uniformly applicable across all SSA nations. Yet, because of the similarities in colonial experience, a transnational approach is vital in providing a framework for designing policies that could be tailored to each country's specific needs and investment priorities. Critical Policy Analysis might be an effective approach to uncover specific differences and similarities. Critical policy analysis involves a critical examination of the education policies of each country, to uncover the power dynamics, interests, and ideologies that shape them. It aims to highlight the ways in which policies may reproduce social inequalities which are quite prevalent in many countries across SSA (Diem et al., 2014). This approach, however, is beyond the scope of this volume.

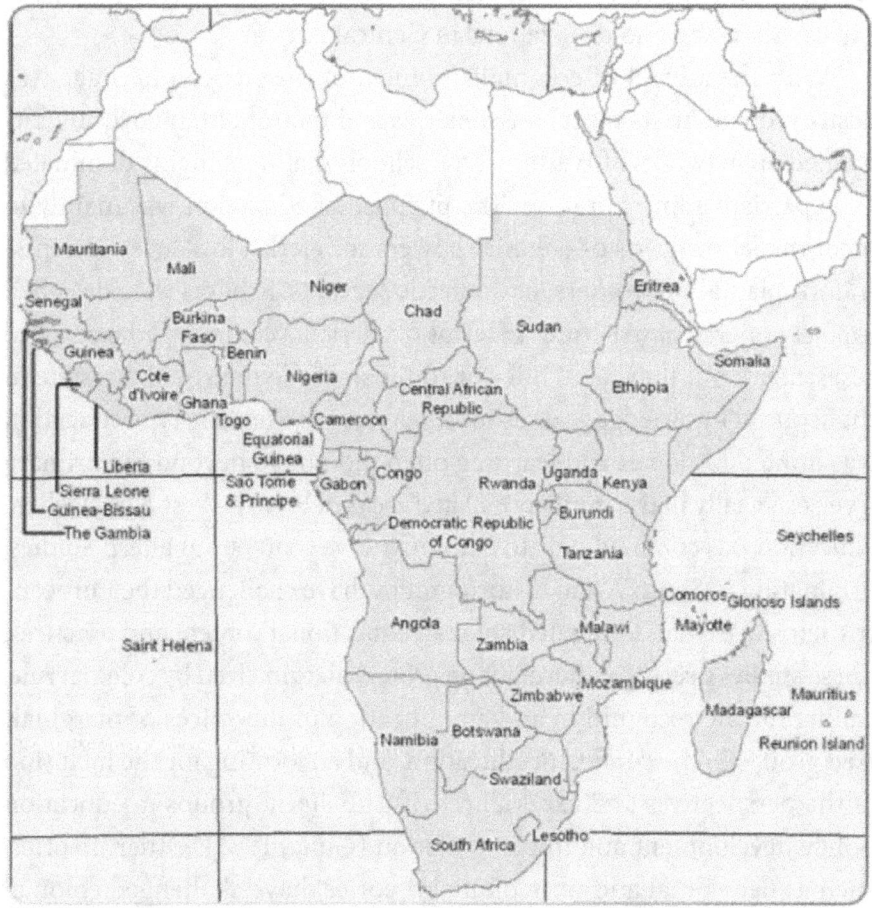

Figure 1.1. Map of Sub-Saharan Africa. Source: Worldmap.org

Historical Perspectives

Contrary to a narrative perpetuated by colonialists that Africa was primitive and inferior, civilization existed in Africa thousands of years before the advent of the Whiteman. African societies had a long and rich history of education: skills, values, traditional norms, culture, and identity that indigenous peoples practiced and passed on from one generation to the next by means of instruction and practical activities. Pre-colonial influence of Christianity and Islam permeated communal life in many regions, including Egypt in the North, Ashanti and Mali in the West, and Tikari, Mani and Sao civilizations in Central Africa.

With the advent of colonialism, most of the African heritage was destroyed and, in its place, missionaries and metropolitan governments opened up networks of Western-type schools that were highly dominated by expatriate administration. The purpose of education was mainly to meet the labor needs of colonial powers for clerks, low-level administrators, plantation workers, or domestic servants. Schools were designed against imperialist structures in terms of curricula content, pedagogy, and assessment, but they were inferior to those of the metropolitan state in the scope of knowledge and resources. Access to Western-type education was limited for locals and learning often did not go beyond the primary level, especially in the thinly populated areas of French West Africa where education was confined only to administrative centers. Subaltern Studies, originating in South Asian historiography, have challenged the Eurocentric narratives that dominated colonial educational content and practices. These studies decry the aftermath on groups marginalized by colonial rule, calling for the recognition and amplification of the voices of marginalized groups in the context of education, and advocating for the inclusion of the perspectives and experiences of "subaltern" groups in education policy development and implementation (Guha, 1982). Other theories, such as decolonial and postcolonial theories, have challenged colonial education systems. Decolonial theory examines the impacts of colonialism on marginalized groups, and challenges the underlying Eurocentric paradigms that inform knowledge production, including in education. It advocates for "decolonizing" knowledge by questioning and moving beyond Western-centric epistemologies and methodologies, to fostering more pluralistic and equitable approaches to education (Mignolo, 2007). Postcolonial theory examines the impacts of colonialism on societies, cultures, and institutions, including education. It critiques how colonial education policies were designed to serve the interests of the colonizer, often at the expense of indigenous knowledge and cultural practices. Postcolonial theory advocates for the decolonization of education systems, emphasizing the need to reclaim and integrate indigenous knowledge systems, languages, and pedagogies into the curriculum (Said, 1978).

At independence, many African countries had literacy rates below 10%, largely inadequate to meet the postcolonial needs of self-governance, economic growth, and sustainability. For example, by the 1960s when countries such as Cote d'Ivoire, Senegal, The Gambia in West Africa, Tanzania, and Somalia in East Africa, were realizing their independence, the gross primary enrollment ratio hovered around 36%; about half the levels found in Asia and Latin America. Despite the low starting point, Africa achieved impressive progress in education, post-independence especially between the 1960s and early 1980s. Enrollment steadily increased by about 9% yearly and the number of students enrolled in African institutions at all levels quintupled to about 63 million in the 1970s; doubling the rate in Asia and tripling that in Latin America. Postcolonial expansions in education granted more groups access and deepened human resource capital, enabling some groups that had previously lacked access to formal education the ability to participate in the political and administrative affairs of their nations. However, educational policies were still heavily steeped in Western traditions and dismissive of indigenous cultural, linguistic, ideological, and philosophical ethos. Indigenous Knowledge Systems (IKS) that emphasized the value of indigenous knowledge, wisdom, and pedagogies were marginalized or completely erased from the curriculum content and pedagogical approaches to teaching and learning, were also not culturally relevant nor responsive to the needs of indigenous communities (Dei, 2000). Postcolonial education did not provide recipients the agency to transform themselves and their political and socioeconomic contexts. In the latter half of the 20th century, expansions in education were seriously threatened by factors outside the realm of education such as poverty, disease, widespread corruption, and ethnic conflicts.

The Unique Case of Cameroon
Precolonial Context

Cameroon was no exception to the rich history of education and culture of precolonial Africa. While the lack of access to education that is widespread in many SSA countries is commonplace in Cameroon, the case of Cameroon is however unique, due to its cultural, colonial, geo-political, and linguistic heritage. Located in the Central African region at the far end of the Gulf of Guinea, Cameroon is highly diversified from the physical, human, economic, and linguistic standpoints. This country has over 200 ethnic groups speaking over 300 maternal languages, besides English and French. Cameroon is the only African country that was colonized by three European powers: Germany, Britain, and France. It eventually inherited two separate systems of education from two of its colonial masters, Britain and France. Each of these colonial systems imprinted a legacy of different institutions, structures, cultures, and norms that influenced the educational policy and practices of Cameroon and shaped the educational outcomes (Meyer & Rowan, 2006) (see Figure. 1.2. Map of the Ten Administrative Districts of Cameroon).

Before the transatlantic slave trade began in the 15th century, the Portuguese had already been exploring the Coast of West Africa. From the 1470s to 1620s, Portuguese explorers transported slaves from parts of Africa to Elmina in the Gold Coast, present-day, Ghana. From 1482 through 1484, Diego Cam, a Portuguese explorer from Fernando Po, sailed through the Congo River and reached the foot of the highest mountain in West Africa: the Buea Mountain in the southern part of Cameroon. From his vessel in the lowlands, and viewing the green scenery, Diego and his men witnessed the active volcano erupting. Their interest piqued by this natural phenomenon, Diego Cam and his sailors explored further up into the River Wouri in Douala, where they found many shrimps and named the area, Rio dos Cameroes (River of Shrimp); from where Cameroon and its derivatives originate.

The transcontinental slave trade has been blamed for many of Africa's woes; among them, the fact that slavery deprived many Africans of their freedom. To get away with the horrors associated with the inhumane trade of human cargo, European slave traders deliberately perpetrated the negative and lasting image of Africa to the rest of the world as the "dark continent" populated by less than humans. Joseph Conrad (1899) in his novel, *Heart of Darkness*, tried to justify that Africans were humans, as if such justification was needed.

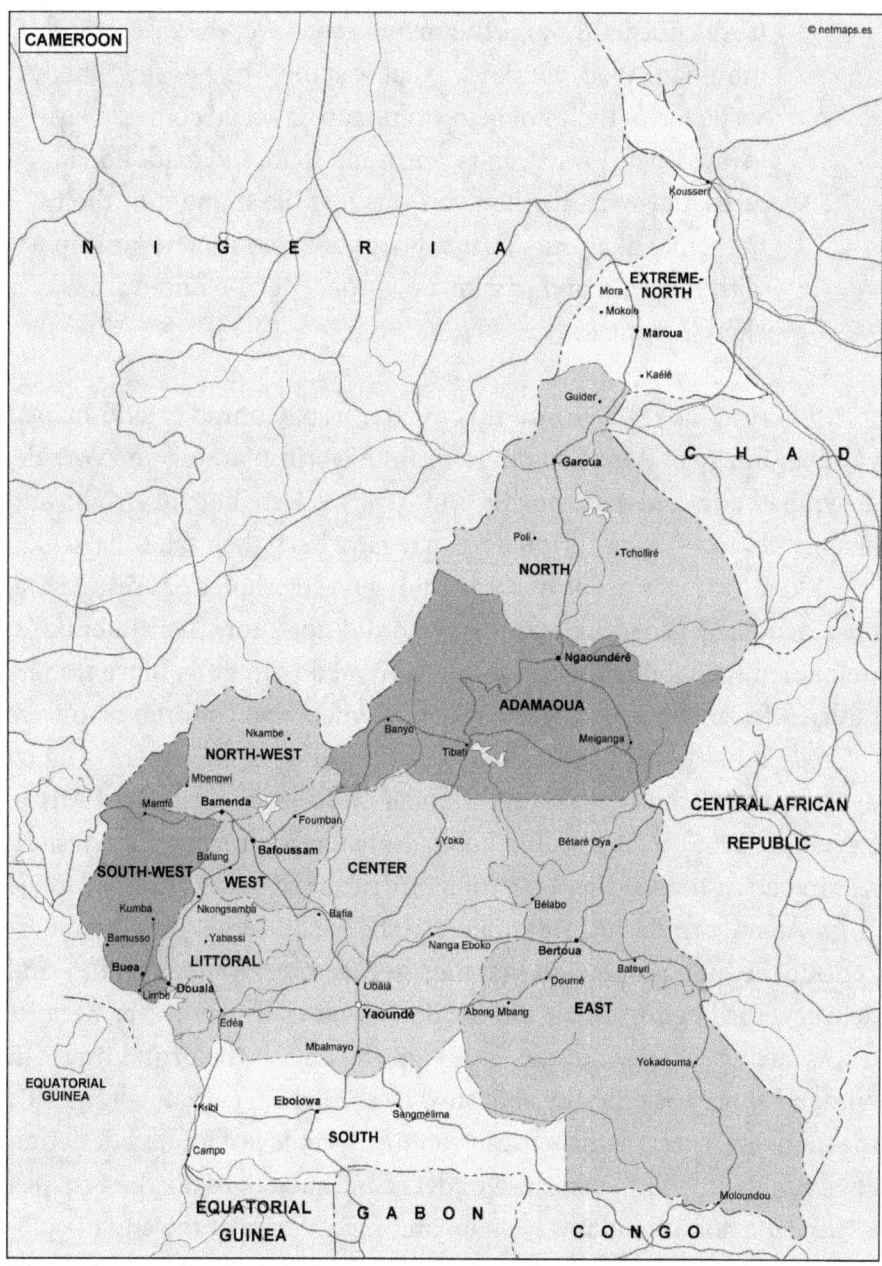

Figure 1.2. Map of the Ten Administrative Districts, Cameroon. Source: Netmaps.net

> It was unearthly, and the men were… No, they were not inhuman. Well, you know, that was the worst of it … this suspicion of their not being inhuman. It would come slowly to one. They howled, and leaped, and spun, and made horrid faces; but what thrilled you was just the thought of their humanity like yours … the thought of your remote kinship with this wild and passionate uproar. Ugly (Conrad, 1899, chap. 2, para. 8).

By luring his readers into this mental trap, Conrad (1899) helped paint an image of Africa to the rest of the world that was unfavorable, unsympathetic, and often hostile. But Africans were human alright, and hospitable; and this, unfortunately, may have been their fatal "flaw."

When the first European ships landed on the shores of West Africa, the legendarily generous Africans, who did not know their intentions, welcomed them, albeit with curiosity. Armed with guns, slave traders raided African villages capturing men, women, and children who were catered off to the West Indies, the Americas, and Europe. There is much debate among scholars about the number of slaves shipped out of Africa. Reynolds (1985), a Ghanaian scholar, using figures from earlier Western researchers, estimates that 11.7 million African slaves were shipped in the cross-Atlantic trade and 9.8 million to the New World. These numbers exclude the high proportion that died between the point of capture and delivery. The huge death toll did not deter slave traders however, because it was such a lucrative trade. Although the end of the brutal traffic in human beings was officially abolished by the British parliament in 1807, the traumatic effect on the African continent would last for decades. After abolition, many European slave traders continued to evade the ban; just like most colonists did not pack up and leave Africa at the end of colonialism. They continued to plunder the continent for its natural resources, perpetrating regional instabilities, and imposing despotic governments that would continue to serve the needs of former colonial masters and sow the seeds of the civil wars that characterize the continent today (Neba-Fuh, 2018; Westmaas, 2012; Klein & Jacob, 1999).

In 1884, without the participation of Africans, European leaders, meeting at the Berlin Conference, divided Africa among themselves into "Portuguese Africa," "British Africa," "German Africa," "Italian Africa," "Spanish Africa," "French Africa," and "Belgian Africa." Parts of Cameroun were sliced up and given to the Germans, who hoisted their flag in Victoria, a town in the southern parts of Cameroon, and established the protectorate of German Kameruns. Through 1914, the Germans continued to extend their protectorate into the hinterlands by conquering various ethnic groups through wars, and by acquiring territories to the east of Cameroon that included the Republic of Congo, parts of Chad, Central African Republic, and Gabon. The new territories were called Neukamerun (Ngoh, 1996).

In 1916, after 30 years as German Kamerun and a world war in which the average people of Kamerun hardly understood the stakes involved, the joint armies of France, Britain, and Belgium defeated the German forces in West Africa. According to Article 119 of the Treaty of Versailles (1919), Germany formally renounced her overseas colonies including Kamerun. The Supreme Council of the Allied Powers decided that France and Britain would partition Kamerun according to how they saw fit for their administrative convenience. France owned 80%, which it Christened French Cameroun, and Britain owned 20%, which it named British Cameroons, and placed it under the Nigerian colonial government. Each territory had separate administrations, but both colonial powers brokered a "carefully balanced" Franco-British agreement over the territories, ensuring joint administrative usage of vital landmarks like the Douala seaport for British merchant vessels and warships (Stoecker, 1986). A period of six months was provided for anybody wishing to join family to migrate to the other side, but very little consideration was given to ethnic, cultural, social, religious, or economic affinities, and the impact that such separations would have on populations clustered around colonial boundaries. The stage for ethnic conflicts had been set, and the populations of the two Cameroons remained restive long after independence. At independence, there were calls to reunite the two colonial territories (French-speaking and English-speaking) that still maintained vestiges of pre-1916 German influence. These calls were based on the premise that such a move was the only path to bring together kith and kin in the divided Kameruns, and foster national integration (Mukete, 2013).

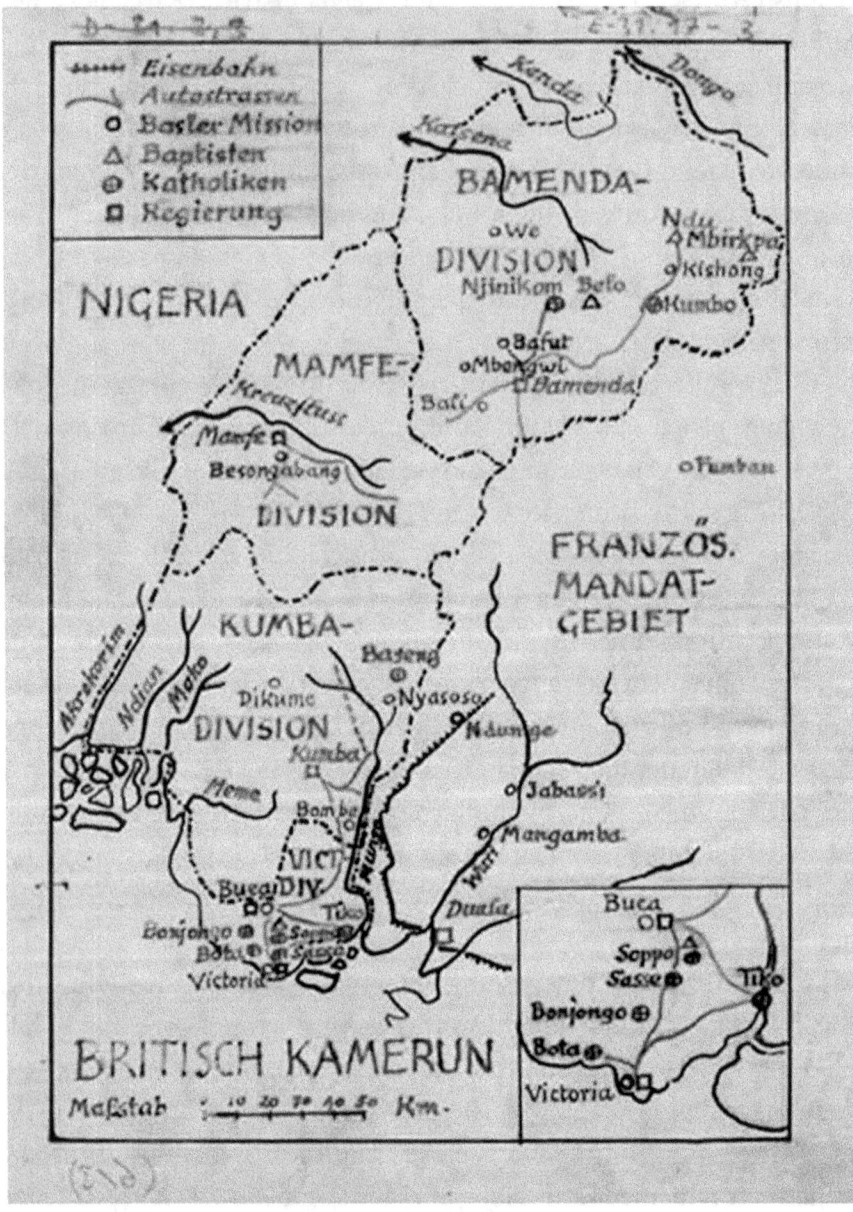

Figure 1.3. Map of British Kamerun, 1916. Map of the Southern part of the trust Territory of British Cameroons. Source: Basel Mission Archives.

Figure 1.4. Map of Present Southern Cameroons. Source: OCHA.org

Postcolonial Tensions

French Cameroun gained independence and became the Republic of Cameron on January 1, 1960. The former British Southern Cameroons got independence on February 11, 1961, through a plebiscite that gave them two options: achieving independence by joining the already independent Federation of Nigeria, or by joining the independent Republic of Cameroun (See Fig. 1.3. Map of British Kamerun, 1916; and Fig. 1.4. Map of Present Day of the Republic of Southern Cameroons/Ambazonia).

By some subversive maneuvers of the colonial empires, the United Nations organization failed to provide a third option for the former British Trust territory of Southern Cameroons to become independent by standing on its own. The 1961 reunification of the former British Southern Cameroons and the French Cameroun was fraught with tensions as Southern Cameroonians were deeply divided on this option. Despite the agreement on a federal system of government, tensions continued to grow as the English-speaking minority felt that the federation existed only on paper, and they were being marginalized by the French majority.

Over the years, the government continued to ignore calls for decentralization, and the many voices of dissent and social upheavals were met with heavy-handedness from the dictatorial government. In 1972, under covert directives of the French government that had an interest in abolishing the federal system and integrating Southern Cameroons to their former colonial territory, the then Cameroonian President Ahmadou Ahijdo, designed a referendum to abolish the federal system. There were only two options on the ballot: "Oui," (*Yes in French*) and "Yes," with no provision for 'No." By an overwhelming majority of 99.99% of votes of the citizens, the president abolished the federal constitution and replaced it with a unitary constitution. He changed the name of the country from the Federal Republic of Cameroon to the United Republic of Cameroon. The assimilation process was intensified; Southern Cameroons economic infrastructures and administrative institutions were dismantled, and in 1984, believing that the assimilation of the Anglophones was complete, President Paul Biya, once again changed the name of the country from the United Republic of Cameroon to the Republic of Cameroon; despite vehement protests from Southern Cameroonians (see Fig. 1.5).

Problems with Southern Cameroons Sub-System of Education
The Impact of Politicization of Education

Education policy in Cameroon is implemented by four ministries namely the Ministry of Basic Education, the Ministry of Secondary

Education, the Ministry of Higher Education, and the Ministry of Employment and Vocational Education. The various educational departments faced serious managerial issues and a possible solution would have been to decentralize management in order to redress the uncertainties noted in aspects such as teacher deployment, lack of sustainable information management systems, lack of reliable information on school statistics, and lack of accountability and transparency in budgetary factors. The decentralization theory in policy design and implementation advocates for the devolution of decision-making powers from central to local authorities, suggesting that such a shift can lead to more responsive and effective education systems, improving education quality by allowing local communities and schools to make decisions that best fit their specific contexts and needs (Hannaway & Carnoy, 1993).

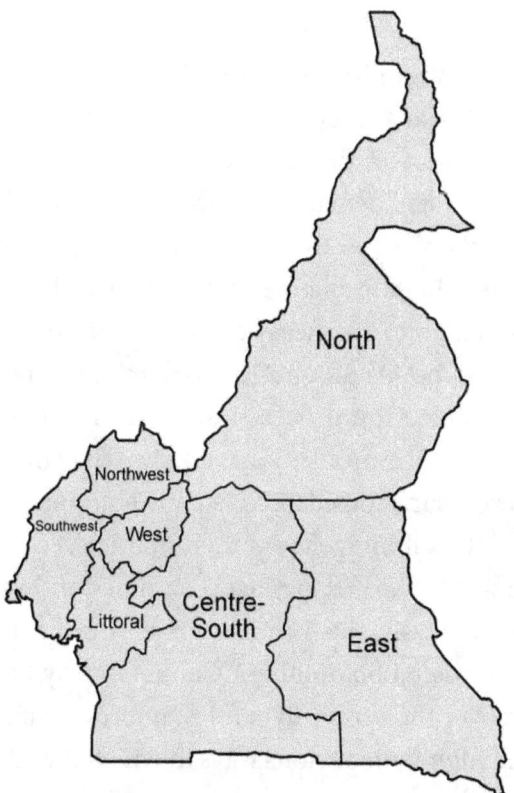

Figure 1.5. Map of Cameroon, 1972- 1983. Source: Golbez Wikipedia.org

Instead, in the early 1990s, the government decided to scrap the General Certificate of Education examination (an assessment system that Southern Cameroonians had inherited from Britain) and created a central education and assessment system. Several meetings and letters to the government indicating that this assessment system was a hallmark of the former British Southern Cameroons' educational system that needed to be preserved, were ignored. The teachers' union called for a peaceful protest in the capital city of Yaoundé. Many teachers, students, and sympathizers participated and sat down in front of the ministry of education, singing songs of freedom and of defiance. The government dispatched military men armed in combat gear to disperse the peaceful protesters with water cannons, spurting toxic sewage waste matter and tear gas. Protesters were severely beaten and many sustained severe injuries. However, the general Certificate of Education was saved, following these protests.

Lack of Goodwill of Administrative Officials

Luminary historians, eager to curry favors from anti-democratic political powers, have over the years, engaged in historical negationism and politically motivated denials of Southern Cameroonians' grievances, which is commonly referred to as the "Anglophone problem." This has given comfort to a dictatorial government which through an iron fist, has managed to maintain an uneasy calm, in a turbulent SSA landscape. However, in 2016, the "Anglophone problem" which originated from a contested decolonization process in the late 1950s and early 1960s, spilled to the surface. The problems have grown over time based on what Southern Cameroonians considered systemic marginalization, economic deprivation, and the submergence of their political, economic, judiciary, sociocultural, and educational heritage. Examined within the framework of critical policy analysis, this is no surprise. A critical examination of the education mandated on Southern Cameroons by La Republique du Cameroun, uncover the power dynamics, interests, and ideologies that shape them, and highlights various ways in which the education policies enacted have produced perceived social inequalities within the Southern Cameroons society (Diem et al., 2014).

Problems can be identified at all levels of the Southern Cameroons educational sub-system: Basic (including Nursery and Primary); Secondary, (General and Technical); Teacher Training; Assessment and Certification; Higher Education and Professional Training; and the lopsided implementation of a national bilingualism policy that serves as a tool for the assimilating of Southern Cameroonians. Specific issues include: the lack of suitable education policies; lack of human and infrastructural resources; acute teacher shortages; poor personnel management; and a perception that the Francophone "La Republique" government is out to obliterate the Anglo-Saxon educational sub-system. English and French were supposed to be the official languages of the federal system, but over the years, French has become the administrative language of preference, and Anglophones have to seek proficiency in it in order to survive.

In October 2016, dissatisfied teachers and lawyers once more took to the streets to peacefully express their frustrations at the infiltration of the Southern Cameroons legal and educational system by the French sub-system. Protesters were again severely brutalized, several arrested and jailed, while many more fearing for their lives, escaped into neighboring Nigeria. In 2014, the Republic of Cameroon government had enacted an anti-terrorism act to combat the spill-over of Boko Haram from Nigeria into the Northern parts of Cameroun. The anti-terrorism law states what may constitute acts of terrorism, without defining who a terrorist is. The government started using this law as a double-edged sword to curtail freedom of expression, freedom of the press, freedom from arbitrary arrests and detention, freedom of association or demonstration, and to perpetrate gross violation of human rights, especially among Southern Cameroonian citizens who have nursed grievances for decades. In November 2017, President Paul Biya, taking advantage of this law, labeled radicals who had been pushed to the fringes by excessive government crackdowns and were clamoring for secession, "terrorists," and declared war on Southern Cameroonians.

Whether Southern Cameroons reverts to its 1961 pre-reunification state or to its post-independence federal state with the Republic of Cameroon is uncertain. What is certain however is that one of the solutions to the ongoing-armed conflict is to design and implement an education policy that meets the personal, sociocultural, and political aspirations of Southern Cameroonians and equips them as equal players in a 21st-century global economy. A suitable education policy for Southern Cameroons and any other SSA African country must accommodate hybridity: integrating the indigeneity of the sovereign state, while closing accelerating globalization needs. Part II of this book will provide a blueprint for such a policy for Southern Cameroons.

CHAPTER 2

Defining Education Policy

Education policies are the principles and government processes in the educational sphere as well as the collection of laws, rules, and regulations that govern the operation of education systems (U.S. Department of Education, 2010). An education policy is usually an embodiment of values, culture, and needs about education as a social institution, and an outline of what regulated practices would look like. The substance of education policy is the stated educational principles and objectives, and the actions that should be taken to achieve those objectives. An education policy is therefore a public policy, designed with the goal of enhancing educational attainment in any nation.

A good education policy must be anchored on the attributes of good public policies that foster principles of citizenship and democracy. A policy is usually a written document, outlining intentions or goals as perceived by policymakers, or "as they would like it to be" (Trowler, 2003, p. 95). Viewing policy as a formal written document that embodies the statements and intentions of policymakers is, however, limited, because this presents policy development, interpretation, and implementation as a static rather than a dynamic entity which is always changing based on a number of factors that include the:

- task of identifying the important issues and goals for the policy;
- various opinions of stakeholders and the potential for conflicts that may arise at every stage of the policy development and implementation process;
- inherent differences in interpretations by those implementing

policy, depending on the perspectives of the people doing the work; and
- complex nature of policy implementation on the ground that could lead to different outcomes than the policy designers intended (Trowler, 2003).

The possibility of mismatch between what is "described" in a policy and what emerges when it is put in effect often occurs because simple policy descriptions do not often capture the multiplicity and complexity of factors that are involved in policy itself. Because of these complexities, Ball (1994) states: "Policy is both text and action, words and deeds, it is what is enacted as well as what is intended. Policies are always incomplete insofar as they relate to or map on to the 'wild profusion' of local practice" (p. 10). These characteristics are true of all policies, including education policy.

Education occurs in many forms for many purposes through many institutions. Formal education usually spans early childhood, kindergarten through twelfth grades, to university and professional education, as well as adult education and job training. Ultimately, education policy directly affects people of all ages, and the aim is always to improve education quality and society. Policy design can be at the school, district, or national level. However, in many Sub-Saharan African (SSA) countries including Cameroon, education policy is designed at the national level. Although the whole society has a stake in the policy outcomes, there is usually no consultation with stakeholders at district or other levels of society that the education policy is supposed to serve. It is incumbent on national education policy designers to carefully examine the present and future needs of society when designing policy. As the needs of society evolve, so too should education policies keep evolving. Rein (1983) posits that three basic steps are involved in policy design at the national level. They include:
- problem or issue identification;
- mobilization of the fine structure of government action; and
- "achievement of settlement (that is, compromises which establish a framework for policy design and practice) in the face of dilemmas

and trade-offs among values" (p. 211).
These can be quite complex processes.

Problems with the Design and Implementation of Education Policy

There are many issues with education policy design and implementation, but the problem of putting into gear the political process that is necessary for effective policy implementation can be the most critical challenge. While the process of designing and implementing policy itself is complex, it is also very political. National policy designers often have multiple agendas, values, and attitudes that often align with the government's ideology on the kind of populace and society that it wishes to establish. Although most policy designers may be civil servants, their views of what education is supposed to be about or identifying "the problem" that needs fixing, may be conflicting. Additionally, the government may not be willing to compromise or to relinquish some of its powers to civil society. The lack of compromise of central governments can render policy design a non-participatory and authoritarian venture, which often puts policy designers and implementers (for example, principals and teachers) at loggerheads.

In the case of Southern Cameroons, efforts have been made by various stakeholders, including teachers and civil society members, to improve education policy, but those efforts have been largely ignored by the central government which has refused to incorporate suggestions for policy improvements from other stakeholders. There is also considerable debate among contemporary Cameroonian scholars as to whether or not Cameroon as a whole has an education policy. Shu (2000) points out the lack of formal policy guidelines in Cameroon, noting that among the top 10 problems, is the problem of "a comprehensive national education policy which can stay, while individual politicians and civil servants come and go" (p. 8). Others like Anja (2000) and Tambo (2003) argue that in a system where there are no good public policies in general, presidential decrees and ministerial orders and regulations, would constitute the Education Policy in Cameroon. Almost all scholars (Tambo, 2003; Tamukong, 2004; Fonkeng, 2010) agree that the problems inherent in the Cameroon education system reveal that there is no comprehensive education policy that can be matched with those of other countries in the world like the 1996 Education Policy of Zambia, the 2002 New Zealand First Education Policy, or the 2004–2005 Federal Republic of Nigeria Policy. What exists as education policy in Cameroon is a myriad of legislations, and presidential and ministerial decrees, that orient educational practices at primary, secondary, higher education, and teacher education. These legislative declarations cannot be described as policy, but rather directives. While the split administrative history of the country and its varied institutional approaches to education pose serious challenges to the design and implementation of harmonious education policies for the two regions, there is no excuse for any nation not to invest in its human capital, given the role of education in enhancing both the individual's and the nation's economic value, productivity, and competitiveness in a global economy (Becker, 1964).

Understanding causes and effects in a social world are always difficult, making the policy design and implementation process more complicated and fraught with unseen and unforeseeable outcomes. Ideally, an approach to policy design which revolves around the central government and is controlled at the national level is not the best approach to policy design and implementation, mainly because it does not take into account the realities of those on the ground. Yet, this is the approach that is often used in many SSA countries; believing that this approach is an "imitation" of American and Western European models that have conducted studies on policy design, change, and implementation. However, early American studies and analyses of central government approaches to education policy have illustrated negative outcomes of government's ability to effectively implement its own programs (Derthick, 1972; Pressman & Wildavsky, 1984; Bardach, 1984). Later studies on American education policy that were more analytical and comparative in nature, sought to examine variations approaches in implementation across programs, and highlighted specific variables that accounted for success (Van Meter & Van Horn, 1975; Sabatier & Mazmanian, 1979; 1980).

Approaches to Policy Design and Implementation

Several approaches to policy design and implementation have emerged over the years, but the two main approaches are:

a). Top-down or Managerial

b). Bottom-up or Phenomenological

Top-Down or Managerial Approach

The top-down approach to policy design and implementation assumes that education policy is too important to be left to chance, or the good intentions of a few individuals (Beckhard & Pritchard, 1992). Based on this assumption, education policy should be formulated in a variety of contexts: the central government, national bodies associated with the government, local authorities, educational institutions, and members of civil society at large. Leaders at the top of organizations set goals within broader policy objectives and get their staff's commitment to them. Managerial perspective is based on the idea that managers know how to create the right conditions for successful implementation of policies. They know the values and expectations of those in the organization, such as teachers, staff, parents, and even students. This approach is generally successful because by tapping into existing organizational cultures there is the sense of "ownership" of policies that emerge, by all stakeholders. Top-down approaches have also been referred to as "culturalism" (Parker, 2000) or as "the new leadership approach" (Bryman, 1999).

Some conditions are necessary for managerial approaches to be successful. Managers in successful top-down approaches need to possess the following skills:

- have clear policy objectives;
- create and sustain the commitment of those involved;
- ensure that there are real expectations of solid outcomes inherent in the policy;
- ensure that the policy innovation has priority over competing demands;
- allocate sufficient financial resources; and
- create a stable environment in which the policy is implemented

(adapted from Cerych & Sabatier, 1986).

Weaknesses of Top-Down Approach

While the top-down approach seeks to develop recognizable patterns in behavior grounded in shared culture across different policy areas, it inherently comes with certain weaknesses. First, culture is not static, but dynamic. Organizational cultures therefore are multiple, and not necessarily unitary. This might render an attempt to configure an organization culture difficult, and even if established, is likely to be unstable. People do not simply act out cultures; they change it too (Tierney, 1987).

Different individuals in the organization may have different value systems and conflicting interests that render compliance problematic. Attempts to engage many perspectives and "stages of actions" *front-of-stage* (the public arena of official statements), *back-stage* (where deals are done behind closed doors), and *under-the-stage* (where gossip and other done in quiet corners, over coffee or near the water cooler), of the various individuals in the organization can be quite complex (Becher, 1999).

There will always be a difference in perspective between those responsible for making policies and those responsible for taking action in implementation. Managers' attempts to manipulate cultures in an attempt to implement policy can be considered unethical (Barrett & Fudge, 1981; Fitzgerald, 1988). Taking statutory language as a starting point for organizational culture is also problematic because it does not consider the significance and impact of previous institutional actions. Even if policy framers are successful, imposing a single set of norms and values in educational settings, goes contrary to the spirit of critical thinking and innovation that should characterize educational institutions like universities. Slavish compliance to approved ways of thinking and doing should not be what educational institutions should be known for (Willmott, 1993). Thus, considering policy framers as the key actors in policy design will always be a source of criticism. This criticism stems from what many consider an elite approach to policy construction. Elite theory suggests that policy that is primarily made by a small group of elites or influential individuals, who possess a disproportionate amount of power and resources, do not often serve the needs and interests of the public. The elite approach to public theory often underscores the gap between the governing elite and the general populace (Mills, 1956).

Bottom-Up or Phenomenological Approach

The bottom-up or phenomenological approach to policy development emphasizes the role of service deliverers such as teachers and others who, though lower down on the ladder, are responsible for putting policy into practice. Bottom-up proponents criticize the top-down approach for placing too much emphasis on governments and other central decision-makers while neglecting the other actors who implement the goals, strategies, and other activities and interactions integrated within policies. Proponents of this approach (Hanf et al., 1978) suggest that a network of service deliverers who are involved in the implementation, execution, and financing of relevant government programs should be identified at various levels. These networks should be used to identify local, regional, and national actors who are engaged in policy planning. Lipsky's (1980) concept of "street-level bureaucrats" would apply here. Street-level-bureaucrats are public service workers, such as police officers, teachers, social workers, and other government employees, who interact directly with citizens and have substantial discretion in the execution of their duties. These individuals effectively become the face of public policy to the general populace as they interpret and implement government policies on a day-to-day basis and effectively act as liaisons between government policymakers and citizens (Lipsky, 1980). Researchers who increasingly acknowledge the importance of the phenomenology of innovation support this perspective on policy design and implementation.

Weaknesses of Bottom-Up

While dealing with service deliverers can ensure that contextual factors are considered, there are some weaknesses with the bottom-up approach. Because of the multiplicity of actors, this approach to policy design has the potential of distorting policy or even rendering it incoherent as it is being put into practice. Critics of the bottom-up approach perceive uncertainties in this approach as policy can become refracted during interpretation and implementation. Some local agents may be novices who are unable to make sense of the complexity of policy messages or comprehend implementation processes. Personal biases, as well as social contexts, may influence the way teachers make sense of policy statements and influence implementation.

This approach also risks over-emphasizing local autonomy or individuals who may not possess much accountability since they are not elected. Some scholars have argued that policy control should be exercised by those who derive their power from sovereign power through elected representation (Matland, 1995). This stipulation comes with its own risks since in the "policy network" politics usually wields a stronger lever. Policy networks refer to the "cluster or complex organizations connected to each other by resource dependencies and distinguished from other clusters or complexes by breaks in the structure of resources dependencies" (Rhodes & Marsh, 1992, p. 182). Rhodes (2017) posits that "central and local officials are maneuvering for advantage when deploying their constitutional-legal, organizational, financial, and political and informational resources, to maximize their influence over outcomes" (p. 42). While political will is always necessary for change to occur, having the political will to change long-standing institutions is usually difficult.

The Combined Approach

Increasingly, the literature has focused on combining top-down (macro-level variables) with bottom-up (micro-level variables) in policy design and implementation, that takes advantage of the strengths of both approaches (Elmore, 1985; Fullan, 2007; Goggin et al., 1990; Matland, 1995; O'Toole, 2000). The combined approach makes sense because a wide range of stakeholders interact at various levels, and validating all of their interactions is necessary. Both policymakers and the local actors who enact the policies on the ground are important for successful implementation. This approach also takes cognizance of the fact that implementation strategies are different in various educational settings (for example, secondary versus higher education), and there is, therefore, the need for a shared vision of all those involved.

Some theories that support this approach include: the Multiple Workstream and the Advocacy Coalition approaches to policy design and implementation. The Multiple Workstream approach examines the formulation of policy that takes into consideration the convergence of three streams: problems, policies, and politics. According to this framework, policy windows open when these streams align, providing opportunities for policymakers to push their agendas or solutions forward. It emphasizes the role of timing and context in policymaking and the importance of policy entrepreneurs adept at recognizing and seizing these opportunities (Kingdon, 1984). The Advocacy Coalition approach suggests that policy changes occur through the interactions and negotiations of various advocacy coalitions that consist of people from different sectors (government, private sector, academia, and other stakeholders) (Downs, 1957).

This book makes suggestions for education policy that, if implemented, would improve the educational systems in SSA countries, with a focus on Southern Cameroons. It remains to be seen if there is the political will and other requisite factors necessary for successful policy implementation. Fullan (2007) suggests nine critical factors that affect education policy design and implementation. These range from factors of change characteristics (for example, need, clarity, complexity, and quality/practicality) to local characteristics (such as district level, community, principal, and teachers), to external factors (government and other agencies).

Conclusion

Policy design and implementation is a multi-dimensional process involving various actors and contexts that render it politically and socially complex. This process looks different across different countries, regions, sub-regions, and geo-political contexts. Despite these differences, a set of conditions is necessary for policy design and implementation. Gornitzka, Kyvi, and Stensaker (2005) identify the following critical variables:
- policy standards and objectives
- policy resources
- inter-organizational communication

- characteristics of implementation
- economic, social, and political conditions
- disposition of implementers

Of course, these descriptive conditions would "look" different in various contexts due to the dynamic interaction of factors that are context-specific. Education policy is not only country-specific but can also be sub-sector-specific. This means that different issues may arise for primary, secondary, and higher education (Gornitzka et al., 2005). This may necessitate a combination of theories for specific policy areas and contexts, stakeholders, and organizational agencies. Adequate time is necessary for the successful implementation of policy. While earlier theorists suggested four years for policy implementation to take hold, Sabatier and Mazmanian (1980) suggest a time span of at least 10 years to enable policy-oriented learning that would guarantee effective implementation. A case-by-case approach to policy design and implementation might be the best approach, as it is difficult to suggest models that would be applicable to all contexts (Gornitzka et al., 2005).

This author has adopted an analytical and comparative approach that examines global systems that work and compares them to some SSA countries while specifically making suggestions for designing policy in Southern Cameroons. Policy design or change, of course, goes hand-in-hand with policy implementation. Designing a policy does not necessarily mean that the policy will be passed or even effectively implemented if adopted. There are many sociopolitical challenges in the situational context of Southern Cameroons. However, providing a blueprint based on examples of systems that work is the first place to start. This is especially important as the SSA region undergoes a series of political movements that seek to establish full sovereignty and build strong nations in the sub-region. The author believes that it is only with strong policies and political will that SSA can be fully equipped to contend with 21st-century global challenges that require the participation of all.

CHAPTER 3

Teacher Selection, Education, Development and Deployment

Teaching is a profession that involves many players, the most important of whom are arguably the teacher and the learners, engaged in an ongoing process of imparting and acquiring knowledge. Teachers are the number one factor influencing in-school student learning; their work with and for students, parents, and society puts them at the frontline of global development. Yet, many countries face critical teacher shortages, a factor that hinders educational progress worldwide and threatens the achievement of international development goals. For example, the United Nations (UN) did not meet its Millennium Development Goals (MDGs) (2000), to eradicate poverty and provide equitable and sustainable education worldwide. In 2015, the United Nations developed a new framework, the Sustainable Development Goals (SDG), to replace the MDGs, Sustainable Development Goal 4 focuses on providing free universal primary and secondary education to all children; eliminating gender disparities in education; and ensuring equal access to all levels of education and vocational training for the vulnerable; including persons with disabilities, indigenous peoples and children in vulnerable situations. An interim report presented in 2023 during the United Nations General Assembly (UNGA) held in New York, indicated that only a mere 12% of the 17 sustainable development goals are on track (Welthungerhilfe, 2023). While factors like the impact of the climate crisis, a weak global economy, and COVID-19 might have hindered the progress of the SDG globally, the poorest and most vulnerable countries, most of which are in the global south, are the hardest hit. It is feared that these goals may not be met by

2030 if drastic measures are not taken to deal with the challenge such as teacher shortages, especially in regions like Sub-Saharan Africa (SSA), where unique political and economic crises make shortages more severe.

The UNESCO Institute for Statistics (UNESCO, UIS, 2016) estimated that 230 million children are out of school; and 25 million (41%) of primary school-age children may never set foot in a classroom. Among those enrolled, about 617 million, or six out of ten children do not meet minimum proficiency levels in reading and mathematics. On October 5, 2016, UIS released its first-ever projections of teacher recruitment needs. The report indicated that to meet the target of 25 students per classroom, countries must recruit 68 million primary and secondary school teachers (24.4 million teachers for primary and 44.4 million for secondary education) in the next 14 years. A holistic approach involving various government agents, stakeholders, and multiple integrative strategies must be deployed to grow the crop of teachers required to meet global targets. However, these projections would be a moving target, if one of the main factors accounting for teacher shortages is not immediately addressed: attrition. The teaching profession must be made attractive enough not only to bring in new professionals but also, most especially, to keep those who are already in the profession from leaving. This is not an option, but an exigency, considering that out of 24.4 million teachers needed for universal primary education (UPE), 21 million are replacement for attrition; and out of the 44.4 million secondary teachers needed, 27.6 million are to replace those who voluntarily leave the profession for reasons other than retirement (UNESCO, UIS, October 2016, No. 39).

The Problem of Teacher Shortages

Teacher shortages is a problem that affects many regions of the world (developed and developing nations alike). In the United States, teacher turnover accounts for 90% of the demand for new teachers each year. While some of this turnover may be due to retirement, two-thirds of U.S. teachers leave the profession due to non-retirement-related reasons such as poor working conditions, low salaries, unfavorable school environments, and general disenchantment with the profession. This makes the teacher attrition rate in the United States about twice as high compared to other developed nations like Finland, Singapore, and Canada (Carver-Thomas & Darling-Hammond, 2017).

Sub-Saharan Africa, however, tops the rest of the world in teacher shortages, followed by Southeastern and Western Asia. Seventy percent of countries across SSA face teacher shortages at the primary level and 90% at the secondary level. In SSA, 17 million teachers are needed to meet UPE and Universal Secondary Education (USE) by 2030 (6.3 million at primary and 10.8 million teachers at secondary levels). Of the 6.3 million primary teachers needed, 2.4 million will fill new teaching posts, and 3.9 million will replace attrition cases. Of the 10.8 million secondary teacher recruits needed by 2030, 7.1 million are for new teaching positions, and 3.7 million to replace those who have left. These statistics indicate that despite some progress made on the United Nations MDGs, the MDGs in general, and the 2000 Dakar Education for All (EFA) resolutions that committed to achieving UPE by 2015 were a failure in SSA.

Some analysts maintain that a large part of the failure of these initiatives could be ascribed to the singular difficulties in recruiting and retaining quality teachers to effectively meet the growing student population in SSA. When the MDGs and EFA were launched, it was projected that more than one million teaching posts would need to be created by 2015, meaning that a total of 350,000 teachers would have to be hired each year to meet the teacher shortage in SSA. However, secondary enrollments did not match primary enrollments in most countries, and the gap between primary school students and secondary graduates to send into classrooms as teachers continued to grow. In Mozambique, for example, teacher recruitment needs have continued to outpace the number of secondary graduates, with only 9.5% of secondary school students enrolling in classes in 2009. Other SSA countries, such as Chad and Niger, are even farther behind, with the teacher workforce continuing to trail targets at the rate of 14% and 18%, respectively, each year. Madagascar still maintains a staggering teacher-student ratio of more than 250 students per trained teacher (Majgaard & Mingat, 2012).

Because of these shortfalls, some analysts have predicted that the number of primary and secondary teachers needed to achieve the SDG by 2030 in Sub-Saharan Africa would be at least 19 million. Such estimates consider various factors, including population growth. The southern three-quarters of SSA (not including South Africa)—has a population of over 800 million. By 2030, the demographics of primary-age children will have grown by 40% to 50%; making SSA the region with the fastest-growing world population (UNESCO, UIS, n.d., Data center). Based on predictions of how many are currently entering the job market and how many intend to become teachers, the current UIS estimated shortage of 17 million teachers will continue to increase. The UNESCO Montreal-based Institute for Statistics report of 2011 stressed that to redress this situation, "policies that effectively address teacher training and retention should be at the core of national education policies [for SSA]" (UNESCO, UIS, 2011).

Following the launching of SDG 2030, the African Union (AU) Heads of State and Government, meeting in Addis Ababa for their Twenty-Sixth Ordinary Session (January 2016), developed the Continental Education Strategy for Africa (CESA, 2016–2025). The framework emphasized the commitment to the future of education in Africa as envisioned by the global development goals. Participants committed to creating a new generation of Africans who are effective change agents capable of driving the continent's sustainable development goals in a manner that is compatible with the continent's needs. The leaders emphasized that teachers were central to the success of the strategies that desire

> to ... set up qualitative systems of education and training [that would] provide the African continent with efficient human resources adapted to African core values.—Those responsible for its implementation will be assigned to reorient Africa's education and training systems to meet the knowledge, competencies, skills, innovation and creativity required to nurture African core values and promote sustainable development at the national, sub-regional and continental levels (African Union, 2016, p. 7).

As stated in the AU's CESA 2016–2025 foreword, "no-one-size fits all when it comes to wants and need" (p. 5).

Policies designed for recruiting, developing, and deploying teachers in SSA cannot simply be "business as usual" strategies that aim to increase the number of teachers. Although cross-country transfer of workable strategies can be valuable, successful policies for SSA will emerge from an in-depth study of each country's specific political, socioeconomic, and cultural contexts. Policy formulation, implementation, and monitoring must consider the complex and interrelated factors that engender teacher shortages in each specific country. Intervention strategies will succeed only through mobilizing financial, human, and technical resources within national, regional, and international platforms and the commitment of multiple players concerned with education in SSA. Once the issues affecting teacher recruitment and deployment have been identified, policy design and implementation must follow. This is usually a discursive process; and not one that logically flows between discrete factors or phases in an orderly manner. This approach has been the key to successful educational outcomes in countries such as New Zealand and Finland, where "directed exploration" and "trialing" models have been employed to engage governmental organizations, teachers, parents, and other stakeholders in open, iterative discussion about reaching goals and resolving problems as a way forward (Carmela & Labate, 2016).

Education Challenges in Sub-Saharan Africa

Apart from political and geographical boundaries, SSA nations share common colonial and postcolonial experiences shaping the region's educational realities. The postcolonial educational systems are similar in that they still maintain neo-colonialist vestiges of imperialism from erstwhile colonial masters that weigh down the region from establishing its place as an equal player in the world arena. SSA must shed the weight of its colonial legacy and eradicate its own tribulations that hold it back from competing fairly with the rest of the world in educational advancements. Problems with recruiting, training, and retaining qualified teachers are endemic across SSA countries due to many factors that include the following: (a) bribery and corruption in recruitment (which often leads to the recruitment of intellectually inferior candidates); (b) a reduction in recruitment standards in many cases to meet shortages; (c) ineffective training and preparation; (d) poor remunerations and incentives for teachers; (e) lack of professional development; (f) unwillingness of teachers to work in rural areas; (g) poor management at the school level which leads to issues of absenteeism; (h) overcrowding (more than 40 students to one teacher); (i) brain-drain of qualified teachers who migrate to countries with better working conditions; (j) lack of teachers' voices and engagement in educational matters; (k) disease such as the HIV/AIDS pandemic that has afflicted countries in SSA at a higher rate than the rest of the world; (l) death from violence and internal conflicts such as the genocide in Rwanda or the on-going violent conflict in Cameroon; (m) severe budgetary constraints; and, (n) the lack of political will.

In 1991, UNESCO established the International Institute for Capacity Building in Africa (IICBA) as one of six Category 1 Institutes and centers specifically created to address the critical shortage of teachers in SSA. Part of IICBA's mandate was to:

- address the educational, technical and professional needs of Africa in teacher development, school leadership and management;
- bring to African institutions the latest research and development in education globally;
- enhance the capacity of Africa's teacher education institutions;
- further the use of technological improvements in teacher development, such as the use of the electronic media in teacher education;
- promote gender equality in mainstream teacher development; and
- enable African education to benefit from work done by our partners by providing a forum for sharing experiences in the above areas (Carmela & Labate, 2016).

Despite these efforts dating back at least two decades, most Ministries of Education still struggle to recruit enough qualified teachers to match the expansion in primary enrollments and deploy teachers to where they are most needed. Thus, the gap between teacher demand and supply continues to widen across the continent.

Problems with Southern Cameroons Teacher Education: A Historical Diagnostic

Like many countries in SSA, Southern Cameroons faces a wide range of challenges in teacher recruitment, training, and deployment that are interwoven with its colonial history and current sociopolitical context. The section that follows will examine major issues affecting the education sector.

Lack of Adequate Teacher Training Colleges

From its early days after reunification, Southern Cameroonians (Anglophones) had emphasized education and developed a robust teacher education and training system. By 1971, the Southern Cameroonian region of the country already had about 85% trained teachers in the field, as opposed to less than 40% for the Francophone sub-system. These Teacher Training Colleges (TTCs) were primarily operated by lay and parochial establishments. However, in 1975, in keeping with its assimilation agenda, the Francophone central government suddenly closed down all ten private TTCs in the country, thus adversely affecting teacher supply in a region that had heavily depended on the private sector for teacher training. These colleges were not replaced with alternative establishments for training teachers. Instead, the government initiated "reforms" that further marginalized and neglected stakeholders in the Southern Cameroons, sub-system of education; strengthening suspicions that the reforms had been initiated to dissolve the much stronger British educational system which Southern Cameroonians had inherited. Following the dissolution of provincial TTCs, a single Higher Teachers' Training College (HTTC), "Ecole Normale Superieure" was instituted in Yaoundé, the capital of Cameroon. This establishment, which offered both first and second cycles for teacher training (the equivalence of undergraduate and post-graduate diplomas), was designed after the much inferior French educational heritage, and almost all programs were delivered in French. Only a first cycle TTC (equivalence of undergraduate degree) had been created in 1967 as an extension campus in the North West Region to serve all of Southern Cameroons. The absence of an HTTC, also known as the second cycle, to train secondary and high school teachers in subject-specific content meant that secondary and high school students in Southern Cameroons were condemned to be taught by unqualified teachers. (See Table 3.1 for student-teacher ratio in government schools).

Eventually, when the extension campus in Bambili was upgraded into an HTTC, Francophones who had not gone through the Anglophone secondary school system and were therefore unfamiliar with the syllabi in chemistry, mathematics, physics, biology, and even history were admitted into this institution by ministerial decrees. Upon graduation, they are expected to teach Anglophone students subjects in which they themselves had no foundational knowledge. With neither a mastery of content nor the English language, Francophone graduates of Teachers' Training Institutions who are deployed to Anglophone regions, resort to teaching students in a language which is now known as "Franglais" (a combination of pidgin/creole, broken English, and word-for-word translation of French words into English). For example, after writing on the chalkboard, a Francophone teacher told a student to "sweep the board." National exit examinations for some subjects, especially in technical education are set in French only, with no adequate English translation. Even when there is an attempt at English translation, it does not make sense to anybody. For example, here is a question on a technical national examination: "What is the function of a *candle* in a car?" This question was supposed to ask the function of "spark plugs" in a car. The questions were initially set in French at the central Ministry. The Francophone teacher/translator administering this examination to Anglophone students opened a French/ English dictionary and looked up "bougie d'allumage" (spark plugs, in English). Too lazy to do the job of translation properly, he stopped his search at the word, "bougie," and "bougie" translates as "candle." So, he translated the question into, "What is the function of a *candle* in the Engine of a car?" Well, if I were a student, I would respond, "To burn up the car!"

These are just a few ways in which the English language, a global language for international communication, commerce, science, technology,

Table 3.1. Student/Teacher Ratio in Government Schools in the North West Region

No	Division	No of Schools	No of Students	No of Teachers	No of Classrooms	No of Periods	Average per Teacher	Student/Teacher Ratio	Requirement by Period
1	BOYO	39	13,781	27	315	1,277	42.2	1 : 510	26 profs
2	BUI	70	33,821	33	408	2,035	62.0	1 : 1,025	66 profs
3	DON / MAN	57	18,115	08	364	1,881	235.0	1 : 2,264	59 profs
4	MENCHUM	30	12,619	20	178	890	74.2	1 : 569	25 profs
5	MEZAM	66	42,764	111	577	2,885	29.7	1 : 385	33 profs
6	MOMO	53	18,018	19	328	1,396	73.5	1 : 948	59 profs
7	NGOKETUNJIA	34	13,161	22	19C	950	43.18	1 : 599	31 profs
	REGIONAL	349	152,279	240	2,350	11,314	559.78	1 : 634	268 profs

Source: Delegation of Secondary Education in the North West Region.

diplomacy, art, and formal education is disdained and misused by Francophone teachers in Southern Cameroons. When students fail to learn concepts due to teacher ineffectiveness, they are branded as having a dislike for core science subjects. Gradually, by one ministerial decree after the other, the Southern Cameroons' system for training teachers inherited from the British was eroded at all levels and replaced by a system with no value for core principles guiding teacher training.

Low Admission Standards into Teacher Training Colleges

Admission of candidates into the Government Teachers' Training Colleges (GTTC) does not follow rigorous standards for control. Candidates write an entrance examination and are admitted only based on the written exams, without the oral component that should accompany examinations into professional schools. The lack of an oral component into TTC means that candidates cannot be screened on some values required of educators, nor evaluated on criteria such as psycho-social maturity or motivation. It is therefore difficult to gauge a candidate's awareness or appreciation of the demands of the teaching profession, which is usually a strong indication of whether a person will commit to the profession or quit. Candidates with disabilities such as speech, hearing, or sight cannot be screened for accommodations (that does not exist anyway). Oral interviews were an integral part of the admission process into TTC in the former British Southern Cameroons sub-system; based on the premise that teaching is a vocation and intellectual capacity alone was not enough to qualify one into the profession. This component has been scrapped.

Short Duration of Training

Following the abolition of private TTC, the government reduced the duration for teacher training from one to three years, depending on the entry qualification. Teaching practice, arguably the most significant aspect of the training process was reduced to two weeks each semester, bringing the duration of the practicum to a total of six weeks in the entire training program for those doing the one-year course. Typically, field experiences are not integrated within coursework to buttress courses. Courses in teacher training and other institutions of education adopt pedagogical approaches that usually overly rely on theories with no hands-on component. These courses are generally disconnected from the authentic classroom environments in which completers are required to teach. Pedagogic practices do not consider the diverse student populations and learning styles teachers will work with within authentic classrooms after graduation. Individualizing instruction and teaching pre-service teachers to accommodate students with disabilities or diverse learning styles is a foreign notion. The insufficient amount of time spent learning in authentic classroom contexts, the ineffective pedagogical approaches to instruction, and the lack of adequate resources to effectively prepare teacher candidates undermine the quality of teacher training institutions. Besides, the lack of meaningful, practical training is in direct violation of the 1998 *Law of Orientation* [Article 16(1)], which stipulated the organization of the Southern Cameroons' sub-system of education (Government of Cameroon, Ministry of Education, 1998).

Elimination and Lack of Emphasis on Key Subjects on the Curriculum

There is an acute shortage of mathematics and science teachers, especially at secondary levels. These shortages lead to a vicious cycle where poor teaching in mathematics and the sciences results in poor performances, and limited availability of student teachers at both primary and secondary levels who have a mastery of mathematics and scientific content. Most teacher training colleges do not have textbooks aligned to the curriculum that teachers would be required to teach upon completion. Instead of trying to resolve this situation in practical ways that might grow the crop of teaching personnel to fill these gaps, the Republic of Cameroon's Ministry of National Education appears to have simply given up on the teaching of these very important subjects (math, English language arts, practical agriculture, and technology); and have consistently failed to give these areas of shortages the adequate and sustained attention that is deserved. Prior to the take-over of the Southern Cameroons' system of Education by the Republic of Cameroon's government, it was obligatory for a pre-service teacher candidate to have passed the following core subjects prior to graduation: Arithmetic, English, Principles and Practice of Education, Practical Rural Science, and Physical Education. The teacher's certificate would not be awarded without a pass in all these compulsory subjects. Currently, less than 10% of teacher trainees in GTTC obtain a passing score in mathematics or French in the General Certificate of Examinations (GCE) Ordinary Levels (O/L), and less than 30% acquire a passing grade in the English language Arts at the GCE O/L. These students cannot be expected to pass these subjects during training, much less teach them upon graduation; yet, all teacher-training students graduate. Upon graduation from TTC, many decline to teach upper primary grades, such as classes five and six, where the mathematical computations become too complex for them to understand. Some teachers have been known to skip teaching these subjects altogether in their classrooms because they could not comprehend the concepts themselves. At secondary levels, the shortages are more acute in science subjects like mathematics, physics, chemistry, and biology. For example, in the sub-district of Pinyin in the Northwestern region of Southern Cameroons, there was only one Anglophone physics teacher for about 1,000 physics students in the 2014 academic year.

Some subjects, such as French, are hardly taught by trained teachers in most Southern Cameroonian schools. French teachers are absent in the nearly 135 secondary schools in the South West Region of Southern Cameroons and in 251 schools in the North West Regions. In the 2014 academic year, the Ndian and Menchum divisions had only five and seven French teachers, respectively. These factors have contributed to the high failure rate in these core subjects and, regrettably, to the overall falling educational standards in Southern Cameroons. Besides, for a country that considered bilingualism the glue for national integration, these lapses smack of a deliberate attempt to keep certain regions from participating in the nation's political, national, and socioeconomic discourse. Tables 3.1 of the 2014 statistics obtained from the Delegation of Secondary Education in the North West Region, one of the two regions that make up Southern Cameroons, graphically demonstrate this problem (see Table 3.1).

Teacher Deployment

Teacher deployment is planned and executed by the central Ministries of Basic Education and Secondary Education. It is unclear what specific management system these ministries use to control deployment to areas of highest need. The distribution of highly qualified teachers, especially in mathematics and science, is highly inequitable and apparently random, with a high concentration in urban areas and acute shortages in rural areas. Several teachers were recently transferred from Higher Elementary Teacher Training Colleges (HETTC) to the Ministry of Secondary Education without a clear rationale or explanation for such cross-ministerial transfers. This was an unnecessary move since, as the name suggests, HETTC is part of basic education. This arbitrary movement of teachers from one level to the other, further exacerbates the inequitable distribution of better-qualified teachers, and teachers of mathematics and sciences.

Issues with Gender Deployment

The distribution of female teachers is highly problematic. Many female teachers do not want to work in remote areas due to the lack of proper housing, safety issues, and lack of other basic amenities in these areas. They tend to do everything possible (including signing fake marriage certificates with ghost husbands in cosmopolitan areas) to avoid being deployed to rural areas. Many teachers assigned to unpopular remote posts often refuse to take up their teaching positions or quickly arrange to be transferred, resulting in many unfilled positions and higher turnover rates that leave only less experienced and untrained teachers in these areas. In a country with multiple linguistic and ethnic groups, these arbitrary practices bedevil the notion of national integration and cohesion.

Overstaffed Administration

Anglophone secondary schools have become flooded with administrative positions (principals, vice principals, and discipline masters) occupied by Francophones who are appointed from the administrative capital, Yaoundé, with neither formal training in administration nor a record of teaching excellence. The main criteria for these appointments are nepotism, cronyism, tribalism, and corruption. In some schools, there are over 13 Vice Principals. Some of these administrators (especially Vice Principals and Senior Discipline Masters) could be classroom teachers filling the gaps created by teacher shortages in subjects like French, but they would rather lobby and acquire administrative posts because of the extra allowances and stipends that accompany these positions.

In some cases, administrators that are appointed to run schools in Southern Cameroons have absolutely no knowledge of the students or the Anglo-Saxon school cultures. For example, a report titled, *Reflection on the Anglophone Sub-System of Education in Cameroon* (2016), compiled by the Cameroon Education Forum (CEF) indicated that the principals of Southern Cameroonian schools such as Government High School (GHS) Idenau, GHS Konye, GHS Bafaka Balue, GHS Motombolombo, GSS Dibanda, Government Bilingual Secondary School (GBSS) 3-Corners Bekondo, were all Francophones whose initial contact with the Anglophone culture was through ministerial appointments. In the North West region, this occurrence was true of at least three schools, including GHS Kedjom Ketinguh. The absence of leadership that can provide proper oversight and accountability leads to a lack of motivation in teachers and poor academic outcomes for students. These administrators, who are far removed from the local populations in language and culture, can also not galvanize the kind of stakeholder participation that Parent Teacher Associations (PTAs) can bring to improve school-community relations and foster a conducive environment for children's education.

In addition to filling most upper administrative positions, Francophones also predominantly fill support staff positions such as security officers, storekeepers, drivers, cleaners, etc. Even when the government attempts to give a semblance of reciprocating by equally appointing a handful of Southern Cameroonians to run Francophone schools, Anglophones still remain apprehensive, perceiving these strategies as a ploy and an attempt to completely assimilate and annihilate the Anglophone minority that comprises only 20% of the population. Such apprehensions are valid, considering the discriminatory implementation of the bicultural policies in other areas of the Cameroonian civil society.

Abuse of Parent Teacher Association (PTA)

Parent Teacher Associations (PTAs) in the former British Southern Cameroons system were established to support teachers as co-partners in the education of students. The Republic of Cameroon government turned this organ on its head, and currently, the PTAs operate almost like public corporations that fund schools, without the voice to impact school policies. Civil administrators like Divisional Officers have been grafted into PTAs as permanent members, and although they do not participate in deliberations and operations, they often call the shots without consultation with the PTAs. Parents are taxed exorbitant levies as PTA fees, and some of the money is used to finance schools, recruit, and pay meager salaries to untrained teachers and other low-level support staff who are hired on a contract basis. Although these are attempts to mitigate the acute teacher shortages, this practice clearly violates the founding principles of PTAs.

The government has taken advantage of parents' eagerness to educate their children to shirk more of its own governmental responsibilities. The less the government does, the more financial tabs the PTAs pick up. So, currently, in many school districts, PTAs provide basic amenities like running water and electricity, building and laboratory equipment, libraries, classroom furniture, and sundry. This blurring of lines between the state and the PTAs reduces the quality of teaching, especially as untrained PTA recruits know that they have no job security, which further reduces teacher morale. Schools in poor districts are disadvantaged when parents in these mostly rural areas cannot afford the PTA levies and have to depend solely on government funding that is not forthcoming. In an attempt to check the abuse of PTAs and other nefarious practices used to fund schools, the government stepped in and grafted the PTAs, which are supposed to be voluntary associations, into the ministries of education, providing them some sort of ministerial statutes to make them appear as legitimate school funders.

CHAPTER 4

Designing Policy for Teacher Education

Designing and implementing effective policy for the teaching profession is imperative in meeting the challenges of both expansion and quality of education in Sub-Saharan Africa (SSA) in general and Southern Cameroons in particular. The teacher policy must provide a comprehensive framework that ensures the preparation of highly skilled and committed professionals and addresses the interrelated factors that impinge upon teacher job performance. Policies that efficiently address teacher quality and development must be integrative and contextually situated within a broader educational improvement agenda that includes cross sectors like infrastructure, curriculum, instruction, assessment, teaching and learning resources, school administration and supervision, a National Learning and Assessment Monitoring Mechanism, and other socioeconomic factors such as health, safety, and the needs for basic amenities for teachers. Some of these sectors lie beyond the scope of this book.

The Case of the Teaching Profession in Southern Cameroons

This chapter examines some specific areas of teacher recruitment, development, and deployment that can ensure that the teacher task force is responsive to a certain extent to the plethora of educational challenges currently existing in Southern Cameroons. These areas include: (a) proper recruitment, (b) adequate supply of teachers, (c) training systems that equip teachers with the required skills, (d) effective deployment, (e) career management that results in consistent teacher welfare and high-quality performance, (f) adequate remunerations, and (g) political will to reform and boost the education sector. It is understood that input models that address these areas as discreet entities cannot resolve current issues. A holistic and integrative approach that connects several government agencies, policymakers, state and district leaders, teacher education institutions, school principals, teachers, and stakeholders in the public sphere is recommended.

From a cursory look at the various areas listed, revamping and improving the quality of teacher education and deployment may seem formidable, but there is hope. Education is a global undertaking, and by comparing successful models around the world, SSA can borrow and contextualize strategies that meet each nation's economic and social imperatives.

Lessons from Singapore

Singapore offers a range of ideas and practices that can inform and shape policy design for many SSA countries, including Southern Cameroons. Singapore is a young nation that only became independent in 1965. Yet, for over a decade, Singapore, has been at or near the top of international measurements of students' performance in reading, math, and science, along with school systems in Asia such as South Korea, Taiwan, Japan, Hong Kong, and Finland. In 2016, Singapore topped global rankings in the Programme for International Student Assessment (PISA) tests run by the Organization of Economic Cooperation and Development (OECD), beating all other nations in the three subjects measured; and coming ahead of school systems across Asia, Europe, Australia, and North and South America that had existed long before its independence. How did Singapore accomplish this remarkable feat, going from one of the world's poorest countries with few natural resources and a mix of diverse cultures, ethnicities, religions, and languages, to becoming number one in education?

Very early in its nationhood, the founding fathers led by the visionary Prime Minister Lee Kuan Yew (2002), in *From Third World to First*, decided to place a high premium on developing the nation's human capital system. Education was highly prioritized, and teachers were regarded as "nation builders" whose role was central to the success of the entire nation. Teaching was accorded the prestige it deserved, schools were highly funded, and substantial investments were made in physical infrastructure, technology, and teacher salaries. There was a push to transform the nation from the pre-colonial model that focused simply on universal literacy and primary education (basic reading, writing, and essential math skills), to universal high school graduation and post-secondary success for all learners. Singapore has undergone four phases of its educational system, each building upon the advances of the previous phase. From 1959 to 1978, the first phase emphasized universal primary education and later universal lower secondary education. The second phase spanned 1979 to 1996 and was oriented toward creating different education pathways to produce a range of required market-relevant skills. From 1997 to 2011, the third phase repositioned the system to deliver the workforce needed to grow a knowledge-based economy. Presently, Singapore's focus is to produce a workforce with the skills and character needed to grow a twenty-first-century knowledge-based economy that will drive expanding companies and generate a more robust entrepreneurial sector. By honing on education, Singapore transitioned its economy from a low-skill, low-pay third-world nation in 1965 to a first-world economy today, which stands as the third richest country in the world, as measured by per capita gross domestic product (GDP). There are jobs for all graduates, and the national unemployment rate hovers around 1%. Singapore's economic success is largely credited to its emphasis on, and investment in education. The small city-state of 5.5 million people has 475,000 pre-tertiary students, 365 schools, 33,000 educators, and 34 students in an average classroom (National Institute of Education, Singapore). In 2013, Singapore spent about 8.7 billion USD on education (including teacher training), or roughly $18,300 per student (Reimers & O'Donnell, 2016).

 At independence, the government of Singapore made a strategic political decision to commit to a long-term, consistent, and sustainable approach to developing an economy based on knowledge and human talents. Education was the process through which such an economy could be cultivated and sustained. A high-quality teaching force and a rigorous career path to teaching were the key to unlocking that vision. The education system in Singapore is run by a hierarchical and integrated system between the Ministry of Education (MoE), the National Institute of Education (NIE) and the Academy of Singapore Teachers. Although centralized, these bodies are aligned and there is relative flexibility in the flow of initiatives from one organ to the other. The MoE is responsible for setting policy, providing direction, and developing the national curriculum; while the NIE is responsible for preparing the workforce—teachers, teacher leaders, school leaders, and others—to deliver on the policy directions set by the Ministry. Rotations between MoE and NIE are commonplace, with top-quality teachers often re-assigned between these institutions to ensure proper feedback and inform policy development, teacher training, and other conditions on the ground. School leaders expect to be reassigned to a new leadership post every five to six years, giving them opportunities to experience different school environments, student demographics, and grade levels. These rotations create a strong sense of system-wide accountability and establish a focus on the entire organization rather than on the independent actors that run them (Reimers & O'Donnell, 2016). SSA countries could learn a lot from the above teacher recruitment, training, and deployment models.

Problems with Teacher Recruitment and Training in Sub-Saharan Africa

As opposed to the integrated system of accountability that drives teacher recruitment and training in Singapore, there appears to be a lack of clear standards for teacher recruitment and development in many SSA countries. In case studies conducted to examine the issue of teacher supply, deployment, training, and management in eight Anglophone African nations: Eritrea, The Gambia, Lesotho, Liberia, Malawi, Uganda, Zambia, and Zanzibar between 2006 and 2008, Mulkeen (2010) discovered that "in all of the case-study countries there was a mismatch between the national requirement for new teachers and the output of newly qualified teachers" (p. 22).

In most of SSA, selection into teacher training is traditionally based mainly on academic performance, through writing and passing a competitive examination. As seen in the case of Southern Cameroons, the oral aspect in the form of interviews that can further screen candidates for suitability does not exist. In many countries, the processes of administering and grading written exams are not transparent and are often tainted with bribery, fraud, and biases. Teacher selection, mainly based on written exams, often favors students from more urban and higher socioeconomic backgrounds who are more likely to perform better academically. This cohort of students is also least likely to stay and pursue teaching in their long-term career goals and less willing to accept posts in remote rural schools. With no structures to motivate teacher performance or retain talents, attrition is often highest among these recruits.

Several factors must be considered to address the issue of inadequate recruitment of teachers. These include proper projection of student enrollment; clear policy on pupil-teacher ratio; clear statistics on the existing number of teachers, broken into their subject specialties; the annual teacher attrition rate; the annual output of newly trained teachers; and the wastage rate (the percentage of newly qualified teachers who do not take a teaching job (Carmela & Labate, 2016). Unfortunately, many African countries lack efficient Education Management Information Systems (EMIS) and the resources that can help link national education needs with regional, continental, and global partners (Mulkeen, 2010).

Lessons for SSA from Singapore on Teacher Recruitment and Deployment

As noted earlier, three competent structures manage education in Singapore: the MoE, NIE, and The Academy of Singapore Teachers. Recruiting and preparing teachers, master teachers, and principals is based on an organized and researched-based transparent process. This process emphasizes clarity between theory and practice, and coherence between policy and program implementation. Around the age of 11, students take the Primary School Leaving Exam (PSLE) in sixth grade. This examination determines the secondary school type of a student (high academic/pre-collegiate, academic/polytechnic, and technical/vocational).

Admission into teaching is through a highly competitive examination run by the NIE. The written examination is followed by interviews and demonstrations of the candidate's desired personal characteristics and values. Only the top third of students are eligible to become teachers, and only around 20% of applicants are accepted into teacher preparation programs. Entrance and progression through the national training program reflect the reported needs of the MoE and the schools. From the beginning of training, three differentiated career ladders are defined, allowing individuals to advance as master teachers, system leaders, or specialists, with new training conducted at each step. Tuition is free, and a job is guaranteed after successfully completing the teacher training program.

To attract a strong talent pool of candidates, starting salaries are roughly comparable to those for entry-level engineers; and top performers have opportunities for bonuses exceeding 25% of the base salary. First-year teachers have a reduced workload (80% of a standard load). All new teachers get 100 hours of professional development per year, and extensive mentorship from a senior teacher. The teaching profession is highly respected, and teachers are seen as nation-builders and innovators who are "expected to be creators of knowledge, facilitators of learning, architects of learning environments, shapers of character, and leaders of educational change" (Reimers & O'Donnell, 2016, p. 113).

Obviously, designing effective policy for SSA countries would require an integrated and coherent approach that encompasses various sectors connected with teacher education: governance, recruitment, education and training of personnel, skills development, access and equity, assessment, financing, and political will. As in the case of Singapore, an efficient, coherent, governance and leadership system is a condition sine qua non for effective education management. "Education is not apolitical in Singapore" (Reimers & O'Donnell, 2016, p. 121). Unlike Singapore, where there is a clear political will and partnerships across systems to boost educational outputs, most SSA countries have top-down, highly centralized, overly bureaucratic systems of government that do not promote efficient sharing of roles between the government and the different partners in education (public and private sectors, parents, civil society, labor unions, and communities).

Cameroon, like many other former French colonies, has a highly centralized system of government designed to facilitate control from

France. Any notion of decentralization between departments consists of de-concentration and segmentation of sub-sectors that lack complementarity. Two ministries are in charge of Education: the Ministry of Basic Education and the Ministry of Secondary Education (referred to as the Center). Both ministries are financed by the Ministry of Budget and Finance. Regional delegations of education mainly implement the vision and regulations defined by the central ministries that directly influence education development within the regions and monitor finances. Consequently, even deconcentrating is not effective since regional delegations do not have the financial autonomy to make decisions that result in critical educational outcomes. Information and vision are not articulated in a two-way upstream-downstream model like that in Singapore. This creates a weak and ineffective compact between the policy maker, the education provider, and the beneficiaries, and of course, a lack of coherence and integration in the development initiatives among various sub-sectors. The teacher education sector is fraught with political interference and irregular conduct in examinations, financing, and infrastructure.

Policy Guidelines for Southern Cameroons

A decentralized system will hold more promise for efficiency and accountability. This is especially crucial at the secondary levels where there is a high need for strategic recruitment and deployment of content area teachers. The ministerial system that manages education needs to be overhauled. An inter-ministerial approach is required to harness the variety of skills and resources needed to systematically redress the educational and socioeconomic failures of the nation. Ministries of Education (MoE) especially, need to be completely transformed from mainly bureaucratic entities into learning organizations, with the Department of Human Resource Management (HRM) acting as a central part of its activities. The role of the MoEs needs to be redefined to include the following tasks:

- Decentralize the appointment of upper administration, such as principals, to regions and counties to eliminate nepotism and ensure strict adherence to criteria on minimum qualifications of members of these bodies.

- Establish a teacher education directorate to coordinate the development of teacher education nationally.
- Establish a clear national picture of the authorized/approved personnel/staff for various levels of the education sector.
- Establish a system to recognize appropriate qualifications for permanent appointments in specific educator posts.
- Establish a department to evaluate qualifications for employment as teachers at technical colleges, Adult Basic Education, and Training Centers.
- Assign Relative Education Qualification Values (REQV) to qualifications recognized for employment in education.
- Design appropriate curricula and list required subjects/fields for Teacher Education Programs.
- Create a list of all vacancy levels, considering operational requirements, geographical context (counties), gender balance requirements, age profile of existing staff, experience and skill profiles of existing staff, and staff required by areas of specialization.
- Establish clear staffing norms taking into consideration all emerging issues, and recruit sufficient and qualified personnel for the education sector at all levels.
- Implement a policy of individual performance contracting linked to annual appraisal and performance pay.
- Evaluate foreign qualifications for employment in education.
- Develop an effective Human Resource management policy throughout the MoE that ensures qualified officials are provided with opportunities for acceptable work-life balance.
- Engage in ongoing in-depth study of teacher education in Southern Cameroons focusing on improving the quality of teachers and teacher educators.
- Develop and implement a nationally approved teacher education policy that centers on Continuing Professional Development (CPD) for teachers and teacher educators.
- Establish a Teacher Service Commission (TSC) to implement a scheme for all teachers and teacher trainers to develop their own

personal CPD plan for two years, allowing for self- and external monitoring, support, and performance-based remuneration.
- Fund CPD based on annual grants to teachers for the exclusive use to buy validated CPD training services; require TSC to manage the CPD process and account for the relevant expenditure annually.
- Require regions to monitor all CPD training for fitness of purpose and assign credit points to each training package, which may be used as credits toward higher diploma or degree awards.
- Make Information and Communication Technology (ICT) a priority area for all teachers by integrating ICT into education, building capacity, and encouraging teachers and administrators to use technology in planning, teaching, and monitoring.
- Provide appropriate and sufficient equipment facilities (for example, connectivity, power) and services to facilitate the use of ICT.
- Create mobile and online education and training platforms and accessibility to make teacher training accessible to all students regardless of their circumstances and locations.
- Expand and improve infrastructure and learning and training facilities especially in rural and other underserved areas.
- Develop quality and relevant, and effective teaching and learning materials.
- Build teachers' capacity for developing and using school-based learning assessment tools, specifically to acquire literacy, numeracy, and inquiry skills.
- Establish organs for scientific research to meet local and global intercontinental challenges as well as technological innovation, creativity, and entrepreneurship that promote global competitiveness. Support educational research and dissemination.
- Provide good remunerations and working and living conditions to teachers in order to enhance their status and value in society.

Adequate Supply and Effective Deployment

Management of teacher supply and quality control in Southern Cameroons will require a multiple-pronged systemic approach that addresses

(a) proper recruitment; (b) adequate supply of teachers; (c) training systems that equip teachers with the required skills; (d) effective deployment; and (e) career management and monitoring that result in consistent, high-quality performance by teachers. Like most SSA countries, Cameroon must develop its own education management system that facilitates data collection, analysis, and dissemination of information to improve the educational sector in all regions, especially in Southern Cameroons.

A comprehensive approach is needed to address the specific challenges that plague the Southern Cameroonian educational sub-system. Recruitment processes in TTC must be revamped, beginning with recruitment to deployment. Admission criteria must be made more rigorous and transparent, and be based on merit, not nepotism (the recruitment of one's relatives outside the established vetting processes); and favoritism (the recruitment of one's friends and known individuals without vetting against established criteria or standards) (Hallak & Poisson, 2005). To ensure that all admissions are offered openly and fairly, the policy should have the force of law behind it. Admission and local authorities must comply, with the policies and consequences for non-compliance clearly spelled out.

Appropriate measures must also be implemented to expand access and enhance equity between male and female candidates, rural and urban dwellers, the poor, and those with disabilities, especially at secondary levels. Other discriminatory practices against vulnerable populations, such as those with known diseases like HIV/AIDS, must be abolished.

Standards and Benchmarks for Performance

Several competencies must be established as prerequisites for admission into teaching programs. These competencies should include practical, foundational, reflexive competencies, and standards/ethics for educators. Appropriate standards must be established across institutions, and consistently and coherently implemented.

Curriculums in teacher training institutions should be designed to provide pre-service teachers the adequate skills and dispositions necessary to perform their profession upon graduation effectively. The main scope of the curriculum should ensure that teaching and learning outcomes optimize mastery and control of instructional and learning theories that candidates can deploy upon completion. While some schools and regional agencies appear to have some standards, these are not often comprehensive enough to support ongoing improvement in training outcomes. Specific teaching and learning objectives of pre-service teacher candidates should include the following competencies, upon completion:

- Demonstration of profound mastery of theories of instruction, learning and child psychology.
- Employment of evidence-based and results-driven methods in classroom management and lesson planning which foster a blend of child-centered approaches that can inspire active student engagement and creativity.
- Demonstrate the ability to use ICT tools and contemporary teaching methods in lesson planning and teaching.
- Successful completion of at least three months of practicum prior to graduation.
- Differentiation of programs for various groups of teachers: PTA-employed, interns, general education instructors, substitute teachers, credentialed educators (especially those in newer fields such as Special Education), and foreign credentialed teachers.
- Adequate personnel training in teacher training institutions and their responsibilities clearly defined.
- Adequate provision of resources to all teachers and administrative personnel in teacher training institutions to effectively develop, analyze, and communicate expectations to those in their care.
- Proper documentation of criteria for evaluation in collaboration with practicing teachers and administrators in elementary and secondary schools.
- Inclusion of school inspectors as part of the training process for teachers.
- Upgrading of the role of the PTAs and proper orientation that positions them in the role of improving quality of education, rather than simply filling financial gaps in recruitment initiatives.
- Set in place a structured system to ensure appropriate and

proportionate teacher deployment that considers the needs and educational outcomes in various regions. Teacher shortages are typically higher in remote parts of the country than in bigger towns and cities; therefore, designing standardized recruitment protocols that consider contextual factors is a must.

Some SSA nations have developed several effective strategies to address the challenge of deploying teachers to difficult locations from which Southern Cameroons can learn. These strategies include:
- Using financial incentives for aspects like housing or rapid promotion to attract teachers to difficult locations.
- Implementing location-specific recruitment systems, that provide teachers with some choice of location.
- Targeting pre-service teacher candidates who are more likely to accept positions in geographical areas with the greatest need and getting a commitment from them to teach a certain number of years in such locations before seeking transfers.

When financial incentives were introduced in The Gambia, ranging up to 17.5% of the salary, based on the geographical location where a teacher was posted, there was a positive impact on deployment to these areas. In 2006, the introduction of hardship allowance, which considered factors like distance from school to main road, was also introduced. The allowances ranged from 30% to 40% of the base salary, depending on the region. Both allowances were paid simultaneously and could potentially bump a teacher's salary in certain regions up to 57% higher than in others. Within two years, 42% of teachers who did not receive those incentives had asked for transfers to hardship schools, indicating that the initiative was working (Carmela & Labate, 2016). In Zambia, teachers in overcrowded urban schools were allowed to teach double shifts for an extra 20% incentive on their salaries, a sort of equivalence for the allowance provided for those working in rural locations.

Including some choice in selecting a location in the recruitment practices may actually have an advantage, as this can enable some teachers to work in areas closer to their hometowns where they have relatives. This would increase the probability of retention, especially for female teachers whose families often worry about safety issues when sent to faraway places.

Countries like Lesotho, Zambia, and Uganda have all had positive experiences in location-specific recruitment. Jobs in specific locations are advertised locally, and candidates can choose what school in the location they would like to work in. Although most candidates may still want to select urban areas, once positions in those schools are filled, they can choose to work in local vicinities where they have relatives and other attractions. In Lesotho, advertising jobs locally, to only candidates willing to work in those regions has increased the retention rate and reduced wastage, compared to when the Ministry of Education Sports (MoES) mandated deployment to completely strange locations.

Career Management and Monitoring

Proper school functioning depends on teachers being present in the classrooms and spending enough time on instructional tasks. Administrators must establish procedures for evaluating and improving teacher performance. Common, mutually generated, and agreed-upon criteria to monitor teacher performance, especially at primary levels with no rigorous end-of-cycle examinations, are critical in improving teacher quality. Performance must be documented and reported regularly to enable administrators to track instructional quality and provide feedback for improvement. Consequences for notoriously poor performance must also be established, and other attitudes, such as chronic absenteeism, must be stamped out.

An effective system of incentives for good performance and sanctions to address shortcomings and violations of the standards at the school level is crucial for improving teacher management and maintaining quality. Administrators also need proper resources, such as well-equipped offices and knowledge and skills for management, data maintenance, and analysis, to effectively perform their roles. Stakeholders in education, the community, and parents must be given a voice to share their perspectives and participate effectively in service delivery (Banerjee et al., 2008).

Ongoing professional development (PD) should be an integral part of teaching. This is especially necessary to support contract teachers whom the PTA hires. PTAs have significantly improved the recruitment and deployment of teachers, especially at primary levels. If properly managed, the practice can significantly meet the current mass recruitment needs in many rural areas. Three studies conducted in South Africa (Kanjee, 2009), Zambia (Kapambwe, 2010), and Malawi (Miske, 2003) indicated that when in-service teachers were trained in the use of specific formative assessments to evaluate students' comprehension, their teaching and classroom instruction improved. More than 80% of experienced teachers who attended the workshops were using techniques taught during PD to collect data on students' learning and provide targeted instructional interventions. Data collected on student performance from these studies also suggested that the training positively impacted students' performance in mathematics and English language.

Better working conditions should be established for teachers in consultation with Teacher Unions and other related organs. Some conditions that impact teachers' morale and welfare include: class sizes and pupil-teacher ratio (PTR), hours of work, workload that allows for work-life balance, school infrastructure, adequate instructional resources, and effective school governance and management, that create school and classroom environment conducive to teacher health and safety, clear guidelines for student behavior and discipline, clear guidelines for professional roles and responsibilities, and autonomy and control (Carmela & Labate, 2016, p. 41).

Financing

Financial resources must be mobilized to meet the growing teacher needs and be efficiently distributed to improve results, reduce waste, and stamp out fraud. Inadequate resources result in underfunding in almost all education sectors, forcing parents to assume heavy financial responsibilities. Fund flows are usually uniform, from the center to the regions, without a clear pattern of correspondence and attention to needs variations in given areas. This renders budget planning, accountability, and reporting difficult, creating room for surplus and duplication in some areas and insufficient funds in others.

Of course, teachers' salaries and remunerations must be more attractive and comparable to those of other professions, such as medicine and engineering. This will improve the prestige of the profession and help boost motivation and retention of quality teachers. The main policy thrust for teacher training and deployment is to prepare new teachers with the necessary skills to be effective classroom practitioners at the start of their teaching assignment, wherever that assignment is. To meet these and other objectives, teacher training programs should provide differentiated pre-service and concurrent training for the following groups of teachers: county-employed teachers, interns, general education teachers, substitute teachers, credentialed educators who are new to neglected fields such as Special Education, and foreign credentialed teachers.

CHAPTER 5

Early Childhood Development and Education

In 2011, UNESCO adopted the International Standard Classification for Education (ISCED) to categorize educational levels and better understand educational outcomes at each level from a global perspective. Early Childhood Education (ECE) and pre-primary education were classified as level 0. Early childhood education is designed for children from birth to two years, while pre-primary refers to children from ages three to the start of primary school. Early childhood education settings are also referred to as early childhood education and development (ECED), play school, reception, pre-primary, pre-school, or daycare centers (UNESCO, Institute for Statistics (IUS), 2011). Early Childhood Education (ECE) refers to programs with an intentional education component that introduce young children to organized instruction outside the family context. These programs provide effective, caring practices that integrate family and community resources to ensure the young child's cognitive, emotional, social, and physical development, nurture their skills for society, and prepare them for school participation. Several studies in the United States indicate that ECE settings present the ideal out-of-home environments for children to interact with other children and adults through play and connections with the academic curriculum (Albright et al., 2011; Downer et al., 2010). Therefore, governments must invest in early childhood education because this environment ensures readiness and builds the confidence to prepare young children for school and a successful life.

Lessons from the United States of America

Some early childhood programs in the United States (US) include:

1). The Early HeadStart and HeadStart programs which are federally funded. Both programs target low-income families and are run by the Department of Health Services (DHS), also referred to as the Department of Health and Human Services (HHS). The Early HeadStart program is focused on teaching pregnant women about child development and enrolling children under three years, while HeadStart enrolls mostly three- to four-year-olds and supports them in their growth and development through individualized learning experiences.

2). The Montessori Preschool program was developed by educator and physician Maria Montessori. The Montessori program aims to develop the child's character, academic ability, and practical life skills through hands-on learning guided by the teacher.

3). The Waldorf Preschool program was founded based on the teachings of the Austrian writer Rudolf Steiner. This program focuses on nurturing the body, spirit, and soul of the child through hands-on and creative group learning. Teachers must be trained and certified in Waldorf teaching methods.

4). The Reggio Emilia Preschool program came into existence in the 1940s. This approach emphasizes self-expression and exploration and the community. Students in this program are allowed to self-direct their own learning and pursue their interests through artistic activities and projects that reflect their own ideas and interests. There is no formal curriculum, and the teacher does not need to have any specific training or credential, but should provide guidance through observations based on theory and practice of the program.

5). The HighScope Preschool Program is a structured and well-organized program where children learn through active participation. Its well-structured academic components, which include reading, math, and science, are based on child development research and theories.

6). The Bank Street Preschool program bases its educational philosophy on the theories of the educational researcher, John Dewey. This program focuses on the child's emotional, physical, social, and mental development through active, self-directed learning and hands-on experiences. Dramatic play and using other resources like building blocks, clay, and puzzles are integral to teaching and learning.
7). The Parent Co-Op Preschool Program incorporates daily parental involvement into the child's education. Children and parents learn together through hands-on, nurturing interactions that promote problem-solving and conflict-resolution skills among preschoolers. Parents are also highly involved in the school's operations and serve in many administrative positions and on the board of directors.

Two components run through most preschool programs described above: (a) exploration and discovery, where the child leads their own learning, and (b) academics, where the child builds foundations for the curriculum in early primary grades.

Because there is cross-classification from ECE to pre-primary, and even early primary grades in terms of age group, orientation, mode, and content of learning, as well as other variables, it is necessary to properly align early childhood education and care (ECE) programs with early primary education. In 2015, the State of Massachusetts in the United States set up a task force to align and integrate the ECE curriculum within multiple standards and curriculum goals in early primary grades. The task force invited input from various professionals (psychologists, higher education faculty and students, family childcare providers, preschool special educators, universal preschool teachers, kindergarten teachers, public school principals, mental health consultants, and community childcare and nursery school directors). One of the main objectives of the task force was to:

> have all children from birth through third grade develop and maintain trusting, healthy, positive interactions and relationships with both adults and peers; develop a positive

sense of self and self-efficacy; express a healthy range of emotions in socially and culturally appropriate ways; understand the role of social interactions and develop the skills needed to regulate attention, impulse and behavior (Massachusetts Department of Elementary and Secondary Education (DESE), 2015a, p. 2).

The Massachusetts Department of Elementary and Secondary Education (DESE), in collaboration with the Department of Early Education and Care (EEC), developed and approved the curriculum standards and guidelines for *Preschool and Kindergarten in the Domains of Social and Emotional Learning, and Approaches to Play and Learning* (Massachusetts DESE, 2015b). Such collaboration is founded on research and evidenced-based practice, indicating a positive connection between young children's emotional and social development and positive academic outcomes through school and later success in life (Domitrovich et al., 2013; US Department of HHS, 2010). The Standards for Preschool and Kindergarten *Social and Emotional Learning, and Approaches to Play and Learning* provide guidelines for Social-Emotional learning in the five areas of emphasis: self-awareness (emotional expression, self-perception, self-efficacy), self-management (impulse control and self-management), social awareness (empathy, respect for others and diversity), relationship skills (communication, relationship building, conflict management, seeking help), and responsible decision making (Massachusetts DESE, 2015b).

In designing early childhood education, much attention must be placed on creating appropriate environments that are responsive to children's social and emotional needs, and support learning and development in academic curriculum areas. The State of Massachusetts provides guidelines for *Building Supportive Environments* that enhance children's social and emotional learning. The environments include: (a) the learning environment (b) the social environment, (c) the physical environment, and (d) the temporal environment. Guidelines are also provided on fostering rich play, family engagements, and building young children's cultural competencies. The Massachusetts DESE (2015a) guidelines for supportive environments are summarized below.

Massachusetts Guidelines for Supportive Early Childhood Environments
The Learning Environment

The learning environment can be a school, a center, or a home; and it incorporates both indoor and outdoor activities. Adults play a vital role in this environment and in their relationships with children. A rich and supportive learning environment promotes children's development in all domains (cognitive, emotional, social, and physical developmental); through warm interactions between adults and children; and children and peers. Using proper materials and resources, this environment should stimulate children's investigative and exploratory skills.

The Social Environment

Positive interactions in the learning environment build trust that positively impacts children's learning and behavior. "Young children benefit from opportunities to develop ongoing, trusting relationships with adults outside the family and with other children. Notably, positive teacher-child relationships promote children's learning and achievement, as well as social competence and emotional development" (National Association for the Education of Young Children (NAEYC), 2009; qtd. in Massachusetts DESE, 2015a).

Adults who work with young children in and out of the classroom (for example, family support professionals, librarians, nurses, specialists, bus drivers, cafeteria staff, etc.) support and enhance learning and serve as role models. They should, therefore, be included in professional development so that together, they can help build strong and caring relationships with children that promote healthy development.

The Physical Environment

The physical environment includes the types of materials, equipment, furniture, and the arrangements and organization of these in learning centers that promote rich and purposeful play.

The Temporal Environment

The temporal environment includes all parts of the day and how this is efficiently planned so that students can spend adequate time learning, playing, resting, socializing, and transitioning from one activity to the next. Proper structuring of temporal time should consider planned and unplanned activities; quiet and problem-solving time should be flexible to accommodate students' strengths and weaknesses.

Play

Play is a voluntary activity for its own sake because it is enjoyable. Through play, young children represent their knowledge of the world by using their imaginations to explore, discover, negotiate, and solve problems. Learning occurs through play as children use various materials, understand their characteristics, manipulate them, and explore how to use them.

Play can be through dramatization, visual arts, movement, dance, constructions, storytelling, drawing, writing, etc. Teachers can provide scaffolding by modeling, coaching, and prompting to produce a blend of enjoyment and learning during play. They can also use structured play engagements to observe and assess children's understanding of concepts. Such assessments may help teachers set new goals and plan subsequent learning experiences to advance children's cognitive, social-emotional, or relationship skills.

Family Engagements

Creating positive partnerships with family and the community is important in empowering parents as their child's first teacher. Good partnerships also facilitate transitions between school and home environments and maintain consistency with what is learned at school, which enhances children's development. Family engagement includes inviting families to share their cultures at school and incorporating children's home culture into the school curriculum. Families that feel welcome at school are more likely to be actively involved in their children's education both at home and in school (Albright et al., 2011).

Building Cultural Competencies

Culture can be defined as "a shared system of meaning, which includes values, beliefs, and assumptions expressed in daily interactions of individuals within a group through a definite pattern of language, behavior, customs, attitudes, and practices" (Maschinot, 2008). Cultures are different yet have some similarities and shared values (for example, love, caring, sharing, friendships, etc.). Educators can help children understand, accept, and embrace various perspectives and outlooks without judgments or stereotyping. Teachers must also be aware of their own cultural norms and how these may affect their interactions with children, as well as their teaching.

Young children's competencies in the domains of social and emotional learning and their approaches to play and learning are critical to their success as learners later in life. It is on this premise that investment in early childhood education is important, since the whole society stands to benefit from it. The National Scientific Council on the Developing Child (2004) summarizes the importance of early childhood education as follows "The foundations of social competence that are developed in the first five years are linked to emotional well-being and affect later ability to functionally adapt in school and to form successful relationships throughout life." More on guidelines and developmental domains for early childhood education can be found in the *Interactive Head Start Early Learning Outcomes Framework: Ages Birth to Five* (US HHS, 2010; 2024).

The State of Early Childhood Education in Sub-Saharan Africa

Early childhood education in Sub-Saharan Africa (SSA) is an area that needs urgent attention. Statistics on *The State of Education in Africa*, by the Africa-America Institute (AAI) (2015), indicate that SSA lags far behind other parts of the world in ECE and pre-primary education. While 104 million children were enrolled in pre-primary education worldwide in 2012, only 11 million had been enrolled in SSA in 2008. Although there were some expansions in enrollment over the years, by 2012, only 20% of young children in Africa were enrolled in ECE programs; falling way short of the 80% or more target. While there are some expansions in a few countries, eight out of the ten countries with the lowest ECE are in SSA, placing SSA at the lowest net ECE enrollment rate in the world.

The Case of Southern Cameroons: Problem Diagnoses

In Southern Cameroons, ECE and Pre-primary education appear to be the least developed levels of education. There is a total lack of government oversight for creating and approving kindergarten and primary schools, leaving this sector mainly in the hands of private providers. Ministry officials often base approval for authorization of kindergarten services on cronyism, bribery, and corruption; thus, enabling greedy business people to operate in the most deplorable circumstances. Facilities often operate in old, dilapidated, poorly maintained infrastructures and lack minimal recreation, hygiene, and safety facilities. Due to this sector's absence of regulation and policies, most kindergarten and pre-primary programs lack trained teachers, structured curricula, and proper materials and pedagogical resources.

The lack of regulations and policy on target age or other cognitive indicators for admission into existing programs has created a negative domino effect that starts from the early childhood level and cascades down to all levels of education in Southern Cameroons. For example, there is an expectation of a two-year duration for nursery schools (which ISCED stipulates is from age three years and up), but the lack of age stipulation has resulted in the admission of premature children as young as two years old into what is called, "prenursery." These facilities are basically babysitting these children in terms of the services provided and have no educational component. Yet, after attending these usually quite costly centers, parents skip kindergarten altogether, and enroll their children directly into primary school. The direct consequence is that underage children, less than five years old, attend primary school (which ISCED states should start at age six years and no less than five years old). These children subsequently move into the rest of the education levels (secondary and university) and are usually developmentally and cognitively unprepared.

Policy Guidelines for Early Childhood Education

Designing policy for ECE will start from reviewing any rudimentary guidelines, standards, and regulations that may have been ignored, and integrating them with effective policies that exist elsewhere (such as in the United States), with a view to arriving at clear standards and articles governing the ECE sub-sector. Borrowing from other systems and contextualizing to suit local needs is unavoidable. NAEYC and other sources in this chapter may provide useful guidelines for designing early childhood policy, training early childhood educators, and providing families with resources for effective early childhood development and care. The overarching objective is to provide equitable access to good-quality, child-friendly Early Child Development Education (ECDE) that improves opportunities for all children in the first cycle of education to succeed at kindergarten, primary, and junior high school levels.

Given the dismal state of ECE and lack of even minimal resources in most programs in Southern Cameroons, policy guidelines to regulate this sector must include the following:

- provision of equitable access to good-quality, child-friendly environment for all children at kindergarten and pre-primary;
- mainstreaming ECDE to facilitate effective transition into primary education in all parts of the country;
- provision of free ECDE based on the unit cost of providing such services at this level, while considering specific standards for school inputs, including teachers, teaching and learning materials, and capacity building;
- increased government financing of ECE services;
- creation of funding modalities for ECE that include start-up grants, capitation grants, school feeding, maintenance, and development of infrastructure;
- recruitment, training, deployment, and proper remuneration of teachers;
- ECE centers to meet a pupil-teacher ratio (PTR) target of 25:1;
- implementation of free and compulsory ECE for all children ages four to five years;

- enforcement of the provisions of the Constitution of child-friendly learning environments;
- promotion of nutritional and health programs at ECE Centers in collaboration with the line Ministries of health, agriculture, and other stakeholders;
- monitoring and ensuring proper transition from ECE to primary education across the country;
- establishing clear criteria for registration of ECE centers and the regulation of fees charged in private ECE centers;
- strengthening partnerships for the development of ECE services through several incentives with private investors;
- identifying and allocating capitation grants for children with special needs and planning for special ECE centers and accommodations in inclusive settings that offer services;
- reviewing the financing of ECE to ensure that ECE funding becomes sustainable, including teacher education curriculum support;
- mobilization of funding for the introduction of appropriate Information and Communication Technology (ICT) across all ECE centers and engage stakeholders;
- ensuring that all primary schools have an ECE unit; and
- providing continuous professional development (PD) to principals, administrators, teachers, and other personnel of ECE so that they can continue to provide effective early learning opportunities that meet the cognitive, emotional, and other developmental needs of early PK-3 grade students.

These goals will provide supportive ECE environments that help young children develop strong foundational language, literacy, cognitive, social, and other essential skills necessary for success in future educational engagements and full participation in society.

CHAPTER 6

Basic Education
Also Known as Elementary or Primary Education in the Lower Grades

The International Standard Classification of Education (ISCED) (UNESCO, Institute for Statistics (IUS), 2011) defines basic education as comprising the two stages of primary education and lower secondary education. ISCED stipulates that age is typically the only entry requirement at this level, with the legal age placed at not below five or above seven years old. Primary education is usually the first level of basic education and typically lasts six years (for example, first to sixth grade), until the child is aged 10 to 12 years. In some countries like Finland, basic education includes lower secondary levels up to age 16 (first grade to ninth grade). Primary education is designed to provide students with fundamental literacy and numeracy skills, and to establish a solid foundation for learning more complex and specialized information at the lower secondary and upper secondary education levels.

The State of Primary Education in Sub-Saharan Africa

With the launching of the 2000 United Nations Millennium Development Goals (MDG), many African nations took important steps toward achieving universal primary education (UPE) by 2015. *The State of Education in Africa*, by the Africa-America Institute (AAI) (2015), notes that Sub-Saharan Africa (SSA) demonstrated the greatest improvement in primary education enrollment compared to other regions of the world, doubling primary school enrollment between 1990 and 2012, from 62 million to 149 million. However, SSA is also the world's poorest region with the fastest-growing population, making progress in steady primary education expansion elusive.

Sociopolitical Context of Southern Cameroons Primary Education

The factors affecting primary education in Southern Cameroons are varied and complex, comprising many overlapping issues, including socioeconomic constraints, institutional ineptitude, and the lack of political will. In the 1970s and 1980s, Cameroon had one of Africa's most effective educational systems, with a literacy rate higher than most other countries in SSA. A major contributing factor to this high literacy rate was the fact that Southern Cameroons' colonial education heritage placed a high value on education. This period also coincided with the period when Cameroon as a whole, experienced significant economic growth and development with real gross domestic product (GDP) growth of 13% annually, primarily due to increases in the prices of agricultural products and petroleum (Government of Cameroon, AFTED, 2012). As prices for these commodities dropped worldwide, revenues declined, and in the 2000s, Cameroon became a highly indebted poor country (HIPC) that was eligible for financial aid.

In 2003, the country established a framework for development by producing a Poverty Reduction Strategic Plan (PRSP) that outlined macroeconomic, structural, and social policies and programs to support growth and reduce poverty. This initiative was unsuccessful, mainly due to mismanagement and widespread corruption. As national revenue declined, education development became uneven, with periods of growth and decline that reflected and were similar to the economy. Although there have been sporadic areas of improvement in the basic education sector, with gross enrollment rates (GER) reaching almost 100% in some parts of the country as opposed to 30% in secondary education, these rates do not tell a comprehensive story of the state of primary education in all of Cameroon. Nation-wide, the primary completion rate increased from 59% in 2004 to 72% in 2008, and the repetition rate decreased from 22% to about 18%, respectively. Still, these apparent improvements hide differences in regional education performance, and mask significant flaws in the educational system of the country as a whole and Southern Cameroons in particular. For example, a 2004 study found that elementary schools had an attendance rate of 2.9 million students; but there were only 1.8 million seats for the almost 3 million students, making learning in such conditions impossible. Fewer girls than boys attend primary schools; mainly due to cultural factors like early marriages, pregnancy, and hands needed to do domestic chores that cause girls to stay at home. Traditional biases against educating girls still exist in many rural areas. The failure of the educational sector in Southern Cameroons must not only be examined within the anachronistic paradigm of scarcity of financial resources but must go beyond that and be situated within the framework of political ill will that the predominantly Francophone central administration has shown toward this region of the country, which is mainly characterized by bad governance dating from the time of the 1961 reunification with Francophone Cameroon.

Problems with Southern Cameroons Basic Education System: A Diagnosis

The main issues with the Southern Cameroons basic education sector can be outlined as follows:

Persistent Policy Snags

Soon after reunification, in 1962/1963, the federal government attempted to restructure and "harmonize" the two sub-systems of education. This attempt failed primarily because the UNESCO team leading the talks could not reach a consensus because the Francophone majority viewed proposals for harmonization as biased. Subsequent attempts at "harmonization" in 1966, 1968, 1971, 1973, 1976, 1983, 1988, and 1989 equally failed, mainly because the reforms were never implemented; as they were viewed by Francophones as skewed favorably toward the Anglo-Saxon system of education, standards, and values. The aversion toward the Anglo-Saxon educational system came to the forefront when, in 2004, the government, without consultations, suddenly passed a decree harmonizing the two systems in a manner that was overwhelmingly skewed toward the

Francophone sub-system of education. The Anglophone primary school system was restructured from seven to six years to match the number of years of school attendance of the Francophone primary school system. The law stipulated that the Francophone lower and upper secondary cycles would move from four 4 + 3 years to 5 + 2 years to match the Southern Cameroonian secondary and high school durations; however, this cosmetic provision never went into effect.

The forced harmonization of the two sub-systems (Francophone and Anglophone) has weakened the quality of primary education in Southern Cameroons. The reduction of primary school years of attendance in 2004 from seven to six years has hurt the mathematics, English, history, and geography syllabi of Classes 5 and 6 students and created cognitive gaps that prevent students from making a smooth transition from Class 6 to Form 1 of secondary school. A revision in the school curriculum did not accompany the reduction to ensure that students met the competencies required to complete primary school. This resulted in many repeaters in Form 1 because a whole year of school appeared to have been skipped, with no provision for transition into the secondary cycle. The high repetition rate of Form 1 students has caused a significant psychological impact on students, added financial burdens on parents, and increased the school dropout rate. Parents have tried to stave off the impact of the shoddy harmonization project by paying for private "make-up" classes in the early mornings and late evenings for their children; and this has further increased the financial and psychological burdens of education on both parents and students.

Another consequence of the shoddy and ill-conceived "harmonization" project is the overload of the school curriculum with too many subjects, some of which are further split into smaller units of study that seem irrelevant. Sixth grade, for example, has 19 subjects on the syllabus, while the nursery level has about 13 subjects. For example, the nursery school curriculum includes: Music, Information and Communication Technology (ICT), National Culture, Civics, Environmental Studies, and other subjects taught to students without any attempt at integration and using ineffective pedagogical procedures that do not foster understanding across these subject areas. Pedagogical methods are limited to forcing students to memorize words, terms, and definitions, and regurgitate them in examinations. The overloaded syllabi do not consider students' physical and cognitive development and often have no clear emphasis on basic skills in numeracy and literacy, which are very important at this level. Young children log heavy school bags to and from school daily, partially due to the absence of resources like proper desks and lockers for students in which they can store their belongings. Parents often have difficulty understanding students' progress reports because of the cacophony of subjects that seem to have no bearing on real life.

In 1967 and 1974, the government created two research institutes, Institutes de Pedagogiques Applique a Vocation Rurale (IPAR). IPAR-Yaounde was created in 1967, and IPAR-Buea was created in 1974, ostensibly with the objectives of conducting educational research and designing and implementing curriculum development for the basic education sector (see Lallez, 1974). A Presidential Order No.277/CAB/PR of October 10, 1974, followed the creation of IPAR-Buea, and outlined four distinct departments for the institute:

- Environmental Studies, (Agricultural and Social Aspects),
- English Language,
- Mathematics, and
- Village Technology (Intermediate Technology).

The creation of IPAR-Buea was a joint undertaking between the Cameroon government and the United Nations Development Programme (UNDP)/United Nations Educational, Scientific, and Cultural Organization (UNESCO) that provided both the financial and human resources to set up the program. The British Council also provided bilateral aid to implement the projects and was poised to collaborate closely with the Cameroonian research team. The work was to be done in two phases: phase one involved extensive research on community needs and expectations in order to make recommendations to the government as to the nature and the form of the reform needed for primary education, while phase two was to use the data collected in phase one, to produce educational materials, and to write textbooks and training materials for primary schools. Based on research conducted in schools and communities of the Northwest, Southwest Region, and Western Regions, I.P.A.R wrote a report in 1977 titled "Report on the Reform of Primary Education." The report, which called for significant changes in curricula, structures, organization, examination processes, teaching methods, and other pedagogical practices of primary teachers, was sent to the government in June 1977. The report's central theme was to prepare pupils during their primary school years to become integrated in their communities and be useful and productive members of those communities. It recommended, among other things, that education should be flexible and take note of differences in pupils' abilities, environments, and social and economic backgrounds. In order to accomplish these goals, a new structure of education based on the concept of community development should be adopted. Therefore, education should:

- meet economic and social needs,
- promote equity, equality, and justice,
- provide more open access to crucial selection processes,
- provide opportunities for further learning, and
- provide the necessary facilities for effective education (IPAR, Buea 1977, p. 8).

Following the report, National syllabi were drawn and submitted to the government for approval. Teaching guides were also prepared for years one to four, and tried out in pilot schools and Teacher Training Colleges (TTC). These initiatives were in preparation for phase two, when the large-scale implementation of recommendations and pilot studies would begin.

Phase two never took off. The syllabi produced failed to meet expected standards and were never approved. In 1989, the mission of both IPARs came to an abrupt end, with nothing to show for its existence, except an extensive drainage on public funds. Resolutions of the "goodwill" education law enacted by the government in 1998 have only been partially implemented, mostly to preserve the Francophone culture and dismantle the Anglophone sub-system of education. Most curriculum reforms and syllabi are promulgated by government law without consultation of teachers, parents, or other stakeholders. They are introduced without any trial period nor professional development to assist instructors in implementing changes in the curriculum. There is hardly any provision for subsequent evaluation during and after implementation.

A Badly Conceived No-Repetition Policy

One of the most controversial policies introduced by the ministerial circular was that of 2006 (No. 15/B1/1464/MINEDUB of February 21, 2006), which stipulated that students in Classes 1, 3, and 5 in primary schools should not repeat a class. This policy implied automatic promotion to the next class, a promotion that was not based on student performance. When this proposal was first suggested by international partners at Kribi in 2002, they had based their recommendations on what obtains in the United States, Britain, France, and other developed European nations. Cameroonian professionals, however, rejected it based on the argument that transferring such a model from more advanced, functional nations with a more erudite culture of scholarship grounded in effective methods of teaching and learning, resources, infrastructure, and use of a variety of approaches such as individualized instruction to ascertain that each child learns at their highest potential, was inappropriate for the Southern Cameroons context. Teachers further argued that automatic promotion may not encourage hard work, excellence, and competitiveness ... qualities that drive student motivation and learning in the Southern Cameroonian context. Despite strong arguments against the policy of obligatory automatic promotion based on attendance only, the policy somehow crept back into primary education practices and is being implemented in many schools. Pedagogues still hold strongly to the position that obligatory automatic promotion to higher classes is out of place in Southern Cameroons, because in addition to a plethora of challenges faced by schools, teachers, and students, this practice does not take into consideration the different pace of learning of each child nor does it make provisions for individualized instruction to accommodate students' differences and bring slower struggling students up to speed. Besides, the socioeconomic

The increased demand for transversal competencies arises from the changes in the surrounding world. Growth as a human being, studying, working and operating as a citizen now and in future require competencies that transcend and integrate the various fields of knowledge and skills (English School Handbook, 2016, p. 10).

The main difference between phenomenon-based learning and learning within the traditional school culture is that students can holistically learn content, as opposed to subject-specific contexts where topics are split into smaller and separate parts that can often be decontextualized. Sheila admits that although phenomenon-based learning can be a robust method of teaching and learning, it requires lots of creativity and can be time-consuming in terms of planning.

Notwithstanding, the advantages and potentials of a phenomenon-based curriculum structure are self-evident. This approach creates better opportunities for integrating different subjects and themes as well as fostering the systematic use of pedagogically effective methods, such as inquiry learning, problem-based learning, project learning, and portfolios. Deeper learning occurs in this environment, as students seek to answer questions about phenomena they have generated themselves and are interested in. The phenomenon-based approach is also key in the versatile utilization of different learning environments (for example, diversifying and enriching learning while using electronic competencies). Skills learned are easily applied across subjects and in authentic and "natural" situations outside of the classroom situations.

Phenomenon-based learning gets students more actively engaged in learning. Children and young people are guided to take responsibility for their studies and each student is supported according to their needs. The student sets goals, solves problems, and evaluates their learning based on their goals. Pupil's experiences, emotions, interests, and interaction with others create the foundation for learning. The teacher's job is to teach and guide students as lifelong learners by considering the unique ways in which students learn and fostering those strengths. Optional materials status of the population does not favor such a policy since most students depend solely on the class teacher for knowledge acquisition. Proponents of this no-repetition policy may have been looking at the economic value of reducing the cost of education; but quality education should be the priority in any policy decision. In rural areas that form the bulk of the school system, and where teacher shortages are most acute, automatic promotion to the next grade often amounts to students facing cognitive gaps in content; and this often surfaces at the secondary school levels. Teachers continue to contest this policy based on their belief that students ought to be evaluated and promoted based on performance, not politics, policy influences, or decisions.

War and Civil Unrests

The sociopolitical context highly complicates the primary education system in Southern Cameroons. Even before the current political crisis, it had been established that many students attending school were not gaining basic skills in reading and math, and those in attendance were often no different than those who did not attend. A system that was already degraded by neglect, abandonment, and corruption, is now in worse shape with the current war that started in 2017 and continues to ravage these two regions. When the war started, schools were closed for over two years following calls of school boycotts by radicals; and some school buildings burned down by government forces as reprisals for boycotts. According to the *Washington Post*, 79 students were kidnapped from a boarding school (Presbyterian Secondary School Nkwen) in the Northwest region of Southern Cameroons on October 30, 2018 (see Kindzeka, 2018). The *Guardian* later reported that although the children were returned to their parents, the kidnappers had not yet been identified. Finger-pointing between government and separatist forces and blaming each side for the kidnappings has left an already traumatized population scared (Maclean, 2018). As reported by *CNN*, the few students attending schools in secret were recalled home by their parents for fear of reprisals from both warring factions and warnings from the separatists for students not to return to school (Tah et al., 2018). Currently, intermittent school closures remain a challenge for both parents and students, who are usually gripped with fear when the separatists declare school closure and the central government in Yaoundé deploys its troops to employ doubtful means to ensure attendance, to demonstrate to the international community that all is well in these regions.

Human Rights Watch stipulates that over 200,000 people, including school children, are internally displaced and hiding in bushes, while the United Nations Human Rights Commission for Refugees estimates that over 50,000 men, women, and children are in refugee settlements in the neighboring country of Nigeria. When people are in refugee camps, basic survival is what preoccupies them, not education. Any effective policy must consider the cognitive gaps students have suffered due to civil unrest while expanding access and improving the quality of primary education. In many countries, primary education is compulsory and free.

Lessons from Finland

Finland could serve as an educational workshop par excellence for informing policy development for SSA countries and even for some developed nations, including the United States. For over a decade, Finland has consistently ranked top among other nations in the Programme for International Student Assessment (PISA), organized by the Organization for Economic Cooperation and Development (OECD) to evaluate educational systems and student performances in mathematics, science, and reading. PISA scores provide comparable data enabling participating countries to improve their education policies and outcomes. These evaluations are often rigorous and American students have often performed below average on these assessments. As part of the research for this manuscript, in 2018, I traveled to Finland to experience what makes the Finnish educational system so successful. In Finland, I visited two schools: the Kirstin Koulo Elementary School in Espoo, Finland (see the back view of the Kirstin School Building in Fig. 6.1) and the English School, Finland.

The Kirstin Koulu school's website describes it as "an inspiring and international primary school [that] appreciates responsibility, appreciation of work, and respect for others.… Special emphasis is on studying mathematics.... The awareness of languages and cultures is our strong area of expertise, and it is part of our daily activities" (Kirstin Koulu, 2018). Figure 6.2 demonstrates the school's motto of emphasizing mathematics skills, as illustrated on some of the charts on the wall of the first grade classroom that I observed.

Figure 6.1. Back view of Kirstin Koulu Elementary School, Espoo, Finland. Source: author.

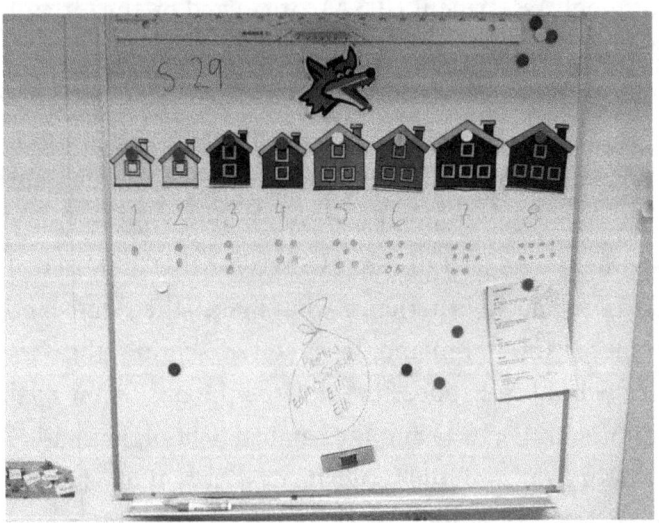

Figure 6.2. First grade classroom wall with math skills. Source: author.

The English School is a bilingual school system that offers instruction in Finnish and English to students from preschool through elementary, middle, and high school. I visited the school campus which serves seventh through ninth grades and is located in Valimotie, Helsinki, Finland (see Fig. 6.3: Picture of the author in the English School building).

Figure 6.3. Author inside the English high school in Finland, 2018. Source: author.

The Finnish formal education cycles are loosely broken into four cycles: (a) Early Childhood and Pre-primary Education, (b) Basic Comprehensive Education, (c) Upper Secondary Education, and (d) Tertiary Education, which is sub-divided into two sectors (traditional universities or universities of applied sciences that focus on vocational educational needs of the world of work and development). Early childhood education includes daycare nursery-kindergarten and continues until the child is seven years old. Just like in the United States, early childhood education focuses on guiding children in developing social skills and encouraging them to get along with others through play and other interactive activities. The Finnish system, however, encourages experimentation and learning through errors in a supportive and positive environment that prepares young children to become independent citizens, capable of taking care of themselves and being responsible and productive citizens. Children in early childhood are given greater autonomy in Finland, and their initiatives and ideas are taken into account more extensively in the learning process. Figures 6.4, 6.5, 6.6, 6.7, 6.8, 6.9, and 6.10 show first-grade students drawing pictures as an extension activity after an oral reading by their teacher and showing off their work to the author. One even drew a picture of me (Fig. 6.9).

Figure 6.4. First grade teacher, reading an excerpt from this open page. Source: author.

Figure 6.5. Students draw various pictures as response to oral reading of text. Source: author.

Figure 6.6. Students draw various pictures as response to oral reading of text. Source: author.

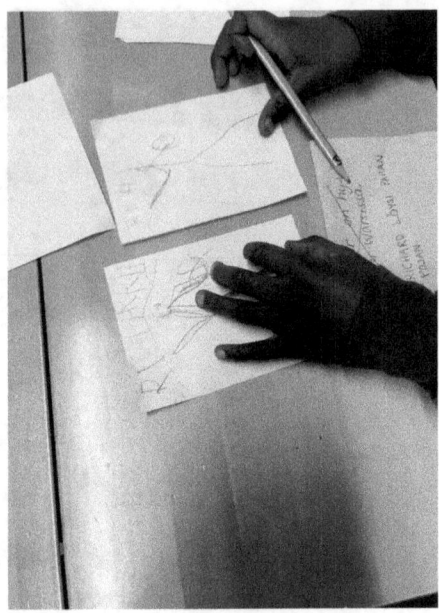

Figure 6.7. Students draw various pictures as response to oral reading of text. Source: author.

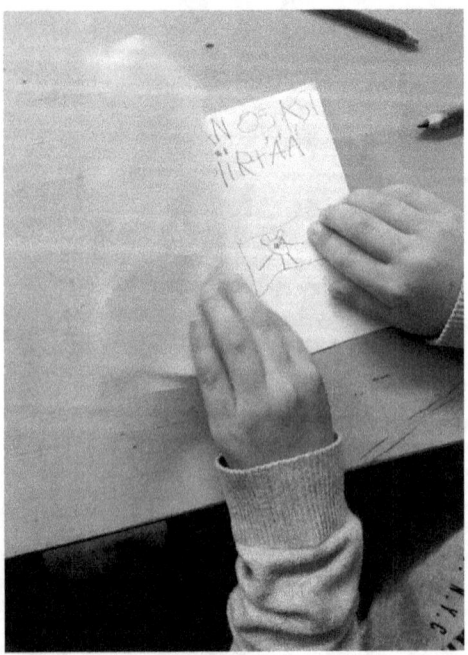

Figure 6.8. Students draw various pictures and write as response to oral reading of text. Source: author.

Figure 6.9. Student drawing of the author. Source: author.

Figure 6.10. First grade students at work in response to oral reading of text. Source: author.

That is the level of creativity and spontaneity I observed among these first graders. The belief is that "each child has the right to be seen, heard, considered, and understood as an individual and a member of the community" (English School Handbook, 2016, p. 6). At this level, possible problems that may affect children's development are identified, and interventions begin to prevent possible problems that may hinder students' learning in the years of compulsory basic schooling.

Basic Comprehensive education starts at age seven years to age 16 years and proceeds from first grade to ninth grade. Students are taught necessary knowledge and skills in basic subjects such as math, science, and reading, and are supported in their growth as responsible members of society (see Fig. 6.11. Finnish Education Model for details).

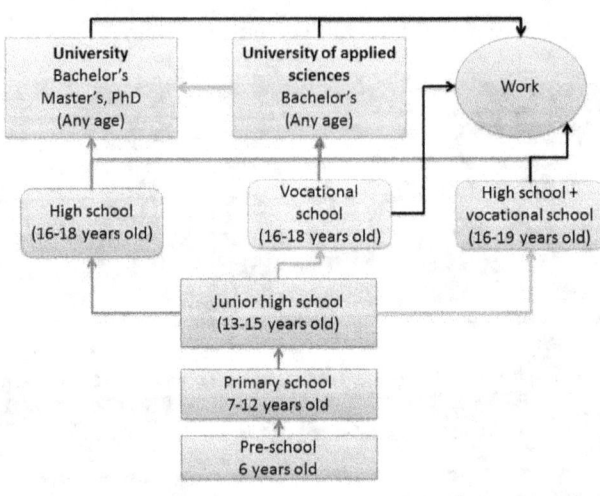

Figure 6.11. Finnish Education Model. Source: Olivia Lucarrelli (blog.hlrnet.net)

Basic education and, in fact, all other cycles of education in Finland are compulsory and free of charge. This includes tuition, textbooks, and other teaching and learning resources. However, compulsory education does not mean a student must attend a formal school setting. Students can study at home to obtain a basic education certificate, because there is no option to leave school in Finland. The emphasis is on the content of compulsory basic education competencies, which remain the same regardless of the method of execution. If a child chooses homeschooling, a custodian or investigating teacher is assigned, who is responsible for organizing the child's studies (for example, acquiring textbooks and other learning materials, teaching materials, providing support or special education, free school meals, school health care, school transportation, and other student services) that are accessible to students attending regular municipal schools. The investigating teacher's task also includes evaluating the student's progress based on the requirements of compulsory education; she/he, therefore, monitors progress in relation to the objectives of the various subjects stipulated in the basic education school syllabus. There is no clear guideline as to how often the investigative teacher should supervise, but typically, custodians may make one or two visits a year and write reports that evaluate the student's competencies as stipulated in the compulsory school subject areas and submit the report to the municipality.

The Finnish School Basic Education Curriculum

The Finish school curriculum is divided into two parts: the municipality-specific part, followed by all the schools in the municipality, and the school-specific parts that the schools draw up for themselves. The government or the municipality designs the core curriculum, but each school can add aspects or modify the curriculum to suit its specific needs. A core/basic curriculum provides a solid foundation of learning for all students and ensures equality in education throughout the country. A blended municipal and school curricula ensures that schoolwork closely aligns with each community's local needs and perspectives. Every stakeholder is a part of designing the curriculum and determining educational goals: parents, guardians, teachers, and students. The *Basic Education Act* mandates that teaching be organized according to the child's age and the conditions of the students and in collaboration with their homes.

School subjects in the common curriculum under the *Basic Education Act* include: Mother Tongue and Literature, Second Language, Foreign

Language, Environmental Science, Health Education, Religion or Lecture History, History, Social Studies, Mathematics, Physics, Chemistry, Biology, Geography, Physical Education, Music, Visual Arts and Crafts, and Domestic Science (or Household) (see Fig. 6.12. Finnish Distribution of Lessons in Finnish Basic Education).

Distribution of lesson hours in basic education 1.1.2020

Subjects	Grades 1 2	Grades 3 4 5 6	Grades 7 8 9	Total
Mother tongue and literature	14	18	10	42
A1-language [1]	2	9	7	18
B1-language		2	4	6
Mathematics	6	15	11	32
Environmental studies	4	10		
Biology and geography [2]			7	
Physics and chemistry [2]			7	
Health education [2]			3	
Environment and nature studies in total		14	17	31
Religion/Ethics	2	5	3	10
History and social studies [3]		5	7	12
Music	2	4	2	8
Visual arts	2	5	2	9
Crafts	4	5	2	11
Physical education	4	9	7	20
Home economics			3	3
Artistic and practical elective subjects		6	5	11
Artistic and practical subjects in total				62
Guidance counselling			2	2
Optional subjects		9		9
Minimum number of lessons				224
(Optional A2-language) [4]		(12)		(12)
(Optional B2-language) [4]			(4)	(4)

--- = Subject is taught in the grades if stated in the local curriculum.

[1] A1 language teaching begins at 1st grade spring term at the latest, for at least 0.5 hours per week.

[2] The subject is taught as a part of integrated environmental studies in the grades 1-6.

[3] Social studies are taught in grades 4-6 for at least 2 hours per week and grades 7-9 at least 3 hours per week.

[4] The pupil can, depending on the language, study a free-choice A2 language either as an optional subject or instead of the B1 language.
The pupil can study the B2 language as an optional subject. The free-choice A2 and B2 languages can, alternatively, be organised as instruction exceeding the minimum time allocation. In this case their instruction cannot be organised using the minimum time allocated in the distribution of lesson hours for optional or B1 language as defined in this paragraph. Depending on the language the pupil receives instruction in a B1 language or optional subjects instead of this B1 language. The distribution of lessons hours would be a minimum of 234 annual lessons for a pupil studying the A2 language as instruction exceeding the minimum time allocation. The corresponding number of annual lessons is a minimum of 226 for a pupil with the B2 language. The total number of annual lessons would be a minimum of 238 for pupils studying both the A2 and the B1 languages as instruction exceeding the minimum time allocation.

Figure 6.12. Finnish Distribution of Lessons in Finnish Basic Education. Source: Finnish National Agency for Education (Oph.fi)

Parents are encouraged to speak their mother tongues to students at home, on the understanding that students will learn Finnish in school as the language of instruction. Both the municipality and the school decide on optional materials for instruction, but the municipality determines the minimum amount of optional materials. The government also decides how many hours of instruction are allocated to each subject area per year, but schools have the flexibility to do the breakdown themselves, as to how many hours per week to meet the distribution of lesson hours each year. One weekly working hour would equal 38 hours of instruction per academic year. The local curriculum is a public document, and most municipalities and schools have web pages from which their curriculum can be read.

Following recent educational reforms, Finland introduced a new *National Curriculum Framework*, beginning in the 2016–2017 academic year, that would apply to all basic schools (grades one through nine) for students ages 7 to 16. This curriculum, known as phenomenon-based learning (PhenoBL), was introduced to run alongside traditional subject-based instructional methods. The reform aimed to ensure that Finnish children and young people obtain skills that will serve them well in the future, both nationally and internationally (Phenomenon-Based Learning, 2017). In addition, the pedagogical guidelines for the new curriculum were to get schools to develop practices that would foster students' motivation, increase interest in learning through active learning, and increase the relevance of the curriculum to students' lives and experiences. See Figure 6.13, where fifth-grade students participate in the Telephone Game, which was used to demonstrate the potential negative effect of spreading rumors at the end of a history lesson that examined the causes of the First World War.

The principal of the English School of Helsinki, Finland describes Phenomenon-based learning and teaching as:

> A transversal competencies and inter-disciplinary curriculum that uses real-world phenomena as a starting point for learning. The phenomena are studied as complete entities, in the real contexts in which they occur. Transversal competencies refer to the skills, knowledge, values, attitudes, and other attributes that constitute the whole child. Lessons

are taught in themes and across subject areas. Phenomena could be holistic topics like, "Time," or "flight." Under the theme of "flight," students would examine all things that fly. For example, they would study birds in biology, airplanes in mechanics, draw an angel in art, and so on and so forth. (Sheila [pseudonym], Principal of English School of Finland, October 30, 2018).

Figure 6.13. Fifth grade students participating in the telephone game. Source: author.

According to Sheila, phenomenon-based learning could also be two teachers working on a project together and bringing students together to do a variety of projects in language, the arts, science, and other subject areas in the curriculum. The advantage of a phenomenon-based structured curriculum is that there are better opportunities for integrating different subjects and themes, fostering inquiry learning, and promoting problem-solving-based learning and projects. Portfolios are an integral tool for students and teachers to organize and evaluate learning.

are provided to promote cooperation and integration within subjects, for example, in arts and crafts (including music, visual arts, handicrafts), sports and household, information and communication technology, consumer and economic education, global education, or drama studies.

Finnish schools have used this form of instruction since the 1980s, but it was not previously mandatory. Changes have been made to the traditional curriculum to allow for more flexibility. For example, social classes are being taught in lower grades more than before, while students have more choice in topics to explore in each subject (for example, domestic science themes can be chosen as part of art at lower grades). There is more flexibility when students begin taking core or optional (electives) subjects. Optional subjects (electives) form their own independent learning levels as the teacher decides, but are evaluated based on the teacher's discretion whether to use numeric grades or verbal/descriptive assessment of performance.

In order to make teaching and learning more relevant, the curriculum objectives and content of subjects can also be modified and even changed to meet the knowledge and skills required for today's society and the future. There is a push to develop ICT skills, and technology is integrated into all subject areas, while well-being is increasingly visible in teaching and learning in all grades across the schools. In addition to in-school learning, the Finnish educational system integrates non-school environments into learning, and students move to authentic places, visiting museums or businesses; and learning from these contexts is naturally incorporated into the curriculum. Exercise and games, even virtual games, are a big part of the learning environments. Because technology has become increasingly more important in everyday life, there is more versatility in teaching and learning, and the outcome is that students develop practical work habits, based on experimentation, exploration, functionality, movement, and play.

The new educational reforms in Finland emphasize safe learning environments and provide guidelines for developing a school culture that promotes inclusion, democratic principles of equality and mutual respect for all, well-being and a sustainable lifestyle, and inspires learning. All school community members are treated as equals, and students call teachers by first name. Students are given opportunities to participate in designing school activities and creating the structures that guide their everyday school life. Much emphasis is placed on developing the culture of the school as a learning community that creates the conditions for all children to learn and thrive together. There are no "good schools" or "low-performing schools" as some school districts are often described in the USA Cultural and linguistic diversity are considered strengths and highly valued, and using different languages is seen as natural in everyday life. In the fifth-grade classroom that I observed at the Kirstin Koulu Elementary School, the teacher asked the students to thank me for visiting their school in their own languages (not Finnish, which is the language of instruction). "Thank Yous" were shouted out in at least 10 different languages in a class of 19 students. When I asked them where they came from originally, they indicated 14 countries of origin including: Kazakhstan, Guatemala, Ghana, Kenya, and France! This linguistic diversity was very impressive to me, because before visiting Finland, I had bought into the myth that one of the reasons for Finnish students' academic success was the lack of diversity in the student body. Nothing could be further from the truth in the Kirstin Koula (school) at Espoo. Since linguistic diversity is valued, every adult is considered a linguistic model (which was demonstrated by the fifth-grade students and their teacher ... a Finnish teacher who was fluent in English). All the teachers I observed in the classrooms were fluent in Finnish and English.

Assessment of Learning

Because phenomenon-based learning is quite versatile, assessment of learning is also versatile, reflecting the eclectic nature of learning and variability in students' interests. The municipality and the school determine at least one clear theme or project for the school to study each year. These themes are called multidisciplinary learning units and combine contents and discussion topics from a variety of subject areas. These units are based on the curriculum objectives of each subject to ensure that set curriculum goals are met. The duration of the study and the time spent on themes may vary according to the schools' local needs and the students' interests. Students participate in designing multidisciplinary learning units; and their work in designing them is assessed as part of course/subject assessment. Parents or guardians are given information about students' progress in thematic units twice a year. The assessment mainly indicates if the student has achieved the goals of the academic year in a given subject stipulated in the curriculum. I visited a seventh-grade English Language Arts classroom when the students were scheduled to take an English quiz. Interestingly, the entire period was not used only for the quiz. The students first reviewed what they had covered before this session, followed by the quiz that lasted about 30 minutes. The classroom environment was quite relaxed even during the quiz (see Fig. 6.14 illustrating the Quiz Questions on *The Catcher in The Rye*, a classic by J. D. Salinger, and Fig. 6.15 that illustrates a student's partial response to some of the questions on the quiz).

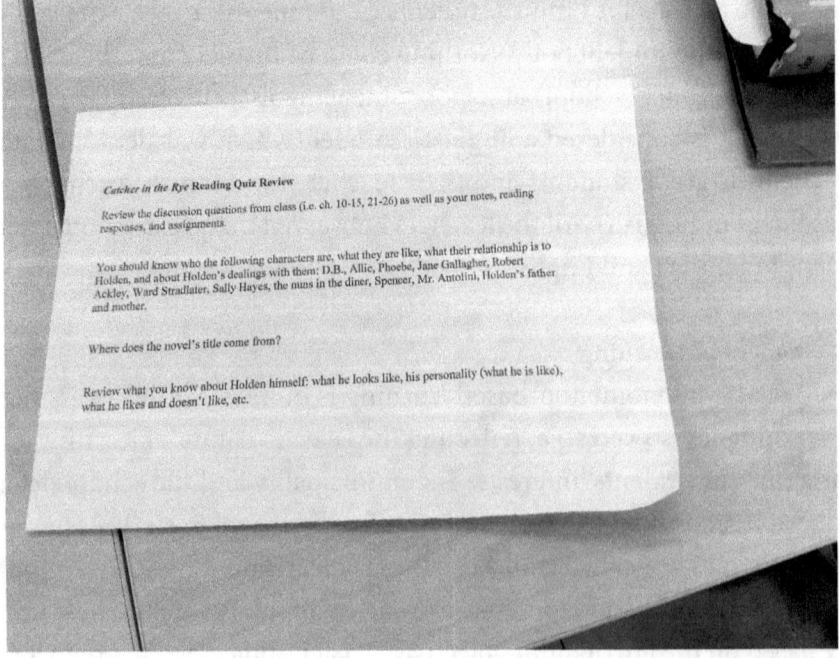

Figure 6.14. English Language Arts seventh-grade quiz on *The Catcher in the Rye*. Source: author.

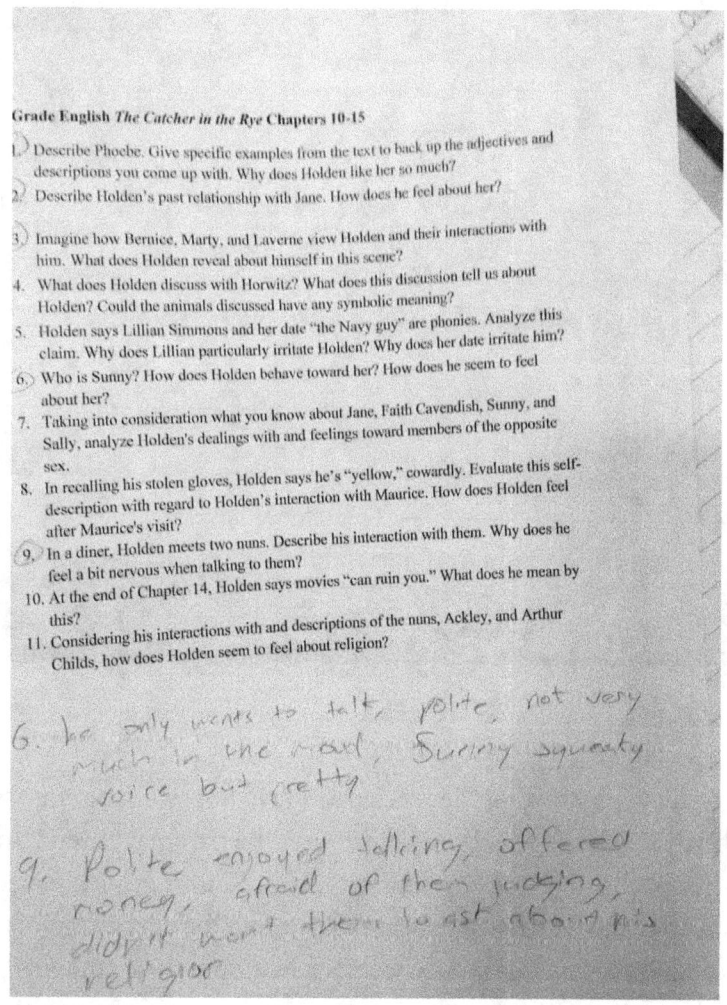

Figure 6.15. Partial student response of seventh-grade quiz on *The Catcher in the Rye*. Source: author.

I later checked some of the students' notebooks to see what lessons they had had that prepared them for this quiz. Figure 6.16, which shows a student's notebook on *The Catcher in the Rye*, shows that they had had many discussions, including character development and life lessons that could be drawn from the relationships among various characters in the novel.

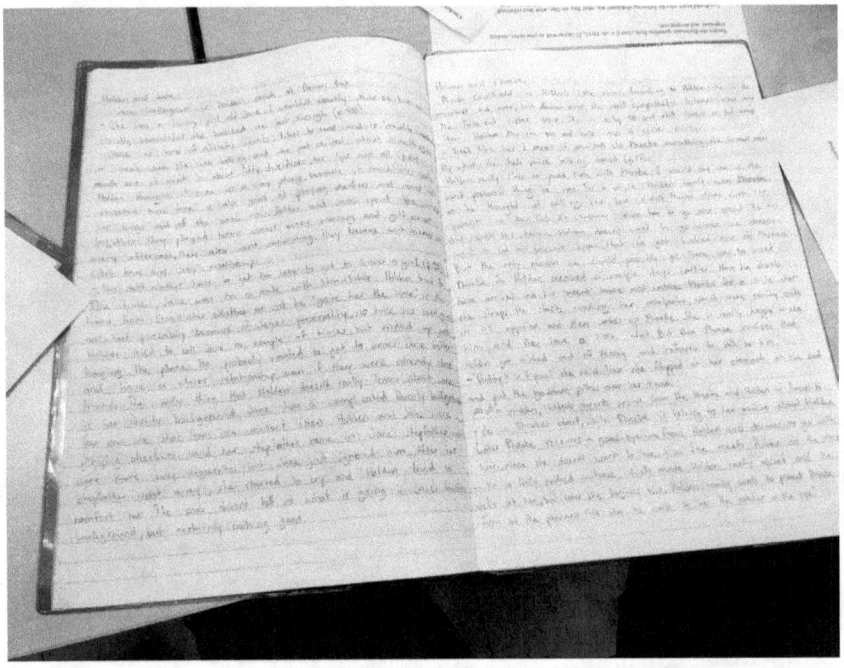

Figure 6.16. Student's notebook on Catcher in the Rye. Source: author.

In order to ensure that there is harmony in how students are assessed in each school, the government determines the national criteria for evaluation for each subject at the sixth grade and ninth grade, respectively (considered grades where students transition into the next cycles). Teachers use these national evaluation criteria when giving their students grades or a sixth-grade certificate of basic education. The emphasis on the evaluations is not so much to determine pass or fail but to serve as a guide to promote learning. Evaluation grades therefore are descriptors of students' performance and competencies based on the objectives of each subject. My observation of a ninth-grade World History lesson showed a very interactive session between the teacher and the students in a relaxed classroom environment. See Figures 6.17, 6.18, and 6.19, which show the ninth-grade students in a World History session on the Contributions of the Romans to History, a picture on the classroom wall that depicted some Roman personalities, and a partial classroom view before the students came into class.

Figure 6.17. Observing a ninth-grade class World History lesson. Source: author.

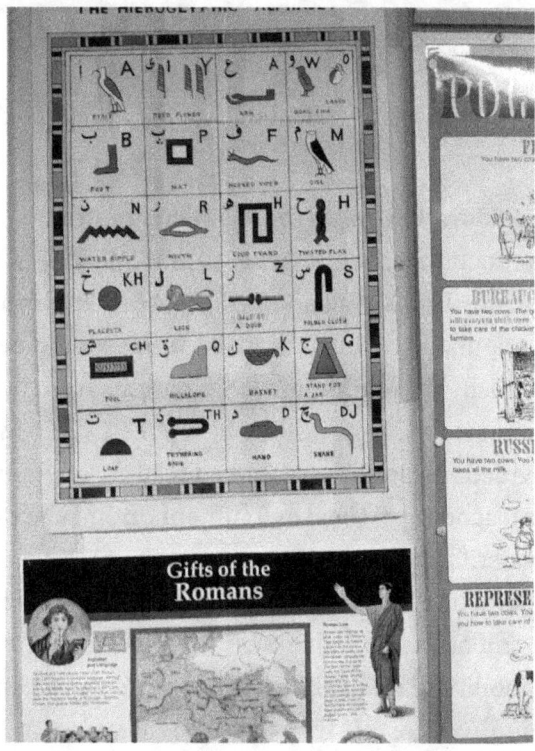

Figure 6.18. Picture on wall of ninth-grade, World History classroom. Source: author.

Figure 6.19. World History classroom at the English School, Helsinki, Finland. Source: author.

Designing Basic Education Policy for Sub-Saharan Africa

There is so much that SSA, in general, and Southern Cameroons can learn from Finland. The 2000 United Nations Millennium Development Goals (MDG) stipulated that primary education should be free, compulsory, and universal. Although many SSA nations have taken important steps toward achieving this goal, they have fallen short in the quality of education provided. To provide quality education, governments must be responsible for teachers' personal emoluments, non-salary costs, teaching and learning materials, and other operating costs. Of course, checks would have to be implemented to hold administrators and teachers accountable for these investments, especially given the high rate of corruption and lack of accountability in many SSA nations. Parents can still be expected to meet some indirect costs if they have the means.

Policy Guidelines for Southern Cameroons

Emulating examples of successful nations like Finland while integrating contextual factors like culture, etc., would be a good place to start policy development. In general, effective policy for Basic Education would include but not be limited to:

- the establishment of a cost-effective system of sustainable financing of primary education,
- review and financing of primary education to ensure that Free Primary Education (FPE) becomes sustainable,
- mobilization of private sector investment in education services,
- ensure that all primary school campuses are child-friendly,
- ensure that teaching, learning, and assessment protocols are effective to ensure that students' transition and transfer between grades and levels of education are based on acquired competencies, and not just on attendance,
- finance primary education through the provision of teachers, teaching, and learning materials, and operational costs,
- build teacher capacity and address issues of cost-effectiveness in the education sector by reviewing teacher quality, terms, and conditions of service, and address teacher absenteeism to obtain greater value for money,
- provide free nutritious meals to all students, especially those in distressed areas,
- ensure budgetary allocations to schools fairly and equitably that especially take into consideration the identified needs of schools,
- review unit cost every five years to take into account emerging trends, such as inflation and other factors,
- establish an ideal school size and class size of no more than 25 pupils per class; revisable as more teachers are trained and recruited into the teaching corps,
- implement enrollment-based staffing norms, with high-potential schools receiving teachers based on no more than a ratio of 1:30 pupils per teacher and no more than 1:25 pupils for distressed and low-performing areas,

- ensure that the development and maintenance of infrastructure is well coordinated and linked to the recurrent budgetary provisions, both by central and county governments, and decentralized units and schools,
- use school mapping and demographic data in planning and providing education, including the establishment of new schools,
- offer rigorous training to administrators and ongoing professional development to all head teachers and members of school management committees (SMC),
- provide recruiting and training budget, accountancy, and procurement management staff,
- change the composition of school procurement committees to include members of the SMC, with the chair not being the same person as the chair of the SMC, as this often creates conflict of interest and waste,
- ensure full enforcement of teacher absenteeism disciplinary measures in the Code of Regulations in order to improve efficiency in teacher resource utilization in schools,
- promote the health and general well-being of students, especially that of female students (for example, provide and integrate the provision of sanitary towels costs to girls into FPE grants to schools for girls),
- Mobilize funding to introduce and integrate ICT across all primary schools and all subject areas.

CHAPTER 7

Secondary Education

Secondary education is the level that follows primary education. Also referred to in the literature as junior, lower secondary, middle, or junior high school. This level is critical, as it prepares students for higher education and other life skills necessary to meet the demands for skilled labor and a workforce needed to grow a global economy (UNESCO, Institute for Statistics (IUS), 2011). Secondary curricula are usually organized around subject-oriented concepts; therefore,to ensure effective delivery, teachers are expected to have specialized knowledge and pedagogical competence in the subjects they teach.

The State of Secondary Education in Sub-Saharan Africa: General and Technical

Although Sub-Saharan African (SSA) countries have made impressive strides toward universal primary education (UPE), expanding greater access to secondary education, improving quality, and ensuring equity remain challenges. Between 1990 and 2006, primary completion grew from 49% to 65%, but the secondary school completion rate only averaged about 30% within the same period. This rate has dropped drastically in recent years due to a severe economic crisis and civil unrest that has affected most of the region. These crises further slowed down the progress in secondary education in SSA compared to other regions of the world's developing regions, such as East Asia, where enrollment stood at 65% to 100% in some places (Verspoor & Bregman, 2008).

Many students in SSA cannot attend secondary school after graduating at the primary level due to high costs and other hardships inherent in the system. Young people living in rural communities are less likely to have access to secondary education than youths in urban areas; children of the poor in most communities are less likely to attend than children of the rich. Boys are more likely to attend than girls since parents would rather have girls stay home to do house chores or get married than send them to school. These systemic disparities exist, although SSA spends about the same percent gross domestic product (GDP) on education; 4.6% in 2004, compared to East Asian countries such as Korea, Singapore, Thailand, and Vietnam that spent 4.3% to 4.6%. To increase output in secondary education, SSA countries must prioritize reform initiatives, efficient resource management, and sustainability in policy design and implementation that are integrated with longer-term goals for national development.

Of the 552 million youths enrolled in secondary schools worldwide in 2012, only about 49 million resided in Africa. According to Lewin and Caillods (2001), two-thirds of all countries with secondary Gross Enrollment Rates (GER) of below 40% are in Africa, and mostly in SSA countries, where only a small minority of students participate in and finish secondary schooling. These unsavory statistics prevail, even though ironically, between 1999 and 2012, SSA was said to have achieved the greatest gains in secondary education participation, compared to all other regions of the world. The World Bank, Department of Secondary Education in Africa (SEIA), recommends sustaining this growth, and an increasing focus on expansion, general improvement on quality, relevance, and equity—"between boys and girls, between urban and rural areas, between the rich and poor, and across regions within countries" (Verspoor & Bregman, 2008, p. 2).

Most secondary education systems in Africa are still based on the literary and academic traditions of schooling that do not reflect the needs of today's rapidly changing society and evolving labor market. Curriculum reforms are slow and often unsuccessful in cases where they have been attempted. Bottlenecks exist in the selection process into secondary schools; and where scholarships are available, they are so poorly targeted that most students who successfully complete primary school are still left behind due to the extremely high cost of secondary education, sporadic tuition hikes, and a variety of formal and informal costs that disqualify prospective students from having access to secondary schools. With the cost of secondary education, three to four times that of primary education per student; and the cost of Technical, Vocational Education and Training (TVET), over 12 times that of primary education, high cost remains among the top challenges for leveling the playing field. Low enrollment and completion rates of the respective age groups, therefore, account for a situation where less than one in two youths enter junior secondary school, and less than one in four enter senior secondary school, with the poorest SSA countries having the lowest participation rates. Secondary education only accommodates 36% of qualifying secondary students in SSA (Africa-America Institute (AAI), 2015). Overcoming the problem of accessibility and affordability of secondary education is the key to preparing students for institutions of higher learning, producing workers who have needed skills for local markets, and having human capital that promotes economic growth in most SSA countries. Other social outcomes, such as better health of mothers and children, the transmission of cultural and ethical values needed for cohesion, active participation in peaceful and democratic societies, and social mobility, are also linked to secondary education acquisition. There is some correlation between macroeconomic growth and expansions in secondary education. Countries with Gross National Income (GNI) per capita of more than $1,200 usually have junior secondary enrollment that rises to about 50% or more and senior secondary of about 30% or more. In fact, six of the ten SSA middle-income countries for which data are available have reached a junior secondary enrollment ratio of 80% or more and have reached or are close to the goal of universal junior secondary enrollment. This has prompted some SSA governments to explore various financing options to boost the quality and capacity of secondary education. For example, countries such as Uganda, where 72% of secondary school-aged children are not in school, are implementing public-private partnerships and enabling more adolescents to gain affordable quality secondary education. Eritrea, The Gambia, Ghana, Sao Tome & Principe, Togo, and Zimbabwe have all enrolled 50% or more of the junior secondary age group. But a large variability still exists among countries, ranging from 14% in the Central African Republic to 32% in Nigeria and 60% in Ghana. It is worth noting that countries with the poorest GNI per capita of around $400 have junior secondary enrollment ratios that hover between 14% and 2% (for example, Tanzania). These variabilities do not suggest that secondary education entirely correlates with increased national income. Other factors, such as government decisions in allocating resources to secondary institutions, strategies of service delivery, and program content that can also have a profound impact on access and quality, must be examined.

While many countries around the globe have moved away from seeing secondary education as the terminal level of education, SSA has only recently begun to see completion of junior and secondary education as the goal for education system management, that is necessary for achieving Education for All (EFA). Gains in secondary education would impact sectors like health, democracy, and governance. SSA must confront the challenge of sustaining growth in primary education while at the same time expanding access and quality to improve secondary education. Among the many challenges confronting the expansion in secondary education are critical factors such as: (a) teacher shortages, (b) inadequate resources for expansion, (c) family networks and household composition, and (d) lack of quality and relevance of the curriculum, and (e) inequitable distribution of secondary school opportunities across different communities.

Teacher Shortage

Teacher recruitment, retention and deployment are issues in all education sectors in SSA. Lewin (2001) indicated that teacher supply must be increased up to four times to achieve the goals of UPE. As goals for UPE are reached and expansion in secondary education becomes a requirement, additional teachers will be needed. Given the stress in training institutions and public expenditures, this challenge seems almost insurmountable, as projected demands for teachers exceed the projected supply needed to meet secondary education requirements. The main challenges with teacher recruitment and retention include (i) high attrition rate, (ii) difficulty attracting and retaining teachers in rural areas, (iii) bottlenecks in recruiting qualified candidates into teacher preparation institutions and systems, and (iv) lack of specialization in specific areas needed for secondary education, especially in mathematics and sciences (Lewin, 2001; Organization of Economic Cooperation and Development (OECD), 2002; 2006; Mulkeen, 2005; Schwille, 2007, World Development Report, 2007).

Inadequate Resources for Expansion

Financing secondary education is a heavy burden to governments, households, and most African countries. Secondary education tends to receive the least state resources, an average of 15% to 20% (World Bank Annual Report, 2005). For most SSA households with low income, the burden of financing secondary education becomes too great to overcome. In Kenya, for example, households meet only 20% of primary and 8% of university education costs, yet the cost of secondary education to households is upward of 60%, making the transition from primary to secondary school impossible for the poorest families.

Family Networks and Household Composition

In SSA, family networks are important since the burden of educating children is shared by extended family members. Household composition is important because a child has a higher chance of accessing secondary education if there are fewer children of secondary school age in the household network and if those networks are strong (Onsomu et al., 2006).

Lack of quality and relevance of the curriculum

As stated earlier in this chapter, secondary curricula across the continent are usually outdated, irrelevant, and poorly implemented. In a continent ravaged by a plethora of issues such as diseases, poverty, and other socioeconomic hardships, curricula content has not changed to integrate factors necessary to confront an evolving labor market that must consider global factors. The lack of relevance in the curricula caused low quality of education across many nations and has given rise to student apathy, school disaffection, and antisocial behavior (World Bank,

Department of Secondary Education in Africa (SEIA), 2007). In Kenya for example, students and teachers spend an average of 18 hours in school per week, which is insufficient time for teachers to cover the curriculum in depth. In a 2003 *Trends in International Mathematics and Science Study* (TIMSS), the average score for eighth graders in mathematics was 466 out of 800 possible points. Students in Botswana, Ghana, and South Africa scored 366, 276, and 264, respectively, while students in Singapore scored an average of 605 in math (United States Department of Education, National Center for Education Statistics, 2003).

Inequitable Distribution of Secondary School Opportunities across Different Communities

There is an uneven distribution of educational opportunities between poor and non-poor regions, both in urban and rural areas (Onsomu et al., 2006; Mugisha, 2003), and the poor tend to have limited access to educational opportunities than the non-poor. These challenges are especially faced at the technical and vocational education levels. For example, in Ghana, an already limited number of technical institutes is further exacerbated by a lack of facilities and materials for training students, inadequate technical teachers or facilitators, difficulty in career progression, mismatch between acquired skills and market needs, and negative attitudes and perceptions toward technical and vocational education (Amedorme & Fiagbe, 2013).

Designing and implementing effective policy goals for Secondary education in SSA must be approached as a network of complex and interrelated factors that include but are not limited to the challenges listed above. These include expansion of access, equity in enrollment between genders, integration of alternative routes and modes of delivery, and expansion of enrollments in selected subjects such as in Science, Technology, Engineering, and Mathematics (STEM).

The Need for Science, Technology, Engineering and Mathematics (STEM) Subjects

For SSA to achieve the Sustainable Development Goals (SDGs) and close the gap between industrialized nations and the region, it must invest in STEM education at secondary levels. STEM education includes the natural sciences: biology, physics, chemistry, mathematics, information and communication technology (ICT), and applied subjects such as technical drawing and agriculture that are linked to the sciences or technology-based industries that are vital for social and environmental sustainability. In SSA, specialization usually starts at upper secondary levels, where typically, students can choose between an academic or a vocational/technical pathway to a career. Although secondary education may only adequately provide some of the skills and knowledge necessary to perform specific professions, it lays the foundation for what students would do in the world of work. At this level where students take their first steps toward specialization, secondary education would logically be the level at which firmer foundations contributing to STEM capabilities and other scientific inquiry at higher tertiary levels should be built. In 2014, the African Union (AU) recognized the severe shortage of STEM skills necessary for driving innovation and boosting African-led development and set an ambitious *Agenda 2063* (African Union, 2014). *Agenda 2063* highlights the value of STEM education and its role in developing human capital to meet various economic, social, and environmental development needs. However, while Agenda 2063 emphasizes agriculture, food security, research for resource exploitation, communications infrastructure, and other biotechnology developments, it fails to highlight the level at which such a knowledge economy should be conceptualized and implemented. With a secondary education curriculum that is currently focused on academic and theory-oriented learning, the vision of *Agenda 2063* is to: "Catalyze education and skills revolution and actively promote science, technology, research and innovation, to build knowledge, human capital, capabilities and skills" (p. 14) may be difficult to accomplish.

The challenges that stand in the way of building a robust STEM sector in SSA, are some of the same that stand in the way of expanding secondary education in general, including:

a). lack of qualified STEM teachers,

b). lack of interest by people with STEM knowledge to go into teaching, c). lack of accessibility to upper secondary education for many,

d). high class sizes resulting in high-teacher-student ratios that are incompatible with effective STEM education,

e). lack of adequate resources, including textbooks, ICT, and infrastructure for effective teaching and learning of STEM,

f). outdated curricula that do not meet 21st-century STEM needs,

g). lack of learner-centered pedagogy that encourages problem-solving, inquiry, critical thinking, and knowledge application,

h). poorly designed high-stakes examination models that do not serve the purpose of effective evaluation, or that are suitable for STEM subjects,

i). assessment reporting systems do not provide adequate data to inform and improve students' or teachers' performance, and

j). gender disparities, especially the underrepresentation of girls in STEM (Tikly et al., 2018).

Policy and curriculum design at secondary levels must consider the role that secondary education should play in preparing graduates for STEM fields.

The current model in most SSA African nations, where discrete science subjects are taught at secondary levels, could be a plus, but this model must go beyond discrete knowledge acquisition to combining the natural sciences, "everyday sciences" such as health and nutrition, and making the connections between science and everyday activities on the environment apparent. Integrating other knowledge skills, such as literacy, the arts, and indigenous knowledge, into the teaching of the sciences would also create relevance and motivate students to pursue STEM fields. A Science, Technology, Engineering, Arts, and Math (STEAM) approach will provide students the opportunity to engage in critical thinking, dialogue, and other creative processes that are necessary for the experiential learning processes that STEM students need to stay engaged as learners and leaders in the 21st century. Because the challenges facing secondary grammar, technical, and STEM education in SSA are widespread and deep-rooted, conceptualizing solutions would also have to be system-wide, yet contextually specific, strategic, and sustainable in the long term.

A SEIA synthesis report supports the idea that secondary education is associated with accelerating economic growth and significantly contributes to national economic performance. Among other benefits, secondary completion equips countries with the human capital threshold that could attract foreign direct investment. It should be noted that the quality of secondary education, especially in STEM, is more important than the number of years of schooling. Equitable access for all students, especially the poor and girls, is necessary to enhance economic growth performance.

Lessons from Some International Education Systems
Characteristics of Systems that Work

Although drawing parallels between SSA educational systems and international models in developed nations may be considered illogical given the different conditions that prevail in both contexts, it is always necessary to draw some lessons from models that work in order to improve nascent systems. The world ranking of best educational systems includes Japan, Barbados, New Zealand, Estonia, Ireland, Qatar, Netherlands, Singapore, Belgium, Switzerland, and Finland as among the top 10. A closer examination of these countries' educational systems indicates certain common characteristics:

- A balanced development of different educational sub-sectors,
- Efficiency in resource availability and spending,
- Government direction and leadership to accelerate and sustain growth, with adequate decentralization and autonomy,
- Public-private partnerships that prioritize and nurture community support and expectations (Verspoor & Bregman, 2008).

Finland, which has routinely scored among the top-ranking countries globally on the Organization for Economic Cooperation and Development (OECD) Programme for International Student Assessment (PISA), has no banding system— that is, all pupils, regardless of ability, are taught in the same classrooms. This accounts for the smallest recorded gap worldwide between the weakest and the strongest pupils. The Finnish secondary education system has two tracks: general upper secondary education and vocational education and training for students 16 to 19 years of age. Schools assign relatively little homework and have only one mandatory test at the age of 16 years (State University Education Encyclopedia, 2024).

Japan, which, according to OECD statistics, is among the top-performing countries for literacy, science, and math, offers a 6-3-3-4, model: six years of elementary school, three years of junior high school, and three years of high school before students decide whether they want to go into four years of university or not. Elementary and junior high schools are compulsory and although high school is not compulsory, enrollment is close to 98% nationwide, with about 46% of all high school graduates going to university or junior college. High school dropout rate is only about 2% (OECD, Education at a Glance, Japan, 2018).

Singapore, which had its independence several years after many SSA countries, is ranked among the 10 best education systems in the world based on PISA test scores. Although primary and secondary schools follow Western models, Singapore started identifying students' abilities and challenges at the primary level and streaming them based on their primary school leaving examinations. Based on this streaming, students can pursue an express track of four years or a normal track of five years that leads to Cambridge General Certificate of Examinations (GCE) "O" Level; they can then choose to pursue either an academic or technical curriculum. The Institute of Technical Training provides technical education, and recently, the Singaporean government pledged the equivalent of 1.6 billion US dollars to prepare competent teachers that will ensure that one in four Singaporean students enters a polytechnic, instead of the current one in five (Singapore, Ministry of Education, 2024).

Barbados, listed among the best global education systems, also benefits from heavy government investment in education. Primary School and secondary education are compulsory for all children. Most schools at the primary and secondary levels are state-owned and heavily subsidized, with the government paying almost all the cost of educating students, including the provision of textbooks, meals, transportation, and uniform grants. There is a wide range of awards and scholarships for students moving on to the tertiary level. These investments have resulted in a 100% participation rate and a 98% literacy rate in Barbados, the highest in the world. The underlying belief is that "every person has a right to education opportunities to help develop his/her abilities to contribute to the social and economic development of the country" (White paper on Barbados Education Reform). Barbados has shifted the focus of education from expanding access to constantly improving quality and meeting the needs of individual students (State University Education Encyclopedia, 2024).

An examination of most systems that work clearly indicates that improving education requires government engagement and leadership, sustainable growth initiatives, efficient resource expenditures and management, and a holistic and integrated approach involving various community stakeholders. SSA must efficiently manage all these factors, if it hopes to compete with the rest of the world in secondary, technical, vocational, and STEM education.

Policy Implications for Secondary Education in Sub-Saharan Africa

In most of the Western world and some of the top ten global education systems examined above, secondary education is designed and implemented for various reasons, including: to provide students with the knowledge and skills necessary to acquire expertise and the capabilities for self-employment; to promote students' development into good and balanced individuals and members of society; the versatile development of personality, and the promotion of lifelong learning. On the contrary, secondary education policies and design in SSA and Southern Cameroons, in particular, are not grounded on these principles. Existing institutions are archaic and lean toward colonial and neocolonial predispositions, thus, necessitating a complete overhaul of secondary education systems at the policy design and implementation levels. There is an urgent need for improvement that emphasizes quality implementation and reform.

Given that the state of education in SSA secondary schools can only accommodate 36% of qualifying secondary students, policies should vouch for universal free or subsidized secondary education. Creating or encouraging collaborative content creation and social media platforms, where teachers can post lesson plans and teaching materials for colleagues to view and give feedback or share materials, could effectively contribute to resource sharing and best practices and encourage more to join the teaching profession. Most importantly, because of the diversity and variability in SSA, factors influencing the transition to secondary school across the continent must be adapted to the context. For example, the rural and urban poor do not share common characteristics. Thus, education policies must be targeted to accommodate these differences.

The Case of Cameroon: French Cameroun versus British Southern Cameroons Systems

As indicated in previous chapters, Cameroon has a bi-cultural educational system modeled after former colonial masters, France and Britain, and attempts at harmonization have been largely unsuccessful. In the French-speaking parts of Cameroon, students generally attend secondary schools between 12 and 19 years old. Under this system, students spend four years at the lower-secondary level (*Collège d'Enseignement General* or *Secondaire*), and three years at the upper-secondary level (*Lycées*). The *Brevet d'Etudes du premier Cycle* is awarded to students graduating after four years of General Secondary School; while the *Baccalauréat* is awarded to successful students who complete the last three years of upper secondary level. The Ministry of Basic Education dictates state policies and programs for basic education, which goes from preschool to primary (elementary) schools, while the Ministry of Secondary Education sets programs, syllabi, and assessments for secondary and technical education, basically dictating policies for the entire country.

In the former British Southern Cameroons (the English-speaking part of the country), students attend secondary education programs between 12 and 19 years old. Typically, the lower-secondary level entails five years of study, culminating in the Cameroon General Certificate of Education Ordinary Levels (GCE "O" Level), followed by a two-year, upper-secondary program for 17- to 19-year-olds, after which students sit for, and if successful are awarded the General Certificate of Education, Advanced Level (GCE, 'A' Level). Previously, primary (elementary) education comprised seven years, consisting of Class 1 through Class 7, but after a forced harmonization project, primary school is currently six years. At the end of class six, students take the *First School Leaving Certificate examination (FSLC)*, certifying that they have completed the primary or elementary education cycle. Students wishing to go on to secondary schools take the *Government Common Entrance Examination (GCEE)*. Students who do well in the examination are placed on a list "A", "qualifying them for competitive admission into the very few, fee-free government secondary schools. With limited classroom sizes, only a small percentage of prospective secondary school students are usually admitted into tuition-free schools. Wealthy families, however, prefer to send their children to private mission-run schools, which have a reputation for quality education but are also very expensive by Cameroonian standards (ranging from $1,000 to $2,000 yearly). Students on list "B" and under, look for admission in private secondary schools, run by for-profit investors.

Secondary school attendance lasts five years, from Form 1 to Form 5, and the curriculum encompasses all subjects from home economics to natural sciences, such as biology, chemistry, and physics. By the end of Form 3 in secondary schools, students select either an arts or science course of study, and the course work between Forms 4 and 5 is more specialized and geared toward the General Certificate of Education Ordinary Level *(Cameroon GCE O/L)* final examination. It is common knowledge that most students who attend private-for-profit secondary schools that are poorly run, resulting in low academic standards, perform poorly in the GCE O/L examinations and are ill-prepared for both local and global markets or high school or tertiary education.

In both the English-speaking and the French-speaking systems, technical secondary schools exist where students can obtain an alternative education to the general and academically oriented course of studies described above. The technical programs are typically seven years in length for students between 12 and 19 years old. In the former British Southern Cameroons system, Technical Secondary School leads to the *City and Guilds Part III*, and some graduates go on to university or higher-level technical studies. Courses offered in the French-speaking technical high schools, *Lycées Techniques* and diplomas awarded upon successful completion, known as the *Brevet de Technicien* and the *Baccalauréat*, qualify graduates to work or pursue higher education.

Challenges in both Systems

According to reports, gross enrollments at the secondary level in 1994 were 32% for boys and 22% for girls, and the failure rate at the secondary level in the same year was 22%, while 24% of the total number of secondary-level students dropped out of school. This dismal situation of secondary education forced a National Forum on Education in May 1995, followed by a National Forum on Technical and Vocational Secondary Education in April 1999. The purpose of these forums was to develop new strategies and modify technical and vocational training to prepare students better to meet the Cameroonian labor market's needs. For the most part, efforts to modify technical and vocational education to make it more relevant to local needs have failed due to the government's lack of follow-up on resolutions and bad faith. The situation in the English-speaking region has deteriorated rapidly due to wanton neglect, attempts at assimilation, lack of proper allocation of limited resources and abandonment by the central government. Cameroon, in general, and the Southern Cameroons region specifically, is therefore among SSA nations that have low rates of enrollment and quality in secondary education. As indicated in Table 7.1 Statistics of Government Secondary Schools in the North West Region of Southern Cameroons (2014), there are not enough government secondary schools in Southern Cameroons to meet the growing population of students who should be attending secondary schools in various parts of this region of the country.

Policy Implications for Southern Cameroons

Secondary education in Southern Cameroons, which, like most SSA countries, inherited a colonial education system, does not provide access to economic viability or grant recipients agency to participate in the political process in their society in meaningful ways. This state of affairs has led to frustrations, rebellion, and an ongoing war that started in 2017 between

SECONDARY EDUCATION

Table 7.1. 2014 Statistics of Government Secondary Schools in the North West Region of Southern Cameroons

No.	Division	Government Schools						Teacher Training	Non-Denominational		Denominational					Total
		GTC	GTHS	GSS	GBSS	GHS	GBHS	GTTC	1st	2nd	Cath	Isla	Bap	Pres	PE	
	BOYO	10	03	16	-	08	02	01	05	02	02	-	03	-	-	52
	BUI	15	04	27	05	11	06	01	06	-	12	04	-	01	-	92
	DON/MAN	11	04	25	-	14	02	02	-	-	02	01	01	01	-	63
	MENCHUM	05	04	12	-	08	01	01	-	02	02	-	-	02	-	37
	MEZAM	16	06	10	09	11	08	04	17	22	05	-	01	06	02	117
	MOMO	10	04	18	02	14	02	02	-	01	02	-	04	04	-	63
	NGOKE-TUNJIA	08	03	09	04	03	08	01	07	06	01	02	01	-	-	53
	TOTAL	75	28	117	20	69	29	12	35	33	26	07	10	14	02	477
	TOTAL	103		117	20	69	29	12	35	33	26	07	10	14	02	477
	TOTAL			137		98		12	68		127		59			477
	TOTAL			338				12				127				477

Source: Statistics obtained from the Delegation of Secondary Education.

Southern Cameroons and French Cameroon, which is ongoing as this book goes to publication, without meaningful prospects of a ceasefire.

In such volatile and conflict-ridden environments, secondary education policy design and implementation are not going to be easy, since fundamental change needs not only financial and technical resources, but also equitability, peace, and justice to take root. To restore basic human rights and the right to education, which millions of Southern Cameroonians believe they have been robbed of, secondary education policy for Southern Cameroons will have to be universal and highly subsidized by the government, emulating successful cases of the best global education systems mentioned earlier in this chapter. Adapting successful case models from the United States, Finland, or other successful nations where students are streamed (tracked) in high schools for academic subjects and the brightest students are put on a "fast track" to support the students' opportunity for lifelong learning and self-development is worth consideration. Students need counseling and professional advice throughout their senior high school years and into college, particularly in a junior college or the first two years of a four-year college program.

Any effective policy must heavily target girls' education at the primary and secondary levels, given that investing in girls' education provides significant yields. In a 2014 report titled "Why Educating Girls Makes Economic Sense," by Jo Bourne (March 6, 2014), it is noted that it is important to educate girls because it is the one consistent determinant of progress for practically every development outcome, from mortality declines to economic growth, democracy, and equity. The report further underscores the fact that the return on one year of secondary education for a girl correlates with as high as a 25% increase in wages later in life, and these effects carry from one generation to the next. Educated girls have fewer, healthier, and better-educated children, and for each additional year of a mother's education, the average child attains an extra 0.32 years of education.

Investing in girls' education also helps delay early marriages and parenthood, which are quite widespread in SSA. It is believed that if all girls had secondary education in SSA, and South and West Asia, child marriage would fall by 64%, from almost 2.9 million to just over 1 million. More educated girls will lead to an increase in female leaders, lower levels of population growth, and subsequent reduction of pressures related to climate change. The power of girls' education on any national economy is undeniable, given that a 1%-point increase in female education raises the average gross domestic product (GDP) by 0.3% points and annual GDP growth rates by 0.2% points. A well-thought-out secondary education policy for SSA and Southern Cameroons must consider all these factors, including a focus on expanding access by providing government grants or universal secondary education for all, including girls and the rural poor, and improving quality and relevance across all regions of Cameroon, especially the contested territories. This long overdue option is necessary for overall economic development and social advancement.

Chapter 8

Conceptualizations of Curriculum for Policy Design

Integral to policy development is the curriculum, a critical factor in students' learning and academic success and a key concern of today's schools.

Definition of Curriculum

The term "Curriculum" is often difficult to define, but generally, it embodies all kinds of instructional materials used in formal and informal settings. The term curriculum is derived from the Latin words "*carrus*" to run, and "*currrere*," a racecourse. This is what Gaius Julius Caesar and his cohorts of the first century B.C. named the oval track upon which the Roman Chariots raced. Literarily therefore, the term meant to run a race on a racecourse. Gaius Julius Ceasar and his friends probably did not know they had bequeathed a word that educators would use almost daily twenty-one centuries later! In fact, more educators are more comfortable with the term curriculum than with the term policy. While policy may have some undertones of politics, many educators believe that curriculum decisions are based on "scientific" evidence of what students need to study. Education policy and curriculum decisions interact, and it can be difficult to determine which influences the other. Without getting into the debate of how education policy, which includes curriculum policy, is influenced by state or government agencies in determining the course of study, textbooks, allotment of time, etc. (an embodiment of curriculum policy), I will state the following as the nexus of the interaction between policy and curriculum, and the rationale for dedicating a chapter on curriculum in this book. While policy governs all aspects of education (why, how, what, to whom, by whom, in what form, and with what resources education is offered), *curriculum deals with what is taught and how it is taught*. Education policymakers have a responsibility to examine curriculum content to ensure that it meets high standards for the education of citizens. Extensive research commissioned by Standards Work, of the Johns Hopkins Institute for Education Policy and its Center for Research and Reform in Education, found evidence that the effect of a high-quality curriculum on students' performance was compelling and persuasive. Steiner (2017) stated in the report that among other factors a "Comprehensive, content-rich curriculum is a common feature of academically high-performing countries" (p. 1).

The Dynamic Nature of Curriculum

Various meanings of the word "curriculum" have emerged over time. In Latin, the curriculum was a "running course." In Scotland in 1603, the curriculum was a "carriageway or a road." In the United States, from 1906, it was a "course of study."

By 1940, in the United States, the term curriculum was used to refer to a Plan for Learning. The meaning of the word curriculum is, therefore, dynamic, ever evolving, and often ambiguous as it can refer to a tangible racecourse or an abstract concept. The quest for a definition of curriculum continues to tax many educators, leading experts like Elizabeth Vallance to observe that, "[t]he curriculum field is by no means clear, as a discipline of study and a practice, 'curriculum' lacks boundaries…." (Vallance, 1983, p. 159). In 1988, Grumet labeled curriculum a "field of utter confusion" (p. 4). In the world of professional education, the word has taken on an elusive, almost esoteric connotation, which often reflects the societal aspects and changes that occur within society. These societal aspects are usually influenced by factors such as: basic needs, cultural factors, individual needs, religions, traditional determinants, and aspirations. Often, these factors form the core of the curriculum in any given context.

State certification laws further compound the problem of defining curriculum because few professionals can become certified in "curriculum."

While a number of curriculum workers, consultants, developers, coordinators, supervisors, and even professors of curriculum can be identified, these specialists, usually hold state certifications in one or more fields, such as administration, guidance, supervision, school psychology, elementary education, and many fields of teaching, but not in curriculum per se, nor can they have endorsement granted in a field called "curriculum."

Although a certifiable field of specialization called curriculum may be lacking, the word itself continues to be treated as if it has a tangible substance that can undergo a substantial variety of processes. In every school in which teachers are instructing students, a curriculum exists. We know that some written plans provide directions of what the school does on a daily basis in the act of teacher-student interactions, as well as the functions of other school personnel. These plans that direct teacher-student interactions can be developed as macro-plans that contains educational content, syllabi, instructional methods, strategies, and assessment protocols that determine students' learning outcomes. They can also be organized, structured, restructured, and reformed. With considerable ingenuity, the curriculum planner can model, shape, and tailor the curriculum to the needs of the students and the context of learning. Curriculum, or its plural, curricula (Latin) or curriculums, can be improved, revised, and evaluated. Based on its evolutionary nature, curriculum can broadly be conceptualized as primarily the instructional and educative program through which students achieve life goals, ideals, and aspirations.

Determinants and Interpretations of Curriculum

Due to the amorphous nature of the word curriculum, many interpretations have emerged over the years. Some are broad, others narrow, depending on the philosophical beliefs of those interpreting the curriculum. Here are some interpretations:

- Curriculum is that which is taught in school,
- Curriculum is a set of subjects,
- Curriculum is content,
- A plan for learning,
- The content of courses in the program,

- Curriculum is a program of studies,
- Curriculum is a set of materials,
- Curriculum is a sequence of courses,
- Curriculum is a set of performance objectives,
- Curriculum is a course of study,
- A pattern of offering a program (scope and sequence),
- Everything that goes on in school,
- Out-of-classroom or out-of-school experiences of the learner,
- Intended outcomes and products of programs,
- The experience through which knowledge is communicated to learners, under teacher guidance,
- Curriculum is everything that goes on within the school, including extra-class activities, guidance, and interpersonal relationships,
- Curriculum is that which an individual learner experiences as a result of schooling (Oliver, 1997, p. 4).

The interpretations have implications for professionals or educators who conceptualize the curriculum and its implementation. The curriculum can be conceived narrowly (as subjects taught) or broadly (as all learners' experiences, both in school and out; directed by the school).

For example, Good (1945) in the *Dictionary of Education* describes the curriculum as: "a systematic group of courses or sequences of subjects required for graduation or certification in a field of study, for example, social studies curriculum, physical education curriculum" (p. 157).

Bobbitt (1918), one of the earlier writers on curriculum, perceived curriculum as: "that series of things which children and youths must do and experience by way of developing abilities to do the things well that make up the affairs of adult life; and to be in all respects what adults should be" (p. 42).

As the years have progressed, the conceptualizations of the school curriculum have continued to be broadened to include non-traditional learning environments, such as museums, community centers, and other contexts that may be virtual, especially in an age of technology, or in real brick and mortar schools, in curriculum development, implementation, and evaluation. Gay (1985), writing on desegregating the curriculum, offered a more expansive interpretation of curriculum: "If we are to achieve equally, we must broaden our conception to include the entire culture of the school—not just subject matter content" (pp. 61–62).

Educational Philosophies that Influence Curriculum Development

Philosophies are statements of beliefs about the aims of education that curriculum designers must consider as they design curriculums. Generally, the aims of education are conceived at a global and regional scale. The United Nations Educational, Scientific and Cultural Organization (UNESCO) provides this leadership and is foremost in providing the aims of education for humanity. Among these aims are the following:

- Fostering international understanding among all peoples of the world,
- Improving the standard of living of people in the various countries, and
- Solving continuous problems that plague humanity, such as war, disease, hunger, and unemployment.

Aims of education are usually derived from philosophies that individuals or groups have about the needs of children in society. No two countries would have the same needs based on historical developments, language, cultural beliefs, and other values. In the United States and other developed nations, four major philosophies have influenced curriculum planning and implementation. These theories and philosophies of education affect all subjects, depending on how they influence teaching and learning. Curriculum designers and educators have attempted to make sense of these philosophies and categorized them from the most traditional to the most liberal. Thus, broadly, these philosophies can be viewed as mainly traditional or progressive. The major philosophies that have influenced the aims and purpose of education and played a role in curriculum design include: Perennialism, Essentialism, Rationalism /Social Scientificism, Liberalism/Progressivism, Reconstructionism, Criticalism/Transformativism, and Accountability Perspectivism.

Perennialism

Perenialists follow the traditions of Plato, Aristotle, and Saint Thomas Aquinas, the Catholic Thinker. Perennialism values knowledge that transcends time. The goal of a perennialist educator is to teach students to think rationally and develop minds that can think critically. A subject-centered philosophy, the classroom has to be a well-organized and well-disciplined environment where students develop a lifelong quest for the truth. Perennialists value a highly academic curriculum emphasizing grammar, rhetoric, logic, mathematics, and great works of literature written by the finest thinkers of the Western World. They are primarily concerned with the importance of mastery of content and the development of reasoning skills. The adage "the more things change, the more they stay the same" summarizes the perennialist's perspective on education. Education was calculated to develop the mind, and school was a preparation for life. In this philosophy, skills are developed sequentially, and the teacher is the leading actor: a sage on the stage. Proponents of this philosophy include Hutchins, former president of the University of Chicago. According to Hutchins (1963),

> the ideal education is not an ad hoc education, not an education directed to immediate needs; it is not specialized education, or preprofessional education; it is not utilitarian education. It is an education, calculated to develop the mind (p. 18).

Essentialism

Essentialism is often referred to in the literature as Academic Scientism or Traditionalism. Essentialism is also a subject-centered philosophy that teaches basic skills and mind training. Essentialists believe that there is a body of knowledge about history, the sciences, and the arts that everyone should know. This body of knowledge, acquired largely through a curriculum of great books, should be emphasized in the curriculum and guide educational thinkers as they apply the knowledge in solving world problems. Essentialist educators focus on transmitting a series of progressively difficult topics and on the promotion of students to the next level. Subjects are focused on the historical context of the material world and culture, and move sequentially to give a solid understanding of the present day. The main purpose of essentialist education is to transmit cultural knowledge. A typical day at an essentialist school is broken up into periods, with students attending different classes during each period. Teaching and learning mainly involve the teacher lecturing while students take notes. Excellent lectures focus on essential knowledge, prescribed lab activities, writing critical essays, grammar, literature, geography, history, natural sciences, and other subjects. Students complete worksheets or hands-on projects, followed by a rigorous assessment of the learning material covered during the process. When assessments show sufficient competence, students are promoted to the next level to learn the next level of more difficult material. Historically, along with progressivism, essentialism has dominated the American educational landscape. This philosophy is also very prevalent in Europe. This philosophy fits in well with the centralized system of education as represented in Europe and most of its colonies, where educational models are mainly Assign-Study-Recite-Test. Ministries of education can select, promote, and control the content that students learn and reward or promote students based on their mastery of the subject matter. William C. Bagley, E.D. Hirsch, and Mortimer Adler, were some of the most influential advocates of essentialism.

Rationalism /Social Scientificism

Rationalism holds the philosophical view that reason is the best test of knowledge. In order to be effective, schools need to be clear about their educational objectives, the design of learning experiences that they provide for students, and how they measure whether the objectives have been met. Furthermore, we can know scientifically how children learn, and design "best practices" based on research. Good education is mainly achieved through lessons with clear behavioral objectives, appropriately sequenced activities, and assessments that indicate clearly whether the student objectives have been achieved. Prominent educators associated with this perspective are Ralph Tyler and Grant Wiggins.

Liberalism/Progressivism

The fundamental work of education is to awaken the mind and unleash the power of human imagination. Borrowing from European philosophers like Rousseau, this philosophy emphasized a child-centered teaching-learning environment. While the subject matter was important, it was secondary to critical skills and learning through experience. Materials that were relevant to students' lives and naturally crossed traditional disciplines would motivate students to want to learn and develop life-long learning habits. Diversity and individualism of learners were valued, and the school was viewed as a social environment to which the learner brought their bodies, emotions, and spirits alongside their minds. Progressive thinking had faith in democracy. Therefore, instead of an authoritarian practice, the teacher was viewed as a coach and partner in the educational process. Prominent educators associated with this perspective are John Dewey, Theodore Sizer, William H. Kilpatrick, and John Childs. According to Dewey:

> The child is the starting point, the center, and the end. His development, his growth, is the ideal. It alone furnishes the standard. To the growth of the child, all studies are subservient: they are instruments, valued as they serve the needs of growth. Personality, character is more than subject matter. Not knowledge or information, but self-realization is the goal.... Moreover, subject matter never can be got into the child from without. Learning is active. It involves reaching out of the mind. It involves organic assimilation, starting from within.... It is he, and not the subject matter, which determines both the quality and quantity of learning (Dewey, 1902, pp. 7–14).

Reconstructionism

Reconstructionists followed progressives and proposed that schools should be used to achieve improvements in society. In essence, schools should not just transmit knowledge or cultural heritage or study social problems but should be used as an agency to solve political and social problems. Subject matter to which all students should be exposed should include: unemployment issues, health needs, housing needs, ethnic problems, and other societal issues. Proponents of this philosophy included Hilda Taba and Theodore Brameld. Brameld described the values of reconstructionism as including:

- sufficient nourishment,
- adequate dress,
- shelter and privacy,
- erotic expression and celebration,
- physiological and mental health,
- literacy skill, information, novelty, curiosity, variation, recreation, adventure, growth, and creativity,
- participation and sharing, and
- steady work and steady income among others (Brameld, 1971 p. 418).

Criticalism/Transformativism

For Criticalists/Transformativists, the fundamental role of schools is to serve as an agent for social and economic justice, to expose patterns of racism and classism embedded in our culture and our economic system, and to especially empower, through education, those who have been denied access to political and economic power. Prominent educators associated with this perspective are Paolo Freire and bell hooks.

Accountability Perspectivism

The accountability perspective is a managerial approach to large-scale enterprises within the public sector. It is characterized by hierarchical authority, rule-based decision-making, production goals, routinization of tasks, accountability through measurement, and rewards and sanctions for performance. Prominent educators associated with this perspective include David Snedden, Marshall Smith, and Jennifer O'Day.

African Philosophies of Education

Like Western philosophies, African philosophies of education consider the context and experiences of the people. African philosophies of education are therefore as varied as the continent itself in geographical, socioeconomic, sociopolitical, cultural, religious beliefs, and colonial histories. In Northern Africa, for example, the philosophy of education is often biased toward the Muslim religion. In parts of West Africa that the French colonized, the philosophies often lean toward Francophone thinking, and in Eastern African regions that were colonized by predominantly the British, the Anglophone mindset often predominates educational aspirations and outcomes. Despite these variabilities, one common thread runs through African philosophies of education: the belief that education is not just about imparting knowledge and skills but is a holistic process that encompasses a person's entire being as well as his/her connections and responsibilities to the larger community. Understanding the various philosophies is important, because they could be incorporated into contemporary curriculum design in Sub-Saharan Africa (SSA).

The main philosophies of education that undergird African epistemologies of education include: *Preparedness/Preparationism, Utilitarianism/Functionalism, Communalism; Holisticism and Perennialism, Ethnophilosophy, Ubuntu, Community, Reasonableness, Moral Maturity, Maat or Ma'at*. A common thread that runs through all these epistemologies is the philosophy of Ubuntu. Higgs (2003) states that "ubuntu is a form of humanism which could engender communal embeddedness and connectedness of a person to other persons" (p. 13). The word "Ubuntu" itself is derived from a Nguni (isiZulu) aphorism: *Umuntu Ngumuntu Ngabantu*, which translates as "a person is a person because of or through others" (Moloketi, 2009, p. 243; Tutu, 2004). In African culture, Ubuntu is the capacity to express compassion, reciprocity, dignity, humanity, and mutuality in the interests of building and maintaining communities with justice and mutual caring (Khoza, 2006; Luhabe, 2002; Mandela, 2006, p. xxv; Tutu, 1999).

Educators like Wiredu (2005) postulate that African philosophies of education, such as Ubuntu, primarily harmonize individual needs with societal interests, encourage putting oneself in the shoes of others, and respect all human and non-human life (p. 8). According to Wiredu (2005), approaching education in this way will produce relevant knowledge for Africa that is both particular (local) and universally applicable (global) (p. 18). Such a philosophy sees an educated person as one who has attained moral maturity and refinement and has acquired a high degree of reasonableness (Wiredu, 2004).

Assie-Lumumba (2005) believes that the African philosophy of education focuses on cultivating self-determined, free and decent citizens who, while integrating fitting aspects of other cultures with theirs, strive to remain in communion with others (p. 23). Virtues like honesty, faithfulness, duty, and empathy for the well-being of others in the community and humanness are highly emphasized. Humanness embodies dignity, compassion, togetherness, community, and respect for human rights. In such a philosophy, the significance of an individual is seen through his/her capacity to commune with others. If, for example, one is faced with the choice of acquiring wealth and preserving the life of another human being, one should choose the preservation of life. The Ubuntu philosophy permeates all facets of life among ethnic groups of Africans or Bantu descent, generally located in SSA. This philosophy of education is a fusion of past and present knowledge to improve people's lives. Understanding this philosophy of education requires adopting a three-pronged approach:

- Reflection—by identifying problems and reflecting on them, one can come up with major problems that negatively affect the African continent and citizens' ways of being and living.
- Justification and Validation—by suggesting reasons for the existence of the problems.
- Determination—by determining the consequences that the problems pose to the educational system, and why failure to fix the problems would be harmful to society.

This approach is cognizant of the main elements that undergird African education policy, which include:
- Bringing individual and Societal interests in concert with each

other,
- Identifying individuals' vulnerabilities and accommodating them,
- Advocating and advancing African people's self-determination and freedom, and
- Fusing the local and global (or universal).

According to Desmond Tutu (2004), Ubuntu symbolizes the backbone of African spirituality and is Africa's greatest contribution to the world.

The various philosophies of curriculum can be interpreted as having general perspectives that are either Prescriptive or descriptive (Glatthorn et al., 2019).

Prescriptive and Descriptive Perspectives of Curriculum

The headings below provide both Prescriptive and Descriptive curriculum perspectives that guide the definitions of curriculum, offered by some past and present leaders in the field.

Prescriptive Perspective Definitions of Curriculum, by Date, Author and Definition

1902: John Dewey—Curriculum is a continuous reconstruction, moving from the child's present experience out into that represented by the organized bodies of truth that we call studies . . . the various studies . . . are themselves experience—they are that of the race.

1918: Franklin Bobbitt—Curriculum is the entire range of experiences, both directed and undirected, concerned with unfolding the individual's abilities.

1927: Harold O. Rugg—The curriculum is a succession of experiences and enterprises that are as lifelike as possible for the learner, giving the learner the most helpful development in meeting and controlling life situations.

1935: Hollis Caswell, in Caswell & Campbell—The curriculum is composed of all the experiences children have under the guidance of teachers.... Thus, curriculum considered as a field of study represents no strictly limited body of content, but rather a process or procedure.

1957: Ralph Tyler—The curriculum is all the learning experiences planned and directed by the school to attain its educational goals.

1967: Robert Gagne—Curriculum is a sequence of content units arranged in such a way that the learning of each unit may be accomplished as a single act, provided the capabilities described by specified prior units (in the sequence) have already been mastered by the learner.

1970: James Popham & Eva Baker—Curriculum is all planned learning outcomes for which the school is responsible.... Curriculum refers to the desired consequences of instruction.

1997: J. L. McBrien & R. Brandt—Curriculum refers to a written plan outlining what students will be taught (a course of study). Curriculum may refer to all the courses offered at a given school or those offered at a school in a particular area of study.

2010: Indiana Department of Education—Curriculum means the planned interaction of pupils with instructional content, materials, resources, and processes for evaluating the attainment (Glatthorn et al., 2008, 2019).

Descriptive definitions of curriculum, provided below, go beyond the prescriptive terms above and force us to think about the curriculum in more than simply what is done in real classrooms. They examine curriculum as an experience, something that is in "action." The definitions vary from the prescriptive definitions of curriculum, primarily in their breadth and in their emphasis on experience, learning, or what students and teachers do.

Descriptive Perspective Definitions of Curriculum, by Date, Author and Definition

1935: Hollis Caswell & Doak Campbell—All the experiences children have under the guidance of teachers.

1941: Thomas Hopkins—Those learnings each child selects, accepts, and incorporates into himself to act with, on, and upon, in subsequent experiences.

1960: W. B. Ragan—All experiences of the child for which the school accepts responsibility.

1987: Glen Hass—The set of actual experiences and perceptions of each individual learner's experiences of his or her education program.

1995: Daniel Tanner & Laurel Tanner—The reconstruction of knowledge and experience that enables the learner to grow in exercising intelligent control of subsequent knowledge and experience.

2006: D. F. Brown—All student school experiences relating to the improvement of skills and strategies in thinking critically and creatively, solving problems, working collaboratively with others, communicating well, writing more effectively, reading more analytically, and conducting research to solve problems.

2009: E. Silva—An emphasis on what students can do with knowledge, rather than what units of knowledge they have, is the essence of 21st-century skills (Glatthorn, Boschee and Whitehead, 2008, pp. 4–5).

Several points worthy of note in the various definitions and perspectives of curriculum, include the following:

1). The term curriculum includes both the plans made for learning and the actual learning experiences provided. (Sometimes plans can be modified or ignored).
2). "Retrievable documents" include all forms of documents, including digitally stored curricula (that is, software and/or shared on the Internet).
3). Some curricular policy statements are very general, while others, for example, daily lesson plans, are quite specific.
4). There are two main dimensions of actualized curriculum: the curriculum as experienced by the learner and that which a disinterested observer might observe.
5). The experienced curriculum takes place in an environment that influences and impinges on learning and constitutes what is usually termed the hidden curriculum.
6). In the written curriculum, when the curriculum is a set of documents that guide planning, instruction is only one relatively minor aspect of the curriculum. Those retrievable documents used in planning for learning typically specify five components: a rationale for the curriculum; the aims, objectives, and content

for achieving those objectives; instructional methods; learning materials and resources; and tests or assessment methods.

However, whatever definition of curriculum that is adopted, curriculum and instruction should co-exist within an intimate relationship that is generally understood by educators and should be useful in helping all stakeholders make operational decisions, and also guide policy-makers design policies.

Part II

Blueprint of Southern Cameroons National Education Policy

Part II provides brief guidelines of various pillars of education policy that are not fully examined in Part I of this book. This part is a blueprint written specifically for the former British trust territory, Southern Cameroons. These and other topics will be expanded upon after experts have convened to generate details when the appropriate time comes. This part is divided into chapters with each chapter indicating an important pillar of education policy.

Some elements of this blueprint were discussed and developed by the Southern Cameroons Education Board (SCEB) Department that was constituted during the early part of the struggle in 2018, when many Southern Cameroonians were clamoring for independence. Other departments were also created as a preparatory step for when this part of the country would get its independence from La Republique du Cameroun or if the pressure that was being put on the central government of Cameroon, could lead to a return to the federal State that was agreed upon at independence. The purpose of the consultative body was to analyze the current education system that is imposed upon the former British Southern Cameroons and suggest new and suitable policy guidelines that could address the issues with the current education system at various levels. The purpose of this policy blueprint is to provide a framework to all counties, departments of education, and governing bodies of public schools for the administration of schools in Southern Cameroons. Without a doubt, there is a "gap" between the education offered to Southern Cameroonians and the 21st-century demands of the workforce.

CHAPTER 9

Mission and Vision of the Consultative Body for Policy Development

Before beginning its work, the defunct Southern Cameroons Education Board (SCEB) outlined its roles which included the following:

- Develop and distribute a National policy with recommendations for who would oversee it.
- Develop a five-year plan for reviewing/revising primary school curricula and textbooks in various subject areas.
- Ensure the quality of the teacher training program at colleges or departments of education at the university and require Teacher Training Colleges (TTC) to offer both initial and in-service teacher training to upgrade and improve the quality of the teaching staff.
- Establish a National Examination Council.
- Establish a proper functioning General Inspectorate of Education.
- Adopt quality and relevant textbooks for schools.
- Develop teaching methodology so that they are geared to real life.
- Reinforce and develop the teaching force and profession through relevant curriculum, professional ethics, and professional advancement.
- Take responsibility for continued evaluation/assessment of the programs that provide advancement to higher levels.
- Encourage the development of school-based assessments and training of teachers in various competencies.
- Provide learning environments (space, equipment, and learning materials) that take into account gender differences (separate

restrooms for boys and girls).
- Reward teachers for excellence in teaching and students for academic excellence.

The board conceptualized the scope of its work as spanning early childhood education, kindergarten through twelfth grades, university and professional education, adult education and job training.

SCEB Vision

All Southern Cameroonian students of the 21st century will attain the highest level of academic knowledge, applied learning, and performance skills to ensure fulfilling personal lives and careers, and their contribution to civic and economic progress in a diverse changing democratic society.

SCEB Mission

Create strong, effective schools that provide a wholesome learning environment through incentives that raise the standard of student accomplishment as measured by a valid, reliable accountability system. Overhaul the entire system and implement an education policy and curriculum befitting of a model 21st-century nation.

SCEB Core Educational Beliefs

Schooling should help all students achieve their highest potential. To accomplish this, students need to be provided equitable access to all areas of the curricula; appropriate high-quality instruction that addresses their needs and maximally advances their skills and knowledge; up-to-date and relevant resources; and settings that are physically and psychologically safe, respectful, and intellectually stimulating. All students—regardless of circumstance—deserve a world-class education. To ensure this, Southern Cameroons will establish itself among the best-educated nations globally, capable of providing one of the most competitive workforces in the world with a high proportion of college graduates. Its citizens will receive a non-discriminatory, all-inclusive, and rewarding education. The quality of a child's education, learning environment, and opportunities to succeed are not to be determined by his or her ethnicity, national origin, tribe, political party affiliation, age, sex, disability, language, and/or socioeconomic status. All students in any learning institution in Southern Cameroons should have an equal opportunity to learn and excel in a safe and supportive environment.

To provide every student with a world-class, 21st-century education, the government of Southern Cameroons must acknowledge the current challenges, including existing inequities in the current educational systems. Analyses of data have revealed persistent discrimination for students from different regions of the country because of their disabilities, language, and ethnic origin. Current evidence also indicates that some groups of students experience low levels of safety and acceptance in schools for reasons including cultural, ethnic, and linguistic backgrounds. Some students have limited access to well-prepared teachers and other educational resources. Having recognized the existence of these inequities, Southern Cameroons will purposefully and strategically take action to prevent and ensure that such inequities, differences, and discrimination do not repeat themselves. All students in every region of Southern Cameroons shall be provided equitable access to education.

SCEB Strategic Goals and Objectives

This policy aims to provide equitable access to good, quality, child-friendly universal education by providing opportunities for all children in the first cycle of education: kindergarten, primary, and junior high school levels. In order to realize this goal, the following will be proposed as general policy objectives:

- Educate a free citizen liberated from all kinds of discrimination, including gender-based discrimination, exclusion, and favoritism.
- Contribute to the promotion of a culture of peace as well as Southern Cameroons and universal values of justice, peace, tolerance, respect for human rights, gender equality, and democracy.
- Dispense a holistic moral, intellectual, social, physical, and professional education through the promotion of individual competencies and aptitudes in the service of national reconstruction

and the sustainable development of the country.
- Promote science and technology with special attention to information and communication technology (ICT).
- Transform the Southern Cameroonian population into human capital for development by acquiring development skills.
- Eliminate all the causes and obstacles that can lead to a disparity in education, be it gender, disability, geography, or social group.
- Ensure that education is available and accessible to all Southern Cameroonians.
- Improve the quality and relevance of education.
- Promote an integral, comprehensive education oriented toward respecting human rights and being cognizant of the country's history.
- Inculcate in children the importance of environment, hygiene, health, and protection against diseases.
- Improve the capacity for planning, management, and administration of education.
- Adopt and support rigorous academic standards in performance in all academic content in all school disciplines, especially English Language Arts and Science, Technology, Engineering, Arts, and Mathematics (STEAM) from kindergarten through upper secondary levels.
- In assessments, maintain policies ensuring that all students receive nationally normed and standards-based assessments.

SCEB Broad Policy Statements and Implementation Strategies

The following are general and broad policy statements for various areas of the education system. They include:

1). Access to Education
2). Quality and Relevance in Education
3). Special Education
4). Education System and Management
5). Financing of Education
6). Disparity in Education

7). Health Education

Other areas examined in this blueprint include:

- school size/class size
- school choice
- graduation requirements
- teacher selection, education, and certification
- teacher pay
- teaching methods
- curricular content
- school infrastructure and investment
- the values that schools are expected to uphold and to model, and
- other areas as seen fit

Access to Education

- Basic education shall be provided to all Southern Cameroonians (boys, girls, women, and men).
- The current six years of basic education shall be progressively increased to nine years, where appropriate, and shall be under the same school administration.
- A specific year shall be stipulated for when Universal Primary Education (UPE) shall be reached.
- Teacher training shall be increased at all levels according to the Pupil-Teacher Ratio (PTR) stipulated.
- Early Childhood Care and Development (ECCD) shall be offered to children by involving various partners, especially communities and encouraging private sector participation.
- Popular education, through functional literacy, shall be provided to all people—women and men, boys and girls—considering their specific constraints, needs, and incentives and in the spirit of life-long learning.

SCEB Objectives

- Take measures to ensure the internal efficiency of the system.
- Increase infrastructure and civil society and faith-based

organizations' initiatives in the construction, management of schools, and equipment in accordance with set standards and laws.
- Encourage private schools at all levels.
- Support private initiatives involved in promoting education.
- Encourage greater parental participation in the efforts to educate their children, including school construction initiatives, donating to schools, volunteering hours in schools, attending parent-teacher conferences, and participating in at least two school events when school is in session.
- Publicize the message that education is free and equal for all Southern Cameroonians.
- Encourage continuing education and distance learning in all types of training (formal, non-formal).

Quality and Relevance in Education
- Develop an outcome-oriented curriculum to be used by all schools, monitored and reviewed as necessary.
- Provide relevant, quality textbooks.
- Strengthen teacher training through both pre-service and in-service methods with the use of distance learning.
- Identify and institutionalize various forms of teacher incentives.
- Inspect all teachers and schools (public or private) to evaluate the performance of students and the implementation of policies.
- Assess all students at the elementary and secondary levels, using a national examination upon completing each education cycle.

CHAPTER 10

Special Education

Special Education (abbreviated SPED) is also known in the literature as Special Needs Education, Aided Education, or Exceptional Education.

Special Education is the practice of educating students in a way that addresses their individual differences and needs. SPED involves understanding and valuing similarities and differences that include: social identities, socioeconomic status, gender, religion, and other factors like disabilities. SPED services are designed to ensure that students with disabilities receive instruction and services specially designed to assist them with access to the general curriculum and allow them to progress in school. All individuals with disabilities and with exceptional needs have a right to participate in free appropriate, public education and special education instruction and services for these persons are needed in order to ensure them of the right to an appropriate educational opportunity to meet their unique needs. Common special needs include learning disabilities (such as dyslexia), communication disorders, emotional and behavioral disorders (such as attention-deficit/hyperactivity disorder (ADHD)), physical disabilities (such as cerebral palsy, muscular dystrophy, spina bifida), and developmental disabilities (such as autism spectrum disorders and intellectual disability).

SPED processes involve individually planned and systematically monitored teaching procedures, adapted equipment and materials, and accessible settings designed to help individuals with special needs achieve higher self-efficacy and success in school and their community. Acquiring certain skills may be too difficult if these students are taught only in typical classroom instructional protocols.

Mark Anderson reported in *The Guardian* (August 18, 2015) that many children with disabilities in poorer countries are left out of primary education, and consequently all other levels of education. This report was corroborated by a US State Department Human Rights Report (2015) stating that over 500,000 children with disabilities were not in education establishments in South Africa, which reflects a trend in other developing nations. In Sub-Saharan African (SSA) countries, Kenya has made commendable efforts by enrolling more disabled students than any other nation: 110 special schools equipped with flexible curriculum, 25,000 teachers and 456 officials trained to cater to the needs of special learners. Ethiopia failed to address disability early on, but newer policies focus on this sector. Currently, there is Federal guidance addressing non-participation. Support centers have been developed to train teachers lacking special education knowledge. Six thousand children with disabilities out of 15 million have access to primary education, mainly in 20 special schools and 130 regular schools. Yet, even in countries that have enacted national policies for SPED, parental involvement is still very limited.

In 2006, the United Nations adopted the Convention on the Rights of Persons with Disabilities (CRPD), officially opened it for signatures to nations on March 30, 2007, and "entered into force," meaning it became law for nations that ratified it on May 3, 2008. Although over 140 nations signed the treaty, they were not obliged not to violate the purpose of the treaty; neither were they bound to uphold the specific obligations of CRPD, until after they had ratified it.

> The Convention is intended as a human rights instrument with an explicit, social development dimension. It adopts a broad categorization of persons with disabilities and reaffirms that all persons with all types of disabilities must enjoy all human rights and fundamental freedoms. It clarifies and qualifies how all categories of rights apply to persons with disabilities and identifies areas where adaptations have to be made for persons with disabilities to effectively exercise

their rights and areas where their rights have been violated, and where protection of rights must be reinforced (Langtree, 2014).

Cameroon signed the treaty on October 8, 2008, and later ratified it. Effective SPED policies and frameworks for implementation are an urgent need in Cameroon as a whole, particularly in Southern Cameroons. The Ministries of basic, secondary and higher education are responsible for implementing inclusive education, while the Ministry of Social Affairs assesses learners with disabilities through its regional delegations, and issues disability cards so that these learners can benefit from free education. SPED Policy Framework in Southern Cameroons is an urgent need because, despite legislation, this continues to be a highly neglected sector with persistent challenges. Although there is national and international legislation that caters to students with special needs in an inclusive environment, many students with disabilities are still unable to realize their education or their social and general human rights in parts of Southern Cameroons due to a number of challenges that include:

- persistent stigma and discrimination that children with disabilities face from birth,
- lack of acceptance by parents, family members, and society in general,
- lack of self-esteem and doubt in their own abilities,
- lack of awareness of the population of the importance of SPED students,
- lack of proper accommodation such as assistive technology, ramps, toilets, etc.,
- lack of trained teachers to effectively teach students with special needs,
- lack of adequate financial resources and basic school supplies, and the lack of education of the community on the nature of disabilities education and the need for inclusion.

Non-governmental organizations, such as Liliane Fonds (2024), have been participating in the sensitization work and lobbying the government, but there continues to be a need for mass sensitization through the media (television, radio, and newspapers), formal and informal meetings with politicians, training of education authorities and school administrators, creation of parent support groups, piloting inclusive education in government schools, and providing specialized advisory support to strengthen government capacity in the field of inclusive education. Attention to SPED policy in Southern Cameroons is nascent and has a long way to go in matters of identification of students with disabilities and ensuring that all students with special needs are served at no cost to parents.

Policy Framework

An effective policy for special education would focus on the following areas:

- Establish a Southern Cameroons Institute of Special Education (SCISE).
- Develop resources for special education (SPED).
- Answer the question of who a child with a disability is.
- Have laws in place that will guide special education.
- Identify services that can be provided to students with special needs.
- Provide adequate venues for students with disabilities to receive special education and related services.
- Ensure that all SPED students receive a Free Appropriate Public Education (FAPE)

Strategies

Strategies will include:

- Establishing a Southern Cameroons Institute of Special Education (SCISE).
- Requiring the efficient utilization of resources, (human and physical, especially with regard to teacher deployment) management and development.
- Introducing Continuing Professional Development (CPD) for

in-service teachers who have had no training in SPED.
- Implementing the policy of inclusive education for special needs pupils.
- Ensuring the disbursement of grants to special schools and units to procure specialized instructional materials and equipment.
- Providing incentives for local production of specialized equipment and instructional materials (assistive devices and appropriate ICT software and hardware) to institutions for learners with special needs.
- Improving the physical and social environments in learning institutions.
- Establishing a Special Needs Education data management system and integration into the Education Management Information System (EMIS) at national and county levels.
- Requiring the efficient utilization of human and physical resources, especially regarding teacher deployment, management, and development, and the introduction of Continuing Professional Development (CPD) for teachers.
- Implementing the policy of inclusive education for special needs pupils.
- Enhancing and continuing disbursing of grants to special schools and units; procure specialized instructional materials and equipment in addition to the capitation.
- Providing incentives for local production of specialized equipment and instructional materials.
- Disbursing operational grants to Education Assessment Resource Centers (EARC) to enable the staff to carry out community mobilization and other outreach activities.
- Improving the Special Needs Education (SNE) data management system and integrating it into the Education Management Information System (EMIS) at national and county levels.
- Providing specialized instructional materials, equipment, assistive devices, and appropriate ICT software and hardware to institutions with learners with special needs,

- Improving the physical and social environments in learning institutions to accommodate students with special needs.
- Developing and funding programs to create public awareness and advocacy on SNE and mainstreaming it into the education programs across levels, and
- Disbursing operational grants to the EARCs to enable staff mobilize the community and conduct other outreach activities involving parents and caretakers.

General Guidelines

All individuals with disabilities and exceptional needs have a right to participate in FAPE. SPED instruction and services for these persons are needed in order to ensure that they have the right to appropriate educational opportunities at no cost to parents and that meet their unique needs. For a child with one or more disabilities to be eligible for SPED, they must have a unique educational need that requires specially designed instruction. Such unique needs are those that indicate that the disability is such that the child's educational performance will be significantly different from those of his/her peers. Specially designed instruction requires adaptation of content, pedagogy, classroom environments, and other instructional necessities that enable the child to access the general education curriculum and meet national and county educational standards.

Chapter 11

Health and Nutrition

The constitution of the World Health Organization (WHO), adopted in 1946, states, among others that:

> Health is a state of complete physical, mental, and social well-being and not merely the absence of disease or infirmity. The enjoyment of the highest attainable standard of health is one of the fundamental rights of every human being without distinction of race, religion, political belief, economic or social condition. The health of all peoples is fundamental to the attainment of peace and security and is dependent on the fullest co-operation of individuals and States (WHO, 1946).

Health and good nutrition are inherently interrelated. According to the Washington State Department of Social and Health Services (DSHS), "Good nutrition prolongs independence by maintaining physical strength, mobility, endurance, hearing, vision, and cognitive abilities" (Washington State, DSHS, n.d., p. 1). According to DSHS, Nutrition education is "any set of learning experiences designed to facilitate the voluntary adoption of eating and other nutrition-related behaviors conducive to health and well-being" (p.1).

Importance of Health and Nutrition Education

For students to perform well at other academic tasks, they should have good nutrition and be healthy. Good nutrition and Health Education involves providing "adequate knowledge and skills necessary for critical thinking regarding diet and health so the individual can make healthy food choices from an increasingly complex food supply and assist the individual to identify resources for continuing access to sound food and nutrition information" (p. 1).

Nutrition education, however, goes beyond providing information to people, to fostering critical thinking, changing attitudes, and adopting practical skills and actions that facilitate healthy living. It embraces a broader vision encompassing educational strategies and environmental support to encourage adopting healthier, sustainable food choices and eating patterns (Piscopo, 2019).

Nutrition problems broadly fall within two categories:
1). Insufficient intake relative to nutritional needs, and
2). Excessive and unbalanced food intake or a particular dietary component.

In Sub-Saharan Africa (SSA), and other developing countries like Southern Cameroons, the problem with nutrition is mostly found in the insufficient intake of nutritious foods. This is due to factors like poverty and other environmental issues. Southern Cameroons recognizes the critical relationship between a healthy student and academic achievement. Students must be healthy to be educated and be educated to be healthy. An increasing number of students are going to school with a variety of health problems that make it more difficult for them to learn at an optimal level and achieve academically.

Goals

The main goal of nutrition education in Southern Cameroons would be to reinforce specific nutrition-related practices or behaviors that would encourage changing habits that contribute to poor health. This will have to occur in multiple settings. The school provides a rich and dynamic environment which can assist in achieving this goal through multiple learning strategies, environmental supports, and collaboration with individuals and groups inside and outside the school, targeting different population groups and utilizing a variety of channels, tools, and materials. The major focus of such education would not only be to acquire knowledge and facts, but rather to lead students to develop permanent behavioral changes. A more integrated approach involves as many groups of the community as possible and uses a variety of educational approaches. These educational approaches that integrate health facilities, lay groups, factories, retailers, and others have been seen to be more effective.

The World Health Organization (WHO) stipulates that health and nutrition education are instinctively interconnected through shared activities, interests, dependencies, and other related aspects, which positively or negatively promote, maintain, and/or restore the individual's health.

Importance of School Health and Feeding Programs

As noted in Blössner's (2008) review of *School Health, Nutrition and Education for All* by Jukes et al. (2008), between 200 million and 500 million school days are lost due to poor child health in low-income countries around the world. Studies show that children who suffer from poor health and poor nutrition, often face learning difficulties. This makes sense because when children are healthy, they can attend school and learn relatively better than their sickly and malnourished peers. Poor health and nutrition affect society from poor school attendance, poor learning, low performance, and lack of growth of the individual, the community, and society at large. Studies conducted among U.S. high school students by the U.S. Center for Disease Control and Prevention (CDC) (2005) show a correlation between health-related behaviors and educational outcomes such as grades, test scores, and academic achievement.

Since health interventions promote positive health behaviors and improve academic outcomes for students, educational and public health institutions should collaborate to promote students' health. The results of such interventions would accrue huge benefits for all countries, especially the poorest and most vulnerable countries, including Southern Cameroons (see Table 11.1).

> **Table 11.1. Characteristics of an Effective Health Education Curriculum for Sub-Saharan Africa**
>
> 1. Focuses on clear health goals and related behavioral outcomes.
> 2. Is research-based and theory-driven.
> 3. Addresses individual values, attitudes, and beliefs.
> 4. Addresses individual and group norms that support health-enhancing behaviors.
> 5. Focuses on reinforcing protective factors and increasing perceptions of personal risk and harmfulness of engaging in specific unhealthy practices and behaviors.
> 6. Addresses social pressures and influences.
> 7. Builds personal competence, social competence, and self-efficacy by addressing skills.
> 8. Provides functional health knowledge that is basic, accurate, and directly contributes to health-promoting decisions and behaviors.
> 9. Uses strategies designed to personalize information and engage students.
> 10. Provides age-appropriate and developmentally appropriate information, learning strategies, teaching methods, and materials.
> 11. Incorporates learning strategies, teaching methods, and materials that are culturally inclusive.
> 12. Provides adequate time for instruction and learning.
> 13. Provides opportunities to reinforce skills and positive health behaviors.
> 14. Provides opportunities to make positive connections with influential others.
> 15. Includes teacher information and plans for professional development and training that enhance effectiveness of instruction and student learning.
>
> *Source.* Centers for Disease Control and Prevention (2020) *Characteristics of an Effective Health Education Curriculum,* https://www.cdc.gov/healthyschools/sher/characteristics/index.htm (accessed June 19, 2020).

The State of Health and Nutrition Education in Cameroon and Southern Cameroons

According to the Himalayan Institute (HI), Cameroonians utilize herbal medicines, natural health products, yoga therapy, lifestyle counseling, and health education awareness to address critical gaps in the overburdened health systems. Amidst the conflict in Southern Cameroons, some rural empowerment programs continue to assist in poverty alleviation through education, health care, and some job creation. Yet in places like the Northwest, the average life expectancy remains at only 54 years, with most deaths stemming from preventable and communicable diseases that are linked to poverty and other controllable lifestyle influences, as well as the lack of health knowledge.

After examining school health, nutrition, and school performance in rural Cameroon, Lengha (2014) states that "there are direct correlations between health and academic performance for learners." No matter the learner's intelligence level, if health and nutritional requirements are not met, academic performance is negatively affected. Poor environmental conditions and unbalanced diets affect health, leading to school absenteeism and negatively affecting academic performance. Other factors, such as the lack of well-constructed toilet facilities, lack of access to drinking water, and lack of sex education in most school curricula, which has led to the prevalence of HIV/AIDS and adolescent pregnancies, have further exacerbated the health issues for school children (Kwachou, 2015; UNICEF, 2012.)

Schools must play a decisive role in supporting and collaborating with communities, institutions, systems, and processes that are void of political corruption, nepotism, tribalism, and occultism, to address the depressing and daunting conditions of health and nutrition that are due in part to an atrocious war currently ravaging the territory since 2017. The war has displaced and killed thousands and destroyed schools, hospitals, homes, property, and many other facilities that were used for promoting healthy lifestyles. In such precarious, calamitous socioeconomic contexts, designing a health and nutrition education policy framework, is an onerous task.

Guidelines

Broad guidelines for such a health and nutrition education policy would involve encouraging and empowering the present generation of youths to make healthy choices, advocate for integration and collaboration among education actors, and improve students' cognitive, physical, social, emotional, and developmental processes. For this to happen certain

factors must be fully present:
- the presence of political will,
- addressing corruption (which is a ubiquitous element in almost all levels of government institutions),
- addressing outdated, harmful traditional superstitious beliefs,
- promoting knowledge and skills, relative to healthy living and good nutritional programs, with governments ensuring regular health/physical examinations and treatment in all education establishments,
- providing adequate and accessible clean and safe water, and conducting regular personal hygiene inspections on learners and their environment,
- delivering appropriate and adequate, safe, clean, and well-maintained sanitary facilities, while making sure that family life and sexuality education are promoted, as well as establishing preventive and mitigating actions to stem the spread and impact of various diseases, including STIs/HIV and AIDS,
- promoting a combination of education and techniques, designed to facilitate the voluntary adoption of food choices and nutrition-connected behaviors, for the furtherance and maintenance of health conditions of the individual,
- focusing on knowledge, attitudes, and values that promote positive health outcomes beyond personal physical health such as early pregnancy and violent substance abuse, to socioemotional and environmental health,
- incorporating nutrition education throughout the school day, in classrooms, farms to schools, school gardens, cafeteria, etc.,
- encouraging healthy eating choices and other nutrition-related behaviors and techniques to enhance awareness, and self-efficacy, surrounding the trigger of risky nutrient-related behaviors through the consumption of proteins, carbohydrates, fat, water, vitamins, and minerals,
- taking advantage of professional and scientific knowledge in designing curricula for effective health education,

- knowing that culinary variances exist across cultures, thereby exposing, endowing, and enhancing understanding and appreciation for diversity; and making sure that the policy framework, content, and curricula are age-appropriate and culturally sensitive, and
- believing that, in infancy and childhood, the family is critical in children's learning and health development preferences and habits; and as children grow and mature, school, community, peers, societal environments, and preferences become important tools; and as they become independent, they start making personal choices.

Strategies
- Institutionalize a government-supported school meals program for needy children.
- Encourage communities to establish community school farms, which would provide the government with discounted commodities for the school meals program.
- Require schools and communities to identify excluded children and to ensure their enrollment.
- Develop and ensure the implementation of an all-inclusive education policy by removing all barriers to disadvantaged groups.
- Sensitize parents on the need to enroll and to retain girls in schools, and to make school environment gender sensitive.
- Address factors that enhance gender parity.
- Conduct a needs assessment to provide baseline data for implementing alternative modes of delivering education.
- Operationalize the Nomadic Education Policy framework to address the challenges in providing education in Arid and Semi-Arid Lands (ASAL).
- Provide low-cost boarding schools in ASAL for both regions.
- Build relationships with community agencies to offer continued supplemental educational campaigns for health.
- Schools will use the adopted health textbooks to promote healthy eating and teach appropriate, long-term eating habits and practices.

- Develop and elaborate nutrition and hygiene strategies for the schools.
- Develop and elaborate a Gender in Education strategy.

Students will be taught, among other factors:
- Acceptance of personal responsibility for lifelong health.
- Respect for and promotion of the health of others.
- An understanding of the process of growth and development.
- Informed use of health-related information, products, and services.

Because there are myriad differences and commonalities regarding school health and nutrition education policies and programs across the regions, it is recommended that school health and nutrition models for Southern Cameroons be carefully examined to fit each community and school. Integrating school programs into community efforts or involving local communities will produce more sustainable results than standalone approaches. As far as health and nutrition are concerned, the overall goal of Southern Cameroons is for students to achieve health literacy and, ultimately, lifelong wellness by mastering the knowledge, skills, and behaviors in the major areas critical to healthy living.

Chapter 12

Character Education

Character education helps solve behavioral problems and improves academic achievements; hence, a comprehensive character education policy may address many tough educational issues while developing a positive school climate.

Norms and Standards for Teachers, Learners, and Parents

Character education includes and complements a broad range of educational approaches, such as whole-child education, service learning, social-emotional learning, and civic education. Because students spend so much time in school, the school environment becomes important to ensure that all students get the support and help they need to reach their full potential. To have successful outcomes in schools and communities, character education must involve everyone—school staff, parents, students, places of worship, and community members.

Why We Need Character Education

Covey (2004), author of *The 7 Habits of Highly Effective People* makes the case for teaching our young people values and virtues in school. According to Covey, character—the foundation of success, includes "things such as integrity, humility, fidelity, temperance, courage, justice, patience, industry, simplicity, modesty, and the Golden Rule" (p. 18). Horace Mann, the Father of American education argued that character development was as important as academics in American schools. In fact, one of the six goals of the U.S. Department of Education (2002) in their *Strategic Plan*,

2002-2007, is to "promote strong character and citizenship among our nation's youth" (p. 16).

Cameroon ranks first among other nations in the world in corruption. Any education policy for Southern Cameroons must include character education. This policy area is necessary to ensure students' mental and moral well-being and enable them to participate peacefully and responsibly as citizens in nation-building.

Policy Goals

Policy goals would be broad and include the emotional, intellectual, and moral qualities of a person or group, tailored after the ethical values of the society and cognizant of the fact that Southern Cameroonians are part of a global community. Tenets will emphasize the role of teachers as professionals, working with parents and community members as partners to positively shape the social, emotional, and character development of the young people entrusted to them each day. Teachers are responsible for assuring that students feel safe, respected, and connected to those around them in ways that ensure that they thrive academically and socially and are motivated to give back to their communities. The policy design will elaborate on the importance of various aspects that include:

- conduct in the teaching profession (examples of such conduct are listed in National Education Association (NEA) (2020) manual;
- ethical conduct toward students; ethical conduct toward practices and performance;
- ethical conduct toward professional colleagues, parents, and community, bearing in mind educators' recognition that quality education is the common goal of the public, boards of education, and educators, and cooperative efforts are essential to attain these character goals.

Chapter 13

Focus on Gender and Culture

In the regional profile of female participation in education in Sub-Saharan Africa (SSA), a gender gap in education increases in severity with each level of education. Although existing data are often incomplete and not always comprehensive, they still provide some direction for informing country-level policy directions about female participation in education, especially if such data are formulated within each country's profile. Because time series data do not exist, it is usually impossible to assess whether conditions change in individual countries or the SSA region.

Eliminating Gender Disparities and Ensuring Gender Equality in Educational Opportunities, with Special Focus on the Girl Child

In the study, Statistical Indicators of Female Participation in Education in Sub-Saharan Africa (Hartnett & Heneveld, 1993) used the concept of Gender Ratio (GR) as a statistical indicator to measure the levels of female participation in education and the disparities that exist between males and females. They considered all 18 indicators that assess performance in education systems, and then, grouped them into the three following categories of educational performance: (a) access, (b) attainment, and (c) accomplishment. *Access* refers to the decision to enter females in school (five indicators); *attainment* to the length of time females remain in school and to the level of education to which they progress (nine indicators); and *accomplishment* to their success once they leave school (four indicators) (Hartnett & Heneveld, 1993, p. 2). Although *Achievement*, an indicator that measures academic performance once a female is enrolled in school, is an important category, these researchers could not include it in their study because cross-nationally comparable data on academic achievement were very limited. The GR for each of the 18 indicators was calculated by dividing the females' rate by the males' rate. A GR of 1.00 for a given country means that females are doing just as well as males on that indicator; a ratio of 0.50 suggests that females are doing half as well as males; and 0.32 implies that females are at a rate that is 32% of the males' rate. Hartnett and Heneveld (1993) organized the GRs by following a student's flow from primary admission to employment and were, therefore, capable of using the GR to pinpoint the levels and areas at which females were disadvantaged, compared with their male counterparts and regional medians.

Generally, females in SSA are disadvantaged in all education sectors, and the gap increases in severity with each level of education. In summary, females are somewhat disadvantaged in both primary admission (GR=0.88) and gross enrollment (GR=0.77); once females are enrolled in primary school, an approximately equal percentage persists to Grade 4 compared to males (GR=0.99). However, only a smaller proportion of females enrolled in Grade 1 complete primary school (GR=0.81), and those enrolled in the final primary grade continue to secondary at nearly the same rate as males (GR=0.92). Class repetition rates are approximately the same as males (GR=1.01). However, despite a primary completion of (GR 0.81), severe disparities exist in females' access to secondary school (GR 0.50). In secondary school, females also repeat at a rate slightly higher than males (GR=1.10). The secondary completion (GR of 0.64) indicates that substantially fewer females than males complete secondary school, and this ratio dips drastically with an under-representation of female enrollment in tertiary education (GR of 0.22), with proportionately fewer females than males enrolled in the sciences. Women generally complete an average of slightly more than three-quarters of a year of schooling, a rate that is 40% that of the males. Only 30% of adult women are literate, accounting for only 32% of women participating in the labor force, compared to 63% of the males, just over half the male rate (GR=0.57). Females comprise 34%, 22%, and 12% of the primary, secondary, and tertiary teaching staff, respectively (Hartnett & Heneveld, 1993).

These data on female participation in education in SSA are helpful to researchers, planners, and policymakers. These data indicate that girls' education is urgent because many world developmental promises cannot be fulfilled without it. Extant research shows that education increases the productivity and earnings of both men and women: with an estimated increase in income of as much as 10% to 20% with each additional year of education (Harnett & Heneveld, 1993). However, the education of females adds not only economic advantage but also social benefits, and experts believe that the completion of high-quality secondary education for girls is the magic solution to combat many of the most profound challenges to human development. Educated females have fewer, healthier, and more educated children, and it is estimated that each additional year of schooling decreases the mortality rate of children under the age of five years by up to 10%. It goes without saying that educated women are more knowledgeable and use better health practices. Since female education and national development are so closely linked, SSA countries that have large gender gaps in enrollments will continue to have lower economic productivity than other nations of the world. Although there is variability among nations regarding females' and males' education, the consensus is that female participation in education is extremely low in most SSA countries. There is, therefore, a great need to close the gender gap in education in SSA if the continent hopes to stay competitive in the global economy. Studies have shown that higher education not only correlates with health but also with individual wealth and with the wealth of not only the individual but also the entire nation. Higher education levels also create a citizenry that is more engaged in civic societies and capable of shared participation in the democratic governance of nations (Verba et al.,1995: 432–437, 445).

The argument for girls' education and gender equality, however, remains based on efficiency rather than on rights. Most arguments advocating girls' education see its value in terms of gains for societies, families, and gross domestic product (GDP), rather than as intrinsically beneficial for girls themselves. It is often not apparent that there is a concern for a girl's right to her own life, education, and the fulfillment of her human existence and potential. There is a greater sense of urgency to view education as a pathway to this goal.

Although a report by Japan International Cooperation Agency (JICA) TAC International Inc, (2015) indicates that the disparity between women and men in education has declined in general, the gender gap is wider in the higher levels of education. According to the World Bank data, the primary net enrollment was 97% for boys and 86% for girls (2012); the primary completion rate was 76% for boys and 68% for girls (2014); the lower secondary gross completion rate was 41% for boys and 38% for girls (2013); and tertiary gross enrollment rate was 14% for boys and 10% for girls (2011). There is a gender gap in literacy rate (adult men 81%, adult women 69%, young men 87%, and young women 80%) (2015). A World Bank Report by Hartnett and Heneveld (1993) explains that the reasons for the gender gaps include the following: some families do not value girls' education as women's roles and jobs would not create much income; poor families might prioritize boys' education over girls', (although primary education is free of charge since 1999, the cost for clothes and learning materials still present a challenge); parents allocate domestic and agricultural work to girls; early marriages of girls and pregnancy; reluctance to send girls to school due to fear of violence at school or on the way between home and school; and the lack of basic and appropriate amenities such as toilets. A policy framework that eliminates all unhelpful stereotypes against women and other challenges faced by girls in Southern Cameroons is necessary.

Chapter 14

Education Planning and Management

The main reason behind the current war in Southern Cameroons is the marginalization of the people and the erosion of the British educational system that was inherited at independence. Effective Education Planning and Management will require decentralizing the management of education and training services within the scope of authority at each management level. Under a decentralized system, County Education Boards will be created, and their role in education planning and data management will be clearly defined.

Goals

With an Education Board acting as the central governing system that is responsible for setting policy, standards, and norms, and for monitoring and evaluating the education program in Southern Cameroons, counties will be involved in the following ways:

- County and District shall be responsible for the implementation of central board policies in collaboration with various stakeholders.
- Headteachers shall be responsible for the general running of schools and ensuring that the academic program meets the standards required by the central government.
- The participation of parents, teachers, and users of educational facilities in their management shall be encouraged so as to achieve transparency, accountability, predictability, and participation in an atmosphere of good governance.
- The cost-efficiency and cost-effectiveness of all activities in the

Education Sector will be improved.
- There shall be proper monitoring and evaluation of the system, and a school-based procedure for monitoring learning.
- Constant review of education policy, statute, rules, and regulations
- Full and regular *dialogue* between the Ministry in charge of Education and all its partners.
- Develop a comprehensive framework and modalities for decentralizing education, training human and financial resource management, and decision-making authority for county and institutional management bodies.
- Establish a national mechanism for consulting and coordinating various providers of education and training services to ensure harmony in education planning and service provision at all levels.
- Strengthen education planning at national, county, and institutional levels.
- Entrench education planning in education laws and policies.
- Establish guidelines for the registration of education and training institutions to ensure that the construction of schools is linked to budgetary allocation and addresses the trend of unplanned school construction and consequent staffing of unplanned schools.
- Develop an effective and harmonized education data management system for the county.
- Develop and institutionalize an efficient financial management system for education customized for national, county, and school levels.
- Establish national Education Management Information Systems (EMIS) with decentralized electronic data management and processing capacity.
- Strengthen Southern Cameroons Education Management Information System (SCEMIS) to offer education planning capacity-building programs in collaboration with relevant institutions at all levels.
- Harmonize and link the collection and processing of education statistics framework at County and Ministry levels with the National

Integrated Monitoring System.

General Objectives
- Reinforce the planning department at central and decentralized levels.
- Review procedures relating to the management and administration of education for their adaptation and modernization.
- Develop and constantly update educational legislation.
- Teach school management and administration to all teachers and ensure that school heads regularly undergo special training.
- Involve parents, communities, elected officials responsible for education and Parents/Teachers Associations (PTAs) in school management.
- Undertake evaluation in every school on achieving government standards and report results to concerned authorities and the general public.
- Teach career guidance and counseling skills to all teachers and practice them at all levels, especially regarding career guidance, school hygiene, reproductive health, and HIV/AIDS.
- Mechanisms for coordination between the Ministry of Education (MoE) and its partners shall be set up and rationalized.
- Constantly review the cost-sharing policy to ensure greater and more predictable contributions from beneficiaries.
- Schools will prepare and submit an annual plan showing income-generating activities.
- Ensure constant and regular dialogue between the government and different partners, including donors, the private sector, and civil society.
- Involve students and parents in institutions' and schools' budget preparation and financial management. (Participatory Budgeting).
- Integrate science, mathematics teaching, and information and communication technologies (ICT) at the heart of the education system. This shall be taught at all levels of education.
- Take measures that promote women and men, girls and boys,

access and performance in science and ICT.
- Train a critical mass of science and ICT teachers.
- Ensure practical skills and provide science equipment and computers to identified schools and progressively to all schools, as the means allow.

Chapter 15

School Admission

This policy includes guidelines for setting out aims, objectives, and other matters related to the discharge of functions relating to admissions by the relevant bodies charged with school admissions. These include:
- Admission authorities of public schools
- Governing bodies and local authorities (when not admission authorities)
- Schools Adjudicators/arbitrators
- Independent Private Schools
- Admission Appeal Panels.

These bodies have a legal duty to act in accordance with the relevant provisions of the policy. The legal responsibility will be enshrined in a Southern Cameroons Education Act, which recognizes the need for a governing body that oversees schools, supports the rights of learners, educators, and parents, and outlines the duties and responsibilities of the State. These guidelines are to ensure that schools and academies are allocated and offered openly and fairly. As with all policies, school admission policies will have the force of law, and when that provision is made, policies will be revised to include the words "must" or "must not" to represent obligatory conditions.

Admission Process

The process will operate as follows:
a). All schools must have admission arrangements that clearly spell

out how children will be admitted, including the criteria that will be applied if there are more applications than places. Admission arrangements are determined by admission authorities.

b). Admission authorities must fix defined admission arrangements each year. Where changes are proposed to admission arrangements, the admission authority must first publicly consult and inform the public of such arrangements. If no changes are made to admission arrangements, they must be consulted at least once every four years. For example, for admission arrangements for entry in September 2025, consultation must be for a minimum of eight weeks and must be completed by March 1, 2024. For all subsequent years, consultation must be for at least six weeks of the school year before those arrangements apply. Another example is for arrangements that are to apply to applications in the academic year 2025-2026. Consultations must be completed by January 31, 2025.); Adequate consultation periods allow parents, other schools, religious authorities, and the local community to raise any concerns about proposed admission arrangements.

c). Once all arrangements have been determined, unsatisfactory arrangements can be objected to and referred to the Schools Adjudicator. Objections to admission arrangements for entry in September 2025 must be referred to the Adjudicator by June 30, 2024. For all subsequent years, objections must be referred to the Adjudicator by May 15 in the determination year. Any decision of the Adjudicator must be acted on by the admission authority, and the admission arrangements must be amended accordingly. The local authority will collate and publish all the admission arrangements in the area in a single composite prospectus.

d). In the regular admissions round, parents apply to the local authority where they live for places at their preferred schools. Parents can express a preference for at least three schools. The application can include schools outside the local authority where the child lives: a parent can apply for a place for their child at any state-funded school in any area. If a school is undersubscribed, any parent who applies must be offered a place. When oversubscribed, a school's admission authority must rank applications in order against its published oversubscription criteria and send that list back to the local authority. Published admission arrangements must make clear to parents that a separate application must be made for any transfer from nursery to primary school and from one level to the other.

e). All preferences are collated, and parents receive an offer from the local authority at the school with the highest preference, where a place is available. For secondary schools, the offer is made on or about August 1, the year the child will be admitted. For primary schools, the offer is made on or about April 16, the year in which the child will be admitted.

f). Parents, and in some circumstances, children, have the right to appeal against an admission authority's decision to refuse admission. The admission authority must set out the reasons for the decision, that there is a right of appeal and the process for hearing such appeals. The admission authority must establish an independent appeals panel to hear the appeal. The panel will decide whether to uphold or dismiss the appeal. Where a panel upholds the appeal, the school must admit the child.

Determining Admission/Enrollment in Schools

Admission authorities are responsible for admissions and *must* act in accordance with this policy, the *School Admission Appeals Act*, other laws relating to admissions, and relevant human rights and equalities legislation. The admission policy of a public school is determined by the governing body, but they must admit learners without unfairly discriminating.

- Learners may not be tested in any way before being admitted, and no child may be refused admission because of inability to pay school fees.
- The MoE may determine age requirements for the admission of learners/students to a school or different grade at a school.
- If an application is refused, the Head of Department must inform

the parent in writing, giving reasons for the refusal. Refused admission to a public school may be appealed.

Required Published Admission Number (rPAN)
- As part of determining their admission arrangements, all admission authorities must set an admission number for each "relevant age group."
- Admission authorities are not required to consult on their rPAN where they propose, either to increase or keep the same rPAN. For a community- or voluntary-controlled school, the local authority (as admission authority) must consult at least the governing body of the school, which proposes either increasing or keeping the same rPAN. All admission authorities must consult in accordance with stipulated guidelines, where they propose a decrease to the rPAN. Community and voluntary controlled schools can object to the Schools Adjudicator if the rPAN set for them is lower than they would wish. There is a strong presumption in favor of an increase to the rPAN to which the Schools Adjudicator must have regard when considering any such objection.
- Admission authorities must notify their local authority of their intention to increase the school's rPAN, and reference to the change should be made on the school's website or public notice board. If at any time following the determination of the rPAN, an admission authority decides that it can admit above its rPAN, it must notify the local authority in good time to allow it to deliver its coordination responsibilities effectively. Admission authorities may also admit above their rPAN in a year.
- Information on variations to the rPAN in-year is set out in the oversubscription criteria.

Oversubscription Criteria
- The school's admission authority must set out, in their arrangements, the criteria against which places will be allocated when there are more applications than places and the order in which

the criteria will be applied. All children whose statement of special educational needs (SEN) or Education, Health, and Care (EHC) plan names the school must be admitted. If the school is not oversubscribed, all applicants must be offered a place.

- All schools must have oversubscription criteria for each "relevant age group."
- Oversubscription criteria must be reasonable, transparent, objective, and procedurally fair and comply with all relevant legislation, including equalities legislation. Admission authorities must ensure that their arrangements will not disadvantage unfairly, either directly or indirectly, a child from a particular social or racial group or a child with a disability or SEN and that other policies around school uniforms or school trips do not discourage parents from applying for a place for their child. Admission arrangements must include an effective, transparent, and fair tie-breaker to decide between two applications that cannot otherwise be separated.
- It is for admission authorities to formulate their admission arrangements, but they must not:
- place any conditions on the consideration of any application other than those in the oversubscription criteria published in their admission arrangements,
- take into account any previous schools attended, unless it is a named feeder school,
- give extra priority to children whose parents rank preferred schools in a particular order, including "first preference first" arrangements,
- introduce any new selection by ability,
- give priority to children based on any practical or financial support parents may give to the school or any associated organization, including any religious authority. The exception to this is where parents pay optional nursery fees to the school or school-run nursery for additional hours on top of their 15-hour funded early education, where children from the school nursery class or school-run nursery are given priority for admission,
- give priority to children according to the occupational, marital,

financial, or educational status of parents applying. The exceptions to this are children of staff at the school and those eligible for the early years' pupil premium, the pupil premium and the service premium who may be prioritized in the arrangements,
- take account of reports from previous schools about students' past behavior, attendance, attitude, or achievement, or that of any other children in the family,
- discriminate against or disadvantage disabled children, those with special educational needs, or those applying for admission outside their normal age group where an admission authority has agreed to this,
- prioritize children based on their own or their parents' past or current hobbies or activities (schools that have been designated as having a religious character may take account of religious activities, as laid out by the body or person representing the religion or religious denomination),
- in designated grammar schools that rank all children according to a pre-determined pass mark and then allocate places to those who score highest, give priority to siblings of current or former pupils,
- in the case of schools with boarding places, rank children on the basis of a child's suitability for boarding,
- name fee-paying independent schools as feeder schools,
- interview children or parents; in the case of sixth form applications, a meeting may be held to discuss options and academic entry requirements for particular courses, but this meeting cannot form part of the decision-making process on whether to offer a place—boarding schools may interview children to assess their suitability for boarding,
- request financial contributions (either in the form of voluntary contributions, donations, or deposits, even if refundable, as any part of the admissions process—including for tests or other academic-related activities,
- request photographs of a child for any part of the admissions process other than as proof of identity when sitting a selection test.

This Policy does not give a definitive list of acceptable oversubscription criteria. Admission authorities should decide which criteria would be most suitable for the school according to the local circumstances. The most common are set out below.

Siblings at the School
- Admission authorities must state clearly in their arrangements what they mean by "sibling" (for example, whether this includes stepsiblings, foster siblings, adopted siblings, and other children living permanently at the same address or siblings who are former school pupils). If an admission authority wishes to give some priority to siblings of former pupils, it must set out a clear and straightforward definition of such former pupils and how their siblings will be treated in the oversubscription criteria (bearing in mind the restrictions set out in the paragraph above).
- Some schools prioritize siblings of pupils attending another state-funded school with close links (for example, schools on the same site, or close links between two single-sex schools). Where this is the case, this priority must be set out clearly in the arrangements.

Distance from School

Admission authorities must clearly set out how the distance from home to the school will be measured, making clear how the "home" address will be determined and the point in the school from which all distances are measured. This should include provision for cases where parents have shared responsibility for a child following the breakdown of their relationship and the child lives for part of the week with each parent.

Catchment Areas

Catchment areas *must* be reasonable and clearly defined. However, catchment areas must not prevent parents who live outside the catchment area of a particular school from expressing a preference for that school.

Feeder Schools

Admission authorities may wish to name a primary or middle school as a feeder school. The selection of a feeder school or schools as an oversubscription criterion *must* be transparent and made on reasonable grounds.

Social and Medical Needs

If admission authorities decide to use social and medical needs as an oversubscription criterion, they *must* set out in their arrangements how they will define this need and give precise details about what supporting evidence will be required (for example, a letter from a doctor or a social worker). Then, they must make consistent decisions based on the evidence provided.

Selection by Ability or Aptitude

All selective schools *must* publish the entry requirements for a selective place and the process for such selection.

Attendance Policy

Education in Southern Cameroons will be compulsory. Children are expected to start schooling at age 4 and continue until age 18.

Education levels

Education levels in Southern Cameroons will be broken down into the following:
- Prekindergarten
- Kindergarten
- Primary School
- Lower Secondary School
- Upper Secondary School

School Admission Age
- Prekindergarten (age 4 years)
- Kindergarten (age 5 year)
- Primary School (age 6–7 years)
- Lower Secondary School (age 12–14 years)

- Upper Secondary School (age 15–18 years)

A student will be admitted into prekindergarten when the child turns four (4) years of age. A child at 44 months old will be admitted to prekindergarten.

	Table 15.1. Suggested Structure of Southern Cameroons Education	
1.	Early Childhood and Basic Education (ECBE)	Pre-kindergarten and Kindergarten (ages 4–5) Duration: 2 Years Primary School: (ages 6–7) Duration: 6 Years.
2.	Secondary Education (SE)	Lower Secondary School (ages 12–14) Upper Secondary or high (ages 15–18) General, technical, and vocational institutes, apprenticeship, and agriculture (3 years)
3.	Non-Formal Education (NF)	Complementary education, training, skills, literacy, adult education; informal apprenticeship
4.	Inclusive and Special Education (IS)	Inclusion of excluded children within mainstream schools, special needs, special schools and units
5.	Tertiary Education (TE)	3rd cycle: colleges of education, professional institutes, polytechnics, universities, open learning
6.	Education Management (EM)	planning, decision-making, accountability, finance, decentralization, capacity building

Table 15.1. Suggested Structure of Southern Cameroons Education.

Language Policy in Public Schools

The Ministry of Education (MoE) will determine norms and standards for language policy in public schools, and the governing body of a school that sets out the language policy of the school would be expected to abide by the norms and standards. No form of linguistic or other forms of discrimination may be practiced in implementing policy determined under this section. A recognized sign language has the status of an official language for purposes of learning at a public school.

Grammar Schools

- Only designated Grammar schools are permitted to select their entire intake on the basis of high academic ability (for example, Magnet Schools). They do not have to fill all their places if applicants have not reached the required standard.
- Where arrangements for pupils are wholly based on selection by reference to ability and provide for only those who score highest in any selection test to be admitted, no priority needs to be given to looked-after or previously looked-after children.
- Where admission arrangements are not based solely on the highest scores in a selection test, the admission authority must give priority in its oversubscription criteria to all looked-after children and previously looked-after children who meet the pre-set standards of the ability test.

Pre-existing or Partially Selective Schools

- Partially selective schools can select a proportion of their intake by ability. Where schools can partially select, they *must* publish the entry requirements for a selective place, and the process for such selection. They *must* offer places to other children if insufficient applicants have satisfied the published entry requirements for a selective place.
- Partially selective schools must not exceed the lowest selection proportion used since the school year.
- In relation to the proportion of pupils admitted on a selective basis,

arrangements provide that only those pupils who score highest in any selection test are admitted.

Selection by Aptitude

Schools that have arrangements to select by aptitude must not allow for more than 10% of the total admissions intake to be allocated on the basis of such aptitude (even if the school has more than one specialism). The only specialist subjects on which a school may select by aptitude are:

    a). physical education or sport, or one or more sports,

    b). the performing arts, or any one or more of those arts,

    c). the visual arts, or any one or more of those arts,

    d). modern foreign languages, or any such language, and

    e). design and technology and information technology. Only schools that selected either of these specialist subjects in the school year may continue to do so.

Banding

Pupil ability banding is a permitted form of selection that can be used by some admission authorities to ensure that the intake for a school includes a proportionate spread of children of different abilities. Banding can be used to produce an intake that is representative of:

- the full range of ability of applicants for the school(s),
- the range of ability of children in the local area or
- the national ability range.
- Admission authorities' entry requirements for banding must be fair, transparent, and objective. Banding arrangements that favor high-ability children that have been continuously used since the school year may continue but must not be introduced by any other school.
- The admission authority must publish the admission requirements and the process for such banding and decisions, including details of any tests that will be used to band children according to ability.

Where the School is Oversubscribed
- Schools that operate admission arrangements, which include both banding and selection of up to 10% of pupils with reference to aptitude, shall clearly state how those two selection methods will be applied in their admission arrangements.
- Looked-after children and previously looked-after children must be given top priority in each band, and then oversubscription criteria must be applied within each band.
- Priority must not be given within bands according to the applicant's performance in the test.
- Children with statements of special educational needs (SEN) or education, health, and care (EHC) plans may be included in banding tests and allocated places in the appropriate bands, but regardless of any banding arrangements, they must be allocated a place if their statement or EHC Plan names the school.

Test for Selection

Tests for all selection forms must be clear, objective, and accurately reflect the child's ability or aptitude, irrespective of sex, race, or disability. The admission authority decides the content of the test, providing that it is a true test of aptitude or ability.

Admission authorities must:
- Ensure that tests for aptitude in a particular subject are designed to test only aptitude in the subject concerned, not ability.
- Ensure that tests are accessible to children with SENs and disabilities, considering the reasonable adjustments for disabled pupils required under equalities legislation.
- Take all reasonable steps to inform parents of the outcome of selection tests before the closing date for secondary applications, October 31, to allow parents time to make an informed choice of school while ensuring that this does not equate to a guarantee of a selective place.
- *Not* adjust the score achieved by any child in a test to take account of oversubscription criteria, such as having a sibling at the school.

Random Allocation

Local authorities must not use random allocation as the principal oversubscription criterion for allocating places at all the schools in the area for which they are the admission authority. Admission authorities that decide to use random allocation when schools are oversubscribed must set out clearly how this will operate, ensuring that arrangements are transparent and that looked-after and previously looked-after children are prioritized.

The random allocation process must be supervised by someone independent of the school, and a fresh round of random allocation must be used each time a child is to be offered a place from a waiting list.

Faith-Based Oversubscription Criteria in Schools with Religious Character

1). As with other maintained schools (schools funded by the Local Education Authority (LEA), these schools are required to offer every child who applies, whether of the faith, another faith, or no faith, a place at the school if there are places available. Schools designated by the MoE as having a religious character (commonly known as faith-based schools) may use faith-based oversubscription criteria and allocate places by reference to faith where the school is oversubscribed.

2). Admission authorities must ensure parents can easily understand how faith-based criteria will be reasonably satisfied. Admission authorities for schools designated with a religious character may prioritize all looked-after children and previously looked-after children regardless of the faith, but they must give priority to looked-after children and previously looked-after children of the faith before other children, not of the faith. Where any element of priority is given in relation to children not of faith, they must prioritize looked-after children and previously looked-after children not of the faith above other children not of the faith.

3). Admission authorities for schools designated as having a religious character must have regard to any guidance from the body or person representing the religion or religious denomination when constructing faith-based admission arrangements to the extent that the guidance complies with the mandatory provisions and guidelines of this Code. They must also consult with the body or person representing the religion or religious denomination when deciding how membership or practice of the faith is to be demonstrated. The church must, as required by the church board, consult with their diocese about proposed admission arrangements before any public consultation.

Children of Staff at the School

Admission authorities may give priority in their oversubscription criteria to children of staff in either or both of the following circumstances where:

1). The member of staff has been employed at the school for two or more years at the time at which the application for admission to the school is made, and/or
2). The staff member is recruited to fill a vacant post for which there is a demonstrable skill shortage.

Children Eligible for Pupil Premium or Service Premium (For example, Grants)

1). Admission authorities may give priority in their oversubscription criteria to children eligible for the early years pupil premium (additional funding), as well as the pupil premium and children eligible for the service premium. Admission authorities should clearly define in the arrangements the categories of eligible premium recipients are to be prioritized.
2). Admission authorities may give priority in their oversubscription criteria to children eligible for the early years pupil premium, the pupil premium, or the service premium who:
   a). are in a nursery class, which is part of the school, or
   b). attend a nursery that is established and run by the school. The nursery must be named in the admission arrangements, and its selection must be transparent and made on reasonable

grounds.

Maintained Boarding Schools

Maintained boarding schools can set separate admission numbers for day and boarding places. A maintained boarding school can interview applicants to assess suitability for boarding, but such interviews must only consider whether a child presents a severe health and safety hazard to other boarders or whether they can cope with and benefit from a boarding environment. To help with this assessment, they may also use a supplementary information form, and information provided by the previous school and the child's home local authority (on safeguarding issues). These processes and their timeline must be clearly set out in the school's admission arrangements.

Boarding schools must give priority to their oversubscription criteria in the following order:
- looked after children and previously looked after children,
- children of members of the Southern Cameroons Armed Forces who qualify for Ministry of Defense financial assistance with the cost of boarding school fees, and
- children with a "boarding need," making it clear what they mean by this.

Consultation

When changes are proposed to admission arrangements, all admission authorities must consult on their admission arrangements (including any supplementary information form) that will apply for admission applications the following school year. Where the admission arrangements have not changed from the previous year, there is no requirement to consult, subject to the requirement that admission authorities consult on their admission arrangements at least once every seven years, even if there have been no changes during that period. For example, for admission arrangements determined in 2024 for entry in September 2025, consultation must be for a minimum of eight weeks and completed by March

1, 2024. For all subsequent years, consultation must last at least six weeks and occur between October 1 and January 1 in the determination year.

Admission authorities must consult with the following:
- parents of children between the ages of two years and eighteen years,
- other persons in the relevant area who, in the opinion of the admission authority, have an interest in the proposed admissions,
- all other admission authorities within the relevant area (except that primary schools need not consult secondary schools),
- whichever of the governing body and the local authority who are not the admission authority,
- any adjoining neighboring local authorities where the admission authority is the local authority and,
- in the case of schools designated with a religious character, the body or person representing the religion or religious denomination.

For the duration of the consultation period, the admission authority must publish a copy of their full proposed admission arrangements (including the proposed rPAN) on their website together with details of the person within the admission authority to whom comments may be sent and the areas on which comments are not sought. Admission authorities must also send upon request a copy of the proposed admission arrangements to any of the persons or bodies listed above, inviting comments. Failure to consult effectively may be grounds for subsequent complaints and appeals.

Determination

All admission authorities must determine admission arrangements every year, even if they have not changed from previous years and a consultation has not been required. Admission authorities must determine admission arrangements for entry in September 2024 by April 15, 2023 and for all subsequent years by August 31 in the determination year.

Once admission authorities have determined their admission arrangements, they must notify the appropriate bodies and publish a copy on their website displaying them for the whole offer year (the school year in which offers for places are made). Admission authorities must send the local authority a copy of their full, determined arrangements. Admission authorities must send a copy of their determined admission arrangements for entry in September 2024 as soon as possible before May 1 of 2023 and for all subsequent years, as soon as possible before March 15, in the determination year. Admission authorities for schools designated with a religious character must also send a copy of their arrangements to the body or person representing their religion or religious denomination.

1). Where an admission authority has determined a rPAN that is higher than in previous years, it must notify the local authority and make specific reference to the change on its website.

2). Local authorities must publish on their website the proposed admission arrangements for any new school or Academy that is intended to open within the determination year, details of where the determined arrangements for all schools, including Academies, can be viewed, and information on how to refer objections to the Schools Adjudicator. Local authorities must publish these details of 2026 by May 1, 2025 and in all subsequent years by March 15 in the determination year.

3). Following determination of arrangements, any objections to those arrangements must be made to the Schools Adjudicator. Objections to admission arrangements for entry in September 2024 must be referred to the Adjudicator by June 30, 2023. For all subsequent years, objections must be referred to the Adjudicator by May 15 in the determination year. Admission authorities that are not the local authority must provide all the information that the local authority needs to compile the composite prospectus no later than August 8, unless agreed otherwise.

Composite Prospectuses

Local authorities must publish online, with hard copies available for those who do not have access to the internet, a composite prospectus for parents by September 12, in the offer year, which contains the admissions arrangements and any supplementary information forms for each of the state-funded schools in the local authority area to which parents can apply (that is, all schools including Academies). They must ensure that this information is kept up to date throughout the period in which parents can apply for a place for their child, and that it is written in a way that makes it clear and accessible to all parents.

Applications and Offers

1). For applications in the regular admissions round, local authorities must provide a Common Application Form (CAF) that enables parents to express their preference for a place at any state-funded school, with a minimum of three (3) preferences in rank order, allowing them to give reasons for their preferences. While parents may prefer any state-funded school—regardless of whether it is in the local authority area in which they live—admission authorities must not give any guarantees that a preference will be met.

2). The Common Application Form (CAF) must allow parents to provide their name, their address (including documentary evidence in support), and the name, address, and date of birth of the child. The child must not be required to complete any part of the CAF. Local authorities must provide advice and assistance to parents when they are deciding which schools to apply for.

3). Regardless of which schools parents express preferences for, the CAF is required to be returned to the local authority in the area where they live (the "home" authority). The home authority must then pass information on applications to other local ("maintaining") authorities about applications to schools in their area. The maintaining authority must determine the application and inform the home local authority if a place is available. The offer to parents must be made by the home local authority.

4). Sometimes, admission authorities must request supplementary information forms to process applications. If they do so, they must only use supplementary forms that request additional information when it directly affects decisions about oversubscription criteria or for the purpose of selection by aptitude or ability. They must not ask or use supplementary forms that ask for any of the information prohibited by the paragraph above or for:

- any personal details about parents and families, such as maiden names, criminal convictions, marital or financial status (including marriage certificates),
- the first language of the parents or the child,
- details about parents' or a child's disabilities, SENs or medical conditions,
- parents to agree to support the ethos of the school in a practical way, or
- both parents to sign the form, or the child to complete the form.

5). Admission authorities may need to ask for proof of address where it is unclear whether a child meets the published oversubscription criteria. In these cases, they must not ask for any evidence that would include the information detailed above. Once a place has been offered, admission authorities may ask for proof of birth date, but they must not ask for a "long" birth certificate or other documents that include information about the child's parents. In the case of previously looked after children, admission authorities may request a copy of the adoption order, child arrangements order, or special guardianship order, and a letter from the local authority that last looked after the child confirming that he or she was looked after immediately prior to that order being made.

Allocating Places

Admission authorities must allocate places only on the basis of their determined admission arrangements, and a decision to offer or refuse admission must not be made by one individual in an admission authority. Where the school is its own admission authority, the whole governing body or an admissions committee established by the governing body

must make such decisions.
1). With the exception of designated grammar schools, all maintained schools, including schools designated with a religious character, that have enough places available must offer a place to every child who has applied for one, without condition or the use of any over-subscription criteria.
2). Admission authorities must not refuse to admit children solely because:
- they have applied later than other applicants,
- they are not of the faith of the school in the case of a school designated with a religious character,
- they followed a different curriculum at their previous school,
- information has not been received from their previous school, or
- they have missed entrance tests for selective places.
3). In the normal admissions round, offers of primary and secondary places must be sent by the home local authority and schools must not contact parents about the outcome of their applications until after these offers have been received. Admission authorities must not provide any guarantees to applicants of the outcome of their application prior to the formal notification of any offers of a place in a suitable school by the home local authority.
4). Where a place is available for a child at more than one school, the home local authority must ensure, so far as is reasonably practicable, that the child is offered a place at whichever of these schools is their highest preference. If the local authority cannot offer a place at one of the parents' preferred schools, it must, if there are places available, offer a place at another school.

Withdrawing an offer or a Place
- An admission authority must not withdraw an offer unless it has been offered in error, a parent has not responded within a reasonable period of time, or it is established that the offer was obtained through a fraudulent or intentionally misleading application.

Where the parent has not responded to the offer, the admission authority must give the parent a further opportunity to respond and explain that the offer may be withdrawn if they do not. Where an offer is withdrawn on the basis of misleading information, the application must be considered afresh, and a right of appeal must be offered if an offer is refused.
- A school must not withdraw a place once a child has started at the school, except where that place was fraudulently obtained. The length of time that the child has been at the school must be taken into account in deciding whether to withdraw the place. For example, withdrawing the place might be considered appropriate if the child has been at the school for less than one term.

Waiting List

Each admission authority must maintain a clear, fair, and objective waiting list until at least December 31 of each school year of admission, stating in their arrangements that each added child will require the list to be ranked again in line with the published oversubscription criteria. Priority must not be given to children based on the date their application was received, or their name was added to the list. Looked after children, previously looked after children, and those allocated a place at the school in accordance with a Fair Access Protocol, *must* take precedence over those on a waiting list.

Infant Class Size

Infant classes (where most children will reach the age of 5, 6 or 7 during the school year) must not contain more than 30 pupils with a single schoolteacher. Additional children may be admitted under limited exceptional circumstances. These children will remain an "excepted pupil" in an infant class or until the class numbers fall back to the current infant class size limit. The excepted children are:
- children admitted outside the normal admissions round with statements of SENs or EHC plans specifying a school,
- children admitted after the initial allocation of places because

of a procedural error made by the admission authority or local authority in the original application process,
- children admitted after an independent appeals panel upholds an appeal,
- children who move into the area outside the normal admissions round for whom there is no other available school within a reasonable distance,
- Children of Southern Cameroons service personnel admitted outside the normal admissions round,
- children whose twin or sibling from a multiple birth is admitted otherwise than as an excepted pupil and/or
- children with special educational needs who are normally taught in a special educational unit attached to the school, or registered at a special school, who attend some infant classes within the mainstream school.

Admission of Children Below Compulsory School Age and Deferred Entry to School

Admission authorities must provide for the admission of all children in the September following their fourth birthday. The authority must make it clear in their arrangements where they have offered a child a place at a school:
- that child is entitled to a full-time place in the September following their fourth birthday;
- the child's parents can defer the date their child is admitted to the school until later in the school year but not beyond the point at which they reach compulsory school age and not beyond the beginning of the final term of the school year for which it was made; and
- where the parents wish, children may attend part-time until later in the school year but not beyond the point at which they reach compulsory school age.

Admission of Children out of their Normal Age Group
- Parents may seek a place for their child outside their regular age group, for example, if the child is gifted and talented or has experienced problems such as ill health. In addition, the parents of a summer-born child may choose not to send that child to school until the September following their fifth birthday and may request that they be admitted out of their regular age group—to reception rather than year one. Admission authorities must make the process for requesting admission out of the normal age group clear in their admission arrangements.
- Admission authorities must make decisions on the basis of the circumstances of each case and in the best interests of the child concerned. This will include taking account of the parent's views; information about the child's academic, social, and emotional development; where relevant, their medical history and the views of a medical professional; whether they have previously been educated out of their regular age group; and whether they may naturally have fallen into a lower age group if it were not for being born prematurely. They must also consider the views of the head teacher of the school concerned. When informing a parent of their decision on the year group the child should be admitted to, the admission authority must clearly state the reasons for their decision.
- Where an admission authority agrees to a parent's request for their child to be admitted out of their normal age group and, as a consequence of that decision, the child will be admitted to a relevant age group (that is, the age group to which pupils are normally admitted to the school) the local authority and admission authority must process the application as part of the main admissions round, unless the parental request is made too late for this to be possible, and on the basis of their determined admission arrangements only, including the application of oversubscription criteria where applicable. They must not give the application lower priority on the basis that the child is being admitted out of their

normal age group. Parents have a statutory right to appeal against the refusal of a place at a school for which they have applied. This right does not apply if they are offered a place at the school but it is not in their preferred age group.

Children of Southern Cameroons' Service Personnel

For families of service personnel with a confirmed posting to their area, returning from overseas to live in that area, admission authorities must:

- allocate a place in advance of the family arriving in the area, provided the application is accompanied by an official letter that declares a relocation date and a Unit postal address or quartering area address when considering the application against their over-subscription criteria. This must include accepting a Unit postal address or quartering area address for a service child. Admission authorities must not refuse a service child a place because the family does not currently live in the area or reserve blocks of places for these children;
- ensure that arrangements in their area support the Government's commitment to removing disadvantage for service children. Arrangements must be appropriate for the area and be described in the local authority's composite prospectus.

Children from Overseas

Admission authorities must treat applications for children coming from overseas in accordance with African Union (AU) law or Home Office rules for non-Southern Cameroonian nationals. Non-statutory guidance on this will be made available on the website of the Department of Education.

Coordination

1). Each year, all local authorities must formulate and publish on their website a scheme by January 1 in the relevant determination year to coordinate admission arrangements for all publicly funded schools within their area. Where the scheme is substantially different from the scheme adopted for the previous academic year, the local authority must consult the other admission authorities in the area and any other local authorities it determines. Where the scheme has not changed from the previous year, there is no requirement to consult, subject to the requirement that the local authority consult on the scheme at least once every seven (7) years, even if there have been no changes during that period. Following any such consultation, which must be undertaken with a view to ensuring the admission of pupils in different local authorities is, as far as reasonably practicable, compatible with each other, the local authority must determine the qualifying scheme and *must* take all reasonable steps to secure its adoption. A local authority must inform the Secretary of State whether they have secured the adoption of a qualifying scheme by, for example, April 15, 2018 for admission arrangements for entry in 2019 and thereafter, by February 28 in the determination year. The Secretary of State may impose a scheme where a scheme has not been adopted. All admission authorities must participate in coordination and provide the local authority with the information it needs to coordinate admissions by the dates agreed within the scheme. Local authorities must make application forms available to parents who wish to apply to a school in a neighboring area that operates a different age of transfer (for example, middle schools) and process these as it would in its regular admissions round.

2). There is no requirement for local authorities to coordinate in-year applications, but they must provide information in the composite prospectus on how in-year applications can be made and dealt with. Local authorities must, on request, provide information to parents about the places still available in all schools within its area and a suitable form for parents to complete when applying for a place for their child at any school for which they are not the admission authority. Any parent can apply for a place for their child at any time at any school outside the regular admissions round. They can apply directly to admission authorities, except where other arrangements are in place locally (for example, the local authority coordinates all in-year admissions).

3). Admission authorities must, on receipt of an in-year application, notify the local authority of both the application and its outcome to allow the local authority to keep up-to-date figures on the availability of places in the area. The admission authority must also inform parents of their right to appeal against the refusal of a place.

Offering a Place

Where schools are oversubscribed, admission authorities must rank applications in accordance with their determined arrangements. The qualifying scheme must ensure that:

1). Only one offer per child is made by the local authority,
2). For secondary school applications, all offers must be made on the same secondary National Offer Day, that is, March 1 or the next working day, and
3). For primary school applications, all offers must be made on the same primary National Offer Day, that is, April 16 or the next working day.

Right to Appeal

When an admission authority informs a parent of a decision to refuse their child a place at a school for which they have applied, it must include the reason why admission was refused, information about the right to appeal, the deadline for lodging an appeal and the contact details for making an appeal. Parents *must* be informed that they must set out their grounds for appeal in writing if they wish to appeal. Admission authorities must not limit the grounds on which appeals can be made.

School Closure

Where a maintained school or Academy is to be closed, the local authority must collaborate with all schools in their area to consider the best way to secure provision for children in other local schools.

Suspension and Expulsion from Public Schools

After a fair hearing, the governing body may suspend a learner from school for no longer than one week. A learner who has been suspended may not go to school.

A public school learner may be expelled only by the Head of the Education Department for serious misconduct (assessed at a fair hearing). Expulsions may be appealed through the provincial department of education.

The Head of Department must make an alternative arrangement for the learner's placement at another public school.

Fairness in Resolving Issues
The School Adjudicator
1). The Schools Adjudicator must consider whether admission arrangements referred to the Adjudicator comply with the Code and the law relating to admissions. The admission authority must, where necessary, revise their admission arrangements to give effect to the Adjudicator's decision within two months of the decision (or by February 28 following the decision, whichever is sooner) unless an alternative timescale is specified by the Adjudicator. An Adjudicator's determination is binding and enforceable.
2). Local authorities must refer an objection to the Schools Adjudicator if they consider or suspect that the admission arrangements determined by other admission authorities are unlawful. If the Schools Adjudicator requests, admission authorities must provide the information set out in the schedule of the School Admissions Regulations.
3). Any person or body who considers that any maintained school or Academy's arrangements are unlawful or not in compliance with the Code or relevant law relating to admissions can make an objection to the Schools Adjudicator. The following types of objections cannot be brought:
   a). objections that seek to remove selective arrangements at a maintained school or a selective Academy;

b). objections about own authority admission's decision to increase or keep the same rPAN;

   c). objections about a decision by the admission authority of a voluntary controlled or community school to increase or keep the same rPAN, unless the objection is brought by the governing body of the school;

   d). objections in respect of an agreed variation from the Policy in relation to admission arrangements for an Academy;

   e). objections to arrangements which raise the same or substantially the same matters as the adjudicator has decided on for that school in the last two (2) years and

   f). anonymous objections.

The Adjudicator may also consider arrangements that come to the Adjudicator's attention by other means which the Adjudicator considers may not comply with mandatory requirements.

Objections to admission arrangements for entry in September 2025, for example, must be referred to the Adjudicator by June 30, 2024. For all subsequent years, objections must be referred to the Adjudicator by May 15 in the determination year. Further information on how to make an objection can be obtained from the office of the Schools Adjudicator.

Variations

   1). Once admission arrangements have been determined for a particular school year, they cannot be revised by the admission authority unless such revision is necessary to give effect to a mandatory requirement of this Code, admissions law, a determination of the Adjudicator, or any misprint in the admission arrangements. Admission authorities may propose other variations where they consider such changes necessary in view of a significant change in circumstances. Such proposals must be referred to the Schools Adjudicator for approval, and the appropriate bodies must be notified. Where the local authority is the admission authority for a community or voluntary controlled school, it must consult the governing body of the school before making any reference. A variation to increase a school's rPAN is not required to be referred to the Schools Adjudicator.

2). Admission authorities must notify the appropriate bodies of all variations and must display a copy of the full, varied admission arrangements on their website until they are replaced by different admission arrangements. Local authorities must display the varied admission arrangements on their website where an admission authority has raised its rPAN.

Children with Challenging Behavior and Those Who Have Been Excluded Twice

1). Admission authorities must not refuse to admit children in the regular admissions round on the basis of their poor behavior elsewhere. Where a child has been permanently excluded from two or more schools there is no need for an admission authority to comply with parental preference for a period of two years from the last exclusion. The twice-excluded rule does not apply to children who were below compulsory school age at the time of the exclusion, children who have been re-instated following a permanent exclusion (or would have been had it been practicable to do so), and children with SNE statements or EHC Plans.

2). Each local authority must have a Fair Access Protocol, agreed with the majority of schools in its area, to ensure that—outside the regular admissions round—unplaced children, especially the most vulnerable, are offered a place at a suitable school as quickly as possible. In agreeing to a protocol, the local authority must ensure that no school—including those with available places—is asked to take a disproportionate number of children who have been excluded from other schools or who have challenging behavior. The protocol must include how the local authority will use provisions to meet the needs of pupils unprepared for mainstream schooling.

3). Fair Access Protocols operate outside the coordination arrangements and are triggered when a parent of an eligible child has

not secured a school place under in-year admission procedures.
4). All admission authorities must participate in the Fair Access Protocol to ensure that unplaced children are allocated school places quickly. Local authorities or admission authorities have no duty to comply with parental preference when allocating places through the Fair Access Protocol.
5). Where a governing body does not wish to admit a child with challenging behavior outside the regular admissions round, even though places are available, it must refer the case to the local authority for action under the Fair Access Protocol. This will typically only be appropriate where a school has a particularly high proportion of children with challenging behavior or previously excluded children. The use of this provision will depend on local circumstances and must be described in the local authority's Fair Access Protocol. This provision will not apply to a looked-after child, a previously looked-after child or a child with a statement of SEN or EHC Plan naming the school in question, as these children must be admitted.
6). Admission authorities must not refuse to admit a child thought to be potentially disruptive or likely to exhibit challenging behavior on the grounds that the child is first to be assessed for special educational needs.

A Fair Access Protocol must not require a school to automatically take another child with challenging behavior in the place of a child excluded from the school.

Chapter 16

Norms and Standards for Educators

The work teachers do with children, pupils, and parents is important. The primary responsibility of educators is to build a trusting relationship with those they work for and with. Norms and Standards for Educators embody the loyalties of the educators that rest with the students and their commitment to do everything to promote what is in their students' best interest. Truthful communication of knowledge and high-quality pedagogical practices are essential to these norms. It is the responsibility of educators to act in accordance with these principles and values.

The roles and associated competencies are meant to describe what it means to be a competent educator. These are not exclusive checklists against which one assesses whether an educator is competent or not. The roles and competencies must be integrated into the learning programs and environments with a blend of theory and practice. They must inform the outcomes of teacher training institutions (qualifications), encompass the practice of the profession, and be associated with assessment criteria for quality control.

Ultimately, norms and standards should reflect applied and integrated competencies. This policy pillar describes the roles, their associated set of applied competencies (norms), and qualifications (standards) for the development of educators. It also establishes key strategic objectives for developing learning programs, qualifications, and standards for educators.

Scope and Purpose

The scope of the policy for norms and standards for educators can be broken down into the following:
- Registration, accreditation and approval of qualifications,
- Evaluation of qualifications for employment in education (including factors that must be taken into consideration when evaluating qualification for employment in education from Early Childhood through Secondary/High School).
- Certification procedures: Recognition of Academic Qualifications
- Professional development for educators with old teacher education certificates and diplomas.
- Evaluation of foreign qualifications for employment in education.
- Recognition of appropriate qualifications for permanent appointment in specific educator posts.
- Evaluation of qualifications for employment in teaching posts at technical colleges.
- Recognition of qualifications for employment in Adult Basic Education and Training Centers.
- Roles for educators in schooling,
- List of appropriate subjects/fields of study for teacher education programs.

Competencies Required for Teachers

Competencies for teachers can be broken down into the following:
1). Practical competence,
2). Foundational competence,
3). Reflexive competence, and
4). Standards/Ethical competence for educators.

Teaching Methodology

The Policy on teaching methodology is premised on the assumption that learning outcomes are optimized when the teacher masters and controls instructional and learning theories and can deploy them on call to respond to student learning needs.

Specific Objectives
- Teachers demonstrate profound mastery of theories of instruction, learning, and child psychology.
- Teachers employ methods that are evidence-based and results-driven.
- Lesson planning uses a blend of child-centered approaches that inspire active student engagement and creativity.
- Teaching practice is assessed or evaluated.
- Evaluation is built on informed analysis and builds on teacher growth.
- The design of school infrastructure and the acquisition of teaching equipment take into consideration the use of Information and Communication Technology (ICT) tools and contemporary teaching methods.
- School management supports the use of innovative methods.

Strategies
- The Southern Cameroons Education Board (SCEB) will be tasked with identifying and preparing practicing schools for teachers in training and recruiting expert supervisors to assess or evaluate teachers during practicum.
- Teacher preparation institutions should ensure that their curriculum reflects standards and objectives.
- Student teachers must complete a full semester (at least four months) of teaching practice before graduation.

Monitoring and Evaluation
The SCEB will:
- Establish an education quality assessment committee that moderates the end of training and certification examinations.
- Design standardized recruitment protocols that enable the board to evaluate the mastery of theories and demonstrate mastery in diverse scenarios.

Chapter 17

Norms and Standards for Learners

The term learner in this policy refers to anyone receiving education or training in an educational institution. These guidelines have been developed to ensure the alignment of minimum standards for learners within all educational institutions in Southern Cameroons so that learners can acquire the highest quality of education or training to improve the quality of their lives and their global communities.

The term "educational institution" in this policy comprises all learning institutions, from pre-nursery to university institutions, teacher-training institutions, and practical and vocational education institutions. The policy also intends to set clear expectations and interventions for all learners with consequences for misconduct that are individualized, consistent, reasonable, fair, age-appropriate, and match the misconduct's severity. Factors such as age, level of education, learner's social, emotional and intellectual development, and learner rights and responsibilities shall be considered at all times. The general guidelines are to be instructive and not punitive and are based on the principle of preventive and positive discipline that addresses the causes of misbehavior, promotes conflict resolution, and takes into consideration the learners' needs and their lives in an educational institution. The goal is to create a safe and supportive education environment, support learners' social and emotional development, and teach self-respect, discipline, and respect for others and the entire community. The policy further aims to ensure that all learners enjoy their time in an educational institution and complete their education or training successfully. All members of the school environment are expected to behave in a manner that does not offend others or make them feel threatened or uncomfortable, both in school and around the local vicinity. They should respect others' property and opinions and treat others fairly and politely. In this respect, the following norms and standards are laid down to guide learners' behavior in and around the school premises, in no order of importance.

In order to facilitate management and ensure consistency, some definitions will be provided.

Definition of a School

School refers to all educational institutions that have the following characteristics:
- have one or more teachers that provide instruction,
- contain enrolled or prospective students who plan to enroll,
- have an administrator, and
- is located within one or more buildings.

Definition of a Public School

A public school is a pre-kindergarten through high school or adult educational institution that:
- is supported with public funds,
- is authorized by action of and operated under the oversight of a publicly constituted local or state educational agency,
- provides educational services to all students who are enrolled,
- has appropriately credentialed teachers who provide instruction,
- has at least one appropriately credentialed administrator, usually a principal, who is responsible for all aspects of school administration, including staff supervision and evaluation, fiscal responsibility, student discipline and safety, curriculum supervision and evaluation, assessment of academic achievement, and school accountability.
- administers statewide assessments to its students at the required grade levels,
- has an administrator, usually a principal, with access to and

responsibility for maintaining official student records for all enrolled students,
- implements a curriculum that fully meets state requirements as specified in the education standards stipulated by the State,
- is non-sectarian,
- contains a budget structure that is consistent with the budget structure of schools operated by the authorizing agency and
- is based in one or more buildings.

Definition of a Private or Parochial School

A private or parochial school is a school that is owned or operated by a private person, firm, association, organization, or corporation rather than by the State or public agency.

It is also necessary to define whether a given entity is a school or a program. Certain factors have to be considered to distinguish schools from programs. For example:
- if the primary purpose of the educational entity is not education, but rather, education is its secondary purpose,
- if students who are enrolled in the entity remain members of the school that referred them or
- if students are enrolled on only a part-time basis.

If the answer to *any* of those three questions is *yes*, then the entity is not a school and may be considered a program.

Other considerations may be as follows:
- Except for State Special Schools, can the entity grant a diploma to its graduates if it accommodates high school students?
- Do the students have full access to all of the facilities and amenities of the entity?

If the answer to *either* of those two questions is *no*, this entity is not a school and may be a program (California Department of Education, 2023).

Expected Behavior and Attitude

The purpose of policy for expected behaviors and attitudes is to create a learning society that is free from discrimination and prejudice and which encourages and helps all who learn and work to reach their full potential while protecting the rights of each individual. To meet this goal, educational institutions should:

- provide a safe and supportive environment where all staff and learners are treated with dignity and respect,
- welcome individuals and groups from local, regional, and international communities,
- value difference and diversity, and strive to create positive relationships so that everyone can work and study to the best of their abilities, free from discrimination, harassment, victimization, or mobbing,
- be all-inclusive and committed to achieving excellence through inclusion and not through segregation; all learners should have a right to equality of opportunity irrespective of race, disability, gender, age, nationality, sexual orientation, religion or belief, marital or non-marital status, pregnancy or maternity status, socioeconomic status, background, or class,
- ensure that both its staff and learners feel comfortable and secure in and outside the educational institution's premises,
- have clear, fair, effective, and consistent procedures for dealing with complaints and well-defined disciplinary measures and
- have an investigation committee to investigate any allegations of rule violations and recommend appropriate disciplinary measures.

Violation could be of clearly stated institutional rules or perceived infringement of a person's rights and privileges. Some examples include:

Bullying and Harassment

Bullying and harassment are defined as any conduct which is unwanted by the recipient or any such conduct which:

- affects the dignity of any individual or groups of individuals,

- causes physical or emotional harm to the recipient or damage to the recipient's property,
- places the recipient in reasonable fear of harm or fear of property damage,
- creates a hostile environment in the educational institution for the recipient,
- infringes on the recipient's rights in the educational institution, and/or
- disrupts the education process materially or substantially or the normal functioning of the educational institution.

Bullying or harassment may be repetitive or an isolated occurrence. It may be:
- physical: comprising of contact, assault, gestures, intimidation, or aggressive behavior,
- verbal: comprising of unwelcome remarks, suggestions, propositions, malicious gossip, jokes, or banter,
- non-verbal: comprising of offensive literature or pictures, graffiti, computer imagery or phone texts, isolation or noncooperation, or exclusion from social activities,
- persistent, offensive, abusive, intimidating, or insulting behavior,
- abuse of power or unfair sanctions that make the recipient feel upset, threatened, humiliated, or vulnerable, and/or
- cyberbullying: through the use of technology and/or any electronic means.

Any learner who feels he/she is being bullied, harassed, or threatened should:
- report any such incidents to the competent institution's authorities,
- keep a note of the date, time, place, and name of the offender, a note of what happened and the offense suffered, and
- keep the name of any witnesses, any action taken, and the name of the person to whom it was reported, and should also keep a

record of any written evidence relating to the incident and any subsequent incidents.

Drugs and Alcohol

The taking of, dealing in, or being under the influence of drugs or alcohol is strictly forbidden for learners in and outside the premises of an educational institution. Possession of any non-prescribed substance, such as opioids, narcotic drugs, hallucinogenic drugs, amphetamines, barbiturates, marijuana, alcoholic beverages, or intoxicant of any kind, may result in short- or long-term suspension from an educational institution. Violating this policy will impede the general welfare and safety of other learners and staff in the educational institution.

If any staff member suspects that a learner is under the influence of alcohol and/or drugs, the learner should be asked to leave the institution's premises with immediate effect, and the learner should be reported to the competent authorities of the educational institution. Learners with ongoing issues with substance misuse should be recommended to attend counseling to receive support and intervention. Any learner suspected of selling, supplying controlled drugs, or bringing them into an educational institution should be suspended with immediate effect, a disciplinary procedure invoked, and the police called to investigate. Any learner who wishes to discuss drug/alcohol misuse issues with someone should contact the disciplinary master or a teacher who can arrange for a private discussion with the learner.

Learners attending the counseling and intervention center shall have the opportunity to make academic progress during the exclusion period, complete assignments and, earn credits missed, including any homework, and take tests or exams missed during the counseling period.

Smoke-Free Environment

All students are required to subscribe to the Smoke-Free Policy. Institutions of learning will not permit smoking in any of their premises and buildings. Some centers may make exceptions and have shelters that smokers may use, but all schools will be completely smoke-free. E-cigarettes are also not allowed on school premises except in designated areas.

Information Technology (IT) Responsible User

All learners must agree to and comply with the institution's IT security and Responsible User Policy before accessing the institution's computer hardware and software or network facilities. The policy covers a range of issues, including unacceptable access and use of the Internet and email, downloading materials, and copyright issues. Users will be informed of the policy when they first log on to the School's IT system. The Policy will also be available in the institution's Learning Resource Centers, if such centers are available.

Health and Safety

When attending school, all learners must take reasonable care for their own health and safety and that of others who may be affected by their actions. This will require all students to:

- observe all instructions, whether written or verbal, to ensure personal safety and the safety of others,
- conduct themselves at all times in an orderly manner and refrain from any form of horseplay that could cause injury to themselves and others,
- treat the building structures and internal fixtures, fittings, and furniture with respect and care,
- use all safety equipment and/or protective clothing as instructed, reporting any loss or defect to their teachers,
- not interfere with or misuse any equipment provided for health and safety purposes,
- report all hazards to their teachers,
- report all accidents to their teachers, whether the injury is sustained or not,
- be familiar with the emergency evacuation procedure, the location of fire alarms and emergency equipment, and
- as part of their health and safety responsibilities, adhere to the smoke-free, drug-free, alcohol, and other controlled substance

policies.

Safeguarding Children and Vulnerable Adults

The policies are designed to keep students up to the age of 18 years and "vulnerable adults" (those students within higher institutions of learning/universities who have severe learning difficulty and/or disability) safe from physical, emotional, financial or sexual abuse and neglect. There will also be an "Abuse of Trust Policy," which forbids staff members working at the institution to have an inappropriate/sexual relationship with a student (even though the student might be over the age of consent). If any member of the educational institution wishes to talk to someone about an instance of abuse, neglect, or abuse of trust happening to him/her or to another student, such a person may speak to a trusted member of staff or a member of the Student Services Team (if those services are available). Students must be assured that they will be listened to and well supported and that, if need be, the school administration will speak to other agencies that can provide further assistance.

Attitude

Students are expected to be exemplary in their actions both in and out of the school premises and do or say things that will discredit them, their families or the reputation of the institution. They are expected to respect the beliefs, manners, and customs of the social and cultural environment and to demonstrate respect for themselves, each other, teachers, administrators, and elderly persons in the community. Students should demonstrate qualities of trustworthiness, honesty, and good citizenship. No student has the right, at any time, to behave in a manner that disrupts the learning process of others or causes another learner or an educator physical or emotional harm.

Chapter 18

Assessment and Other Procedures

Assessment is a systematic way to collect and analyze information on students' academic development and progress. Effective assessments should be guided by some basic principles that include but are not limited to the following:
- Assessments should be an ongoing process.
- Assessments should assess processes as well as products.
- Assessments should be integral to instruction (integrated with teaching).
- Assessments must be authentic, reflecting "real" content in the various courses.
- Assessments should be a collaborative, reflective process between teachers and learners.
- Assessments should be multidimensional (using triangulation).
- Assessments should be developmentally and culturally appropriate.
- Assessment should identify students' strengths and use their strengths to build upon areas of weaknesses.
- Assessments should be both formal and informal (such as observations, etc.).
- Assessments should be formative and summative.
- Assessments must involve students, parents and other school personnel.

Assessment is a significant aspect of teaching and learning. Because it has to be authentic, specific guidelines may not be appropriate for all settings and all student demographics. However, policy can guide some general areas of the assessment procedures.

Examination

Failure to complete coursework could result in students not being entered for an examination. Students will be entered for examination only if they have excellent attendance throughout the course. If students have questions about the courses and exams entered, they have to talk to the school's principal. If students have any other queries about exam dates or regulations, they can contact the examination office.

Plagiarism

All students are required to carry out their assignments, tests, examinations, or any school projects without copying the work of others (that is, students are required to submit work that is uniquely their own). It's crucial to understand that copying the work of others, also known as *plagiarism*, is academic dishonesty or academic fraud, and offenders will be subject to academic censure, up to and including expulsion from school.

Textbooks and Stationaries

While the goal is to provide free and appropriate public education to all Southern Cameroonian children, students may sometimes be expected to provide their own equipment, especially for specialized tasks. Course textbooks will be provided, and copies of all course textbooks will be available in the school libraries in book and digital form, if available.

Coursework and Certificates

Students must comply with the school's policies regarding the retention of their work (artwork, portfolios, and other such artifacts), certificates, and coursework. Student progress reports, report cards, and other certificates will be mailed home or picked up from school when students have completed their courses.

Electronic Devices

All electronic devices not required for lectures, such as cell phones, are to be turned off before entering the classroom. Except with special approval for certain examinations, students must hand in their devices to the Examination Officer (not just switched off) if they are sitting for an examination. Failure to do so may disqualify a student from the examination.

Money and Valuables

Students should not bring unnecessary valuables, including large quantities of cash, into the institution's premises. An educational institution cannot accept responsibility for loss or damage to personal possessions.

Lost Property

Lost property should be handed in at the center's main Reception, and all inquiries about missing items may also be made here. Any lost property not claimed within one month will be disposed of. Any school identification cards found on the premises will be stored at the main Reception.

Identification Cards

A student's identification card shows that he or she is a student at the institution, which should be worn at all times or be ready to be shown to a staff member when asked. Students will need their identification card to access Digital Learning Zones, use the institutions' transport facilities, and access the educational institution's canteen (where applicable). If a student loses their identification card, a replacement can be obtained from the Digital Learning Zone at a charge. The identification card will also allow them to receive discounts from some shops.

The Local Community

Students should always respect the school neighbors and not cause a nuisance to neighbors by creating excessive noise, using foul language, being anti-social in their behavior, or engaging in other dangerous activities where applicable.

Leaving School

At the end of the course, students will be expected to return all borrowed books and equipment in undamaged condition to their last examination. Students will be given detailed information about the procedures for collecting examination results, references, and other documents needed after completion. If students are considering leaving before their course is completed, they should first discuss this with their teachers and administrator.

Chapter 19

Disciplinary Structure and other Expectations

This policy is based on the provisions of laws and principles that protect the rights and dignity of individuals and ensure that all learners have access to education. The disciplinary system should be fair, flexible, and consistent. The institution's staff, learners, parents/guardians, and the entire community are responsible for contributing to an environment that promotes a safe, healthy, and supportive learning environment. Therefore, preventive and positive discipline is a shared responsibility of learners, administrative and non-administrative staff, parents/guardians, and the entire community.

This policy applies the principle of preventive and positive discipline to address the causes of misbehavior, resolve conflicts, meet learners' needs, and keep learners in a safe educational institution. Preventive and positive discipline involves interventions, skill building, and consequences. This policy sets clear expectations and defines levels of support and intervention for all learners for misbehavior that are individualized, consistent, reasonable, fair, age-appropriate, and match the severity of the learner's misconduct. Disciplinary measures should support all students' social and emotional development by teaching alternatives to violence and respect for all members of the learning environment. Disciplinary measures should not be aimed at depriving a learner of his/her sense of dignity and self-value but should have the ultimate aim of understanding and addressing the causes of misbehavior in order to resolve conflicts while teaching new skills and repairing the harm done, restoring relationships, and reintegrating learners into the community.

Minor misconduct and first-time offenses shall be treated in a manner consistent with progressive discipline. Factors such as age, level of the learner, social, emotional, and intellectual development, and overall learners' rights and responsibilities shall be taken into consideration at all times. Each educational institution has to tailor local solutions, which shall include non-exclusionary, preventive, and positive approaches to discipline, to address the needs of its learning environments.

Stages of Disciplinary Measures

Disciplinary measures may be applied in the following stages:

First Stage
- verbal warning,
- a letter home (if under age 18 years) with written notice informing that the commission of an additional offense will lead to a particular disciplinary measure and
- monitoring by a personal tutor.

Second Stage
- formal verbal warning,
- a letter home (if under age 18 years). A learner may be required to repair, restore, replace, or pay for damaged, vandalized, lost, or stolen property. Payment may be required either in cash or if appropriate, agreed-upon services, depending on the learner's financial means.
- loss of school privileges, for example, field trips, after-school activities, etc., and
- monitoring by the Curriculum Leader.

Third Stage
- written warning by the Program Manager, then,
- final written warning by a member of the Disciplinary Committee, and
- a letter home (if under age 18 years).

Final Stage
- final review meeting with the Principal and/or Head of School, and/or
- student may be asked to leave the school indefinitely.

Student, Parent/Caregiver, and Institution Contract
What the School Expects from Students
The school expects students to:
- attend regularly and punctually, and to notify the school of any absence immediately,
- meet school standards for appearance and dress/uniform regulations,
- show respect to others regardless of their ethnic background, gender, age, religion, or personal circumstance,
- show respect for others' property and to respect the school environment,
- work hard to achieve their goals,
- uphold the school policies,
- subscribe to high standards of behavior, becoming role models,
- take responsibility for their own learning and progression,
- complete and hand in on time all work sets, and complete all academic work honestly and responsibly, rejecting all forms of cheating, plagiarism, or dishonest presentation of one's work,
- seek help from school staff if needed,
- meet assessment and examination requirements,
- take responsibility for their own and others' health and safety,
- behave safely and responsibly by refraining from all forms of misconduct or aggressive or disrespectful behavior toward individuals or property,
- refrain from the use of disrespectful communication to or about others,
- reject all forms of discrimination or harassment toward others,
- refrain from the use of mobile phones and extraneous electronic equipment while in classes or when doing educational activities,

- not engage in any behaviors involving the use of drugs, alcohol, addictive substances, or smoking,
- participate as required in all school activities and functions, including all lessons and sporting activities,
- refrain from any political party campaigning or promotion in the school,
- refrain from the display or use of symbols that are intended or liable to be offensive to others, and
- always act in a manner that will not discredit themselves, their family, and their school.

What Students Can Expect from Their Educational Institution

It is impossible to provide an exhaustive list of a learner's rights and expectations. The following list should, therefore, not be construed as denying or limiting other rights provided to learners in educational institutions:
- No learner shall be excluded from or discriminated against admission into any educational institution in Southern Cameroons or from obtaining the advantages and privileges of such educational institutions (including the rights to participate fully in classroom instructions and extracurricular activities) on account of race, color, ethnicity, national origin, religion, sexual orientation, gender, handicap, disabilities, age, marital, and/or military status.
- Learners have a right to:
  - an induction onto the course and institution, and to have their rights and responsibilities as members of the institutional community clearly explained to them,
  - high-quality learning programs delivered by well-qualified and experienced staff,
  - opportunities to express their views about the school,
  - full access to all institution's privileges; for example, field trips, after-school activities, transport system if available, and other amenities,
  - physical safety and the protection of personal property,
  - student government, and the right to seek and hold posts in

student government,
- participate in free elections of their peers by secret ballot,
- have their voices heard in matters affecting them,
- participate in the development of rules and regulations to which they are subject and to be notified of such rules and regulations,
- freedom of speech, assembly, press, and association,
- access procedures for formal complaints and procedures for those situations in which they believe themselves to be victims of discrimination,
- access to procedures to appeal a decision pertaining to misconduct, charges, or sanctions on their part,
- expect safety, confidentiality, and privacy when being considered for misconduct or when reporting the misconduct of others,
- written work/assignments returned promptly, with written feedback that can help them in their studies,
- a safe environment with access to sanitary facilities.

What Parents/Guardians or Caregivers Can Expect from an Institution

All parents, guardians, caregivers, and family members have a right to be included in all aspects of their child's education. This includes:
- the opportunity to contact the school with any concerns, and the right to
- regularly access information about their child's progress and education records, including discipline data, any information on education programs and opportunities,
- being given every available opportunity for meaningful participation in their child's education,
- opportunities to file complaints and/or appeals regarding matters affecting their child's education,
- participation in decision-making processes affecting school policies and procedures,
- monitoring and evaluating school policies and practices, including

but not limited to the right to visit schools and classrooms,
- being contacted by teachers or the school administrator if any issues are causing concern, and
- provide feedback about the school.

Responsibility of Parents and Guardians

Parents and guardians have the responsibility to:
- share the responsibility for the behavior of their child in an educational institution and educational-sponsored activities,
- prepare the child to assume responsibility for attending classes and for his or her own behavior,
- foster in the child a positive attitude toward himself or herself, others, the educational institution, and the community,
- communicate with the educational personnel about the child,
- behave in a civil and non-disruptive manner when visiting an educational institution,
- ensure that their child brings to school only those things that are allowed and
- encourage appropriate conduct and hard work.

CHAPTER 20

Instructional Time

In Southern Cameroons, local public and private schools must be open for at least 380 sessions (the time during which the school conducts classes) and 190 days during a school year. The school day is divided into two sessions: morning and afternoon.

Term dates are determined by school employers. The local authority is the employer for community, voluntary-controlled, and community special or maintained nursery schools. The employer is the governing body for foundation, voluntary-aided and foundation special schools.

The Southern Cameroons Education Board (SCEB) determines term dates and communicates these to school governing bodies at county and other community levels. However, these provisions may not be entirely enforced due to other considerations that may be specific to certain environments. The head administrator may recommend the length of a school day, including session times and breaks. The governing body must agree with the administrator's recommendations. Some academies may set their own term dates and school days.

Guidelines to Setting School Hours

This section provides information on the rules relating to the setting of school hours and term dates.

Number of Days for Schools to be Opened Each Year

Schools must open for at least 380 sessions (190 days) during a school year. The school year begins after December. If a school is prevented from meeting and it is not reasonably practicable for arrangements to be made for it to make up the lost session(s), it can be deemed to have been opened for the required 380 sessions.

Term dates are determined by school employers. As noted above, the local authority is the employer for community, voluntary-controlled, and community special or maintained nursery schools. The employer is the governing body for foundation, voluntary-aided, and foundation special schools.

Determination of the Length of a School Day

The head teacher of a state-funded school will recommend the length of a school day, including session times and breaks. The governing body must agree to the recommendations. As with term dates, academies set their own school day. As noted, academies have the freedom to set their own school day and term dates.

Procedures for Changing the Pattern of the School Day

These procedures must be followed when the governing body of any community, voluntary, controlled, or community special school proposes to change the time of school sessions. The school day is divided into two sessions: morning and afternoon. The procedures set out in the Session Times apply to proposals to change the start or finishing time of the school day and, secondly, to change the lunch break by altering the length of the morning session or the beginning of the afternoon session. Proposals which alter the length of the lunch break are also dealt with.

Provisions for Changing School Session Times

Regulation 1

Where the governing body proposes to make any change in session times, it must consult the Local Education Authority (LEA), the head-teacher, and all teaching and non-teaching staff employed in the school before taking any of the actions mentioned in subparagraphs (a) to (h) below:

a). Prepare a statement
- i). indicating that they propose to make a change in session times;
- ii). specifying the proposed change and when the proposal would take effect;
- iii). drawing attention to any comment on the proposal included as an appendix to the statement by virtue of sub-paragraph (b) below and including such response to the comment as they may consider appropriate and
- iv). giving details of the date, time, and place of the meeting which they are required to hold by virtue of sub-paragraph (e) below;

b). if required by the LEA, include an appendix to that statement, such written comments on the proposal as the authority may provide for that purpose;

c). produce that statement and any appendices in such language or languages if any (in addition to English) as they consider appropriate or as the LEA may direct;

d). take such steps as are reasonably practicable to secure that the parents of all registered students at the school and all persons employed at the school are given (free of charge) a copy of the statement and any annex not less than two weeks before the meeting which the governing body is required to hold by virtue of sub-paragraph (e) below, and that copies of the statement and any appendices are available for inspection (at all reasonable times and free of charge) at the school during the two-week-period immediately preceding that meeting;

e). provide an opportunity for discussion of the proposal at a meeting which is open to:
- all parents of registered pupils/students at the school, and
- the headteacher and such other persons as the governing body may invite;

f). consider any comments made at the meeting on the proposal before determining whether any change in those times should be made (and if so);

g). whether the proposal should be implemented with or without any modifications: and except where paragraph (j) below applies, not less than six weeks before any change in those times is to take effect;

h). inform the LEA of the change and of when it is to take effect;

i). take such steps as are reasonably practicable to ensure that the parents of all registered pupils/students at the school are well-informed; and

j). where the proposal concerns the times a school session begins in the morning or ends in the afternoon (or both, as the case may be), the period referred to in paragraph (g) above shall not be less than three months.

Regulation 2

No change in the times of a school session shall be made as to take effect: where paragraph (j) above applies, otherwise than at the beginning of a school year; in all other cases, otherwise than at the beginning of a school term.

Minimum Weekly Teaching Times

In order to prioritize instructional offerings that comprise the formal curriculum, the Instructional Times Policy sets out the following suggested minimum weekly teaching times as a guide for schools:

- Ages 5–7 years, 21 hours
- Ages 8-11 years, 23.5 hours
- Ages 12-16 years, 24 hours

The above guidance does not outline the standard minimum hours schools must operate. It is non-statutory and has advisory status only. In addition, attempts may be made to increase the length of school sessions to accommodate new developments in the National Curriculum. At the discretion of the headteacher, an extension could also be granted for classes preparing for national end-of-year examinations. Any extensions will solely depend on the needs of the learners, resources available, and approaches applied at a given school.

Implications for Teachers

Firstly, the governing body is required to consult all teaching and non-teaching staff in the school, the headteacher and the LEA about any proposed changes before taking any further steps.

Where a proposed change in school session times affects the times at which the school day begins or ends (or both), the period of notice that the governing body must give to the LEA and parents remains at least three (3) months, and the change can only take effect from the beginning of the school year. However, where a proposed change affects only the time of the end of the morning session or the start of the afternoon session, consequently affecting the length of the students' lunch break, the governing body has to give only a six-week notice and the change can take effect from the beginning of any school term.

All teachers should be at school during the formal school day (as stipulated by their individual timetables), except for special reasons, with prior permission of the headteacher, who shall apply his/her discretion in this regard based on policies put in place.

A Pay and Conditions document would be developed, and provisions would entitle classroom teachers to a reasonable break between school sessions.

CHAPTER 21

Education Financing, Resource Mobilization, School Infrastructure and Investment

The financing and resource mobilization of education and training will be guided by the principles of affordability, needs-based resource allocation, including grants, efficiency in resource utilization, partnerships, strongly decentralized financing and accountability systems, and effective coordination. Overall, education and training financing sources will include financial outlays by central and county governments, private sector providers of educational services, religious organizations, civil society, foundations, the private sector, non-governmental organizations (NGOs), households, communities, and other stakeholders.

The government shall maintain the overall policy for quality improvement and aim to:

- Finance education at all levels;
- Include other partners such as the private sector, civil society, religious organizations, communities, donors and beneficiaries in the financing of education.
- Review budget allocation proportionately for each sub-sector of education.
- Ensure each head of an institution is accountable for finances in his/her organization.
- Reduce the cost of education to households by providing teachers, teaching and learning materials, and grants to schools to cover operational and maintenance expenses under the Free Primary Education (FPE) and Free Day Secondary Education (FDSE)

policies.
- Establish Needs-based grants for learners in Early Childhood Education and Development (ECDE), primary, secondary, special needs education (SNE), adult education, and not-for-profit non-formal schools that meet set criteria.
- Build new schools/classrooms, rehabilitating and maintaining existing facilities, and encouraging the collaboration of the (central and county) government, communities, and households, based on agreed-upon guidelines and aimed at reducing the cost burden of education on the stakeholders.

School Infrastructure and Investment

The policy on school infrastructure examines and describes minimal infrastructure at each level of schooling to ensure that schools produce well-rounded individuals capable of transitioning to the next level of schooling or becoming productive citizens who can contribute to their community and society.

Levels of Schooling Supported by the Policy

This policy covers nursery, primary, secondary, tertiary, and post-tertiary education, as well as technical/vocational education and SNE.

Infrastructure Imperatives

The primary imperative for the infrastructure policy is to provide a safe and conducive environment for learning of all forms and for teachers and administrators to be their best selves so that the best and brightest of our human resources can be attracted to the profession and help develop our future generation.

Education Stakeholders

In deciding on infrastructure imperatives, the following stakeholders in education are primarily considered in order of priority:
- Learners
- Teachers

- Administrators
- Parents/Community

Components of the Education Infrastructure
Learning Infrastructure

Infrastructure must be capable of providing the whole learning experience for learners. Every school must include facilities to support learners in achieving their potential at the level for which education is being provided. Minimal infrastructure for learning must include:
- Classroom blocks
- Desks and chairs
- Book lockers
- Computing labs
- Science/Language/Other labs
- Library (physical or virtual)
- Infirmary
- Internet Access
- Learning Aids
- Cafeteria
- Playground
- School Clubs' meeting areas

All schools must have a constant power supply available for at least 80% of the school day.

School premises must include adequate provisions for safe Water, Sanitation, and proper Hygiene (WASH), including separate male and female toilets.

In addition, area secondary and high schools must provide comprehensive sports and physical education facilities that include but are not limited to:
- Football/handball fields
- Basketball court
- Volleyball court
- Lawn Tennis court

- Tennis/Ping Pong (optional)
- Track & Field
- Swimming pool
- Coaches

Furthermore, area secondary and high schools should include music programs and provide studios, musical instruments, and music instructors.

Teaching Infrastructure

Infrastructure must facilitate instruction preparation and delivery to enhance learning. *Minimal* infrastructure for teaching that must be provided at each facility to include:
- Whiteboards
- Markers
- Textbooks
- Teaching Aids
- Computing facilities
- Internet Access
- Projectors (for high school classrooms)

Administration Infrastructure

Infrastructure must support the basic administration of the learning institution, such as admitting learners, preparing transcripts/report cards, processing payments, and interacting with the community. Minimal administrative infrastructure for each school must include:
- An administrative block
- A meeting room
- Auditorium
- Administrative computing systems
- A school website
- A staff common room
- WASH facilities

Security and Safety Infrastructure

Infrastructure must protect learning spaces against internal and external threats. Minimal security infrastructure for each school will include:
- Perimeter fencing
- A painted and visible signboard
- Permanent security guards
- A water hose and other firefighting equipment
- Smoke alarms
- A designated and well-publicized muster point

Social Infrastructure

Infrastructure must provide direct communication and interaction between the school and its surrounding community. Minimal social infrastructure for each school must include:
- A Parent/Teachers Association (PTA)
- A School-Based Management Committee (SBMC)
- Local city council representative will be on the SBMC
- A Student Leadership Organization (for secondary and high schools)

Investing in Infrastructure

All school zones will be classified into urban and rural communities using the most recent national census data.

Budgeting

A local school governing committee led by the principal will prepare the school's budget, which will be presented to the school board for ratification and adoption. This will apply to all levels of schooling.

Funding

Funding for infrastructure will come primarily from taxes. A special school infrastructure levy would be imposed on all workers, businesses, visitors, tourists, and travelers.

Funding Models

The initial pace of education infrastructure buildout will have to be very rapid to compensate for almost 60 years of underinvestment by both the colonial authorities and La Republique du Cameroun. The costs may be beyond what the revenue sources available to the government can sustain. Different funding models must be considered to ensure sustained investment in education.

- Direct Government Funding: the government will contract and pay for education infrastructure based on reference designs using funds from the treasury and education levies.
- Public-Private Partnership: Private sector actors will be encouraged to enter into Public-Private Partnerships (PPPs) to develop school infrastructure using either a cost recovery or Build, Operate, and Transfer (BOT) model. In such models, the government will provide guaranteed student enrollment numbers and cover the cost of education for each student to private investors until their costs have been recovered.

National

The federal government must budget for free education from kindergarten to twelfth grade.

Maintenance

A percentage of the initial capital investment (not below 20%) will be budgeted each year as operational funds for the maintenance of school infrastructure.

Local communities will have a defined tax levy percentage that will be used to maintain school state-of-the-art facilities.

CHAPTER 22

Monitoring and Evaluation

Monitoring is a continuous process of data collection, analysis, and measurement of progress toward projected objectives. Evaluation is assessing a project to determine the relevance and fulfillment of objectives, effectiveness, impact, and sustainability. When the national and county government agencies consider Monitoring and Evaluation (M&E) as a learning and development process, they will embrace and take ownership of it. Previously, when M&E was seen as a punitive instrument, users developed negative attitudes toward the process. However, employing M&E should serve to improve quality performance, not to punish. M&E should help employees grow. This should be the department's outlined goal.

Policy Strategy

The national and local governments will establish an Independent Education Standards Quality Assurance Commission. This commission will develop the following strategies that undergird its work:

- Standardize M&E procedures,
- Synchronize the M&E framework with education outcomes,
- Develop and implement quality assurance measures and standards,
- Build capacity of personnel at county and institutional levels,
- Establish a sustainable M&E funding mechanism,
- Ensure the coordination process to avoid duplication of efforts,
- Establish the process of obtaining comprehensive baselines to link all M&E activities,
- Establish the Education Management Information Systems (EMIS)

- Introduce a centralized information tracking system and complementary reporting systems,
- Continuously improve data gathering and the dissemination of results and
- Develop and implement a scorecard system on key basic education indicators (access, participation, internal efficiency, and learning achievements) at all levels.

A general principle that undergirds this blueprint will be the development of legislation that will have the force of law behind it to ensure enforcement.

Appendix

Southern Cameroons Colonial Timeline

1858:	Alfred Saker (British Missionary) and the Baptists arrived in Bimbia (a seaside settlement of Southern Cameroons), and renamed it Victoria, after the reigning British Empress.
1884:	The Berlin Conference: Germany hoisted its flag over the Ambas Bay Colony of Victoria and the territory was ceded over to the Germans in July.
1885:	Britain transferred territory to Germany per the Treaty, and on April 21, Southern Cameroons became part of the German Protectorate of Kamerun.
1916:	Defeat of Germany in World War I, Southern Cameroons coveted by Britain.
1922:	Southern Cameroons became League of Nations Mandated Territory under United Kingdom rule.
1923:	Southern Cameroons appended to Nigeria by United Kingdom.
1946:	Southern Cameroons made United Nations Class B Trust Territory under United Kingdom as Administering Authority.
1951:	First Parliamentary Elections organized in Southern Cameroons to choose representatives to Eastern Nigeria House of Assembly in Enugu and the Federal House in Lagos.
1953:	Southern Cameroons Representatives walked out en-masse in protest from Eastern House of Assembly in Enugu.
1954:	Southern Cameroons achieved Self-Governing status with Dr. Emmanuel M. Endeley as first Premier.
1956:	Southern Cameroons organized parliamentary elections for the second time.

APPENDIX

1957: London Constitutional Conference increased the number of elected membership of the House from 13 to 26, and created a House of Chiefs for prominent Traditional Rulers.

1959: Southern Cameroons organized democratic elections for a third time and effected the first peaceful and democratic transfer of power in Sub-Saharan Africa (SSA). The government party was defeated and first Premier became Leader of Opposition in the House.

September 30: After his defeat, the new Premier John Ngu Foncha and the defeated Premier Emmanuel M. L. Endeley traveled together to the United Nations Trusteeship Committee to put the case for the independence of Southern Cameroons.

1960: The United Nations imposes the Two Alternatives on Southern Cameroons: "independence by joining" either La Republique du Cameroun or the Federal Republic of Nigeria.

1961: Southern Cameroons was federated with La Republique du Cameroun as autonomous state of West Cameroon.

1972: End of federation imposed on Southern Cameroons and territory annexed as the 9th and 10th Provinces of La Republique Unie du Cameroun (United Republic of Cameroon) and occupied militarily.

1984: Annexation is completed with change of country's name by Presidential Decree to revert to Republique du Cameroun, the name by which French Cameroon gained its independence from France on January 1, 1960.

1985: Emergence of Southern Cameroons Liberation Movements, arrest and detention of Fon Gorgi Dinka.

1993: Southern Cameroons Liberation Movements convened under the banner of the All Anglophone Conference (AAC I) in Buea and issued the "Buea Declaration," which called for constitutional amendments to restore the 1961 federation.

1994: Southern Cameroons organized the second All Anglophone Conference (AAC II) in Bamenda and issued the "Bamenda Proclamation," which stated that if the federal state was not restored within a reasonable time, Southern Cameroons would declare its independence.

August 6: AAC I was re-baptized Southern Cameroons Peoples Council (SCPC); the Anglophone Council became Southern Cameroons People's Organization, (SCAPO), with the Southern Cameroons National Council (SCNC) as the governing body; and the advisory body renamed Southern Cameroons Advisory Council (SCAC).

1995: SCPC issued the Buea Peace Initiative (BPI) and sent a delegation to the United Nations to petition against annexation. BPI envisioned a modality for the peaceful separation with La Republique du Cameroun.

Delegation issued the London Communiqué to alert the world on the annexation and occupation of Southern Cameroons by Republique du Cameroun and its implications on peace and security in the Gulf of Guinea.

1996: **January**: Government of La Republique du Cameroun published the country's third Constitution with no mention of Southern Cameroons.

September: Southern Cameroons conducted a Signature Referendum on the future of the territory.

1999: **December 30:** Justice Frederick Alobwede Ebong proclaimed the Restoration of Sovereignty and Independence of Southern Cameroons.

2000: Southern Cameroons filed an application for membership of the United Nations, the Organization for African Unity, the Commonwealth, the Francophonie, the Economic Community of West African States, and the Non-Aligned Movement.

2002: Southern Cameroons Peoples Organization (SCAPO) took the Nigerian Government to the Federal High Court of

Nigeria in Abuja to require Nigeria to take the Southern Cameroons case before the International Court of Justice to establish the right of the people of the Southern Cameroons to self-determination. The Federal High Court of Nigeria ruled in their favor on March 5.

October 10: International Court of Justice ruled that sovereignty over the Bakassi Peninsula rested with Cameroun, ignoring the interplay of Southern Cameroons claiming Bakassi Peninsular.

2003: Representatives of the People of the former United Nations Trust Territory of the Southern Cameroons under United Kingdom Administration submitted the case *v. La Republique du Cameroun to the African Commission on Human and people's Rights* (Communication 266/2003).

2005: Southern Cameroons becomes a member of the Unrepresented Nations and Peoples Organization (UNPO).

2006: **August 14:** SCAPO responded to the handover of Bakassi to Cameroun by proclaiming the independence of the Republic of Ambazonia (Southern Cameroons), including the territory of Bakassi.

2009: African Commission on Human and People's Rights (ACHPR) issued ruling on Communication 266/2003—recommending dialogue between La Republique du Cameroun (Respondent State) and Southern Cameroons, which the Commission recognized as a people.

2016: Lawyers and Teachers protest over government use of French in Southern Cameroons systems and replacement of Southern Cameroonians with Francophones.

2017: **January:** Leaders of the protesting lawyers and teachers are arrested and jailed by the regime in Yaounde.

October: Southern Cameroons/Ambazonia declares its Independence.

November: President Paul Biya declares war on Southern Cameroons/Ambazonia.

2018: **January:** Southern Cameroonian/Ambazonian leaders are abducted in Nigeria.

2024: At the time of publication of this book, the armed conflict between La Republique du Cameroun and Southern Cameroons is ongoing.

Glossary

Achievement Gap: A consistent difference in scores on student achievement tests between certain groups of children and children in other groups.

Average Class Size: The number of students in classes divided by the number of classes. Because some teachers, such as reading specialists, have assignments outside the regular classroom, the average class size is usually larger than the pupil-teacher ratio.

Bottom-up Approach: A bottom-up approach gives all teams a voice in decision-making.

Cameroon: Officially called the Republic of Cameroon, is a country situated in Central Africa, sharing boundaries with Nigeria to the west and north, Chad to the northeast, the Central African Republic to the east, and Equatorial Guinea, Gabon, and the Republic of the Congo to the south.

Combined Approach: The combined approach consisting of a wide range of stakeholders who interact at various levels and validating the interactions of all. In this approach, both policymakers and the local actors who enact the policies on the ground are important for successful implementation.

Cooperative Learning: A switch from more traditional, curriculum-focused methods of education. Cooperative learning environments support students learning, both as self and within the group.

Comparative Education: Using data from the educational practices and situations of one geographical area to examine the educational practices in another.

Computer Based Learning (CBL): A structured environment where computers are primarily used to teach as a key component, both in and out of a classroom situation.

Continental Education Strategy for Africa (CESA): A framework emphasizing the commitment to the future of education in Africa as envisioned by the global development goals committed to the creation of a new generation of Africans who are effective change agents capable of driving the continent's sustainable development goals.

Continuing Professional Development (CPD): Is a combination of ideas, techniques, and approaches that are designed to help manage and enhance the growth, abilities and learning of professions in an ongoing, systematic and outcomes-focused approach that results in lifelong learning that can be applied to practice.

Critical Thinking: The mental processes used when evaluating information that has been put forth as true. Critical thinking consists of reflection, examination, and formation of judgement. Information is gathered through communication, experience, reasoning and observation. While based in values of intellect, critical thinking goes beyond subject/matter division.

Curriculum: The courses of study offered by a school or district which can comprise of activities in and outside the classroom that enrich learners' experiences.

"Ecole Normale Superieure" (ENS): Following the dissolution of provincial Teacher Training Colleges in the Anglophone (English Speaking) region, or Southern Cameroons, a single Higher Teachers' Training College was instituted in Yaoundé, the capital of Cameroon, called "Ecole Normale Superieure."

Education Policy: Education policy is usually an embodiment of values, stated rules and regulations, culture and needs about education to control and modify the behavior of schools and social institution, and an outline of what the practices would look like. Education policy is therefore a public policy, designed with the goal of enhancing educational attainment in any nation.

Education Reform: A movement or plan that brings or attempts to bring an entire change of the system of educational theory and practice across society or community lines.

Exam/Examination (a.k.a. Test): An assessment of an individual meant to determine his or her knowledge, skill, or other classification on a subject. Exams may be oral, written or performance-based, and could be formal or informal.

Government Teacher Technical College (G.T.T.C): As the name indicates, these are teachers' colleges run by the government as opposed to private teachers' colleges run by individuals or the private sector.

General Certificate Examinations (GCE): These are examinations that students take at the end of secondary schools (GCE Ordinary levels) and high, schools (GCE Advanced Level).

Higher Education: The education provided by institutions such as colleges and universities that reward academic degrees upon completion. The term higher education refers to both teaching and research activities of universities. In the teaching sphere, it refers to both undergraduate and graduate level (sometimes referred to graduate school). Higher education is different than other types of post-secondary education such as vocational institutions.

Human Resource Management: Is the process of employing people, training them, compensating them, developing policies relating to them, and developing strategies to retain them.

International Standard Classification of Education (ISCED): Maintained by UNESCO, the ISCED, provides a comprehensive framework for organizing education programs and qualification by applying uniform and internationally agreed definitions to facilitate comparisons of education systems across countries.

Managerial Perspectives: Managerial perspective in an organization refers to the study of how individuals, groups, and structures within an organization affect behaviors, outcomes, and the organization's performances.

Millennium Development Goals (MDGs): The United Nations Millennium Development Goals (MDGs) are 8 goals that UN Member States agreed to try to achieve by the year 2015. The Declaration, signed in September 2000, committed world leaders to combat poverty, hunger, disease, illiteracy, environmental degradation, and discrimination against women.

Philosophy of Education: The study behind the nature, ideal content, and purpose of education. Questions include problems of authority, the nature between the human subject and the knowing mind, and the relationship between society and education. The philosophy of education has long been linked to the theories of human development.

Policy-design: Policy design looks at a problem or issue identification, mobilization of the acceptable structure of government action, compromises which establish a framework for policy planning and practice in the face of dilemmas and trade-offs.

Post-Secondary Education: Any education following the attendance of secondary school. This can be in the nature of vocational training and education or to prepare for careers and professions through higher education.

Secondary Education: The period of education directly following primary education, as defined in contemporary systems. It can be followed by tertiary, post-secondary, or higher education.

Southern Cameroons: The Southern Cameroons (also known as Ambazonia) was the southern part of the British League of Nations mandate territory of the British Cameroons in West Africa. Since 1961, it has been part of the Republic of Cameroon, and is made up of the Northwest Region and Southwest Region.

Special Education: The purposeful intervention, designed to accommodate, overcome or eliminate the obstacles that keep students with disabilities from learning.

STEM Fields: Science, Technology, Engineering and Mathematics (STEM). Collectively they are considered an advanced society's core. The strength of a STEM workforce is, in many societies, seen as the indicator of a nation's self-sustainability.

STEAM Fields: are the areas of Science, Technology, Engineering, the Arts, and Mathematics. STEAM is designed to integrate STEM subjects with arts subjects.

Student: An individual who attends school or classes, from primary, secondary to higher education. Sometimes primary students are referred to as pupils.

Substance of Education Policy: The substance of education policy is the stated educational principles and objectives, and the actions that should be taken to achieve those objectives.

Sustainable Development Goals (SDG): The Sustainable Development Goals (SDGs), also known as the Global Goals, were adopted by the United Nations in 2015 as a universal call to action to end poverty, protect the planet, and ensure that by 2030 all people enjoy peace and prosperity.

Syllabus: The outline and summary of topics that will be covered during the length of a course. It can be set by an exam board or by the instructor.

Teacher Service Commission (TSC): Is a body that is responsible for the appointment and registration of teachers and principals that provide instruction to students at preschool, primary, secondary and Post-secondary institutions

Tertiary Education: The level of education that follows secondary education. Most commonly refers to higher education, such as university or master programs.

References

Africa-America Institute (AAI). (2015). *The state of education in Africa report 2015: A report card on the progress, opportunities and challenges confronting the African education sector.* https://www.aaionline.org/wp-content/uploads/2015/09/AAI-SOE-report-2015-final.pdf

African Union (AU). (2014). *Common African Position (CAP) on the post-2015 development agenda.* Addis Ababa.

African Union (AU). (2016). *Continental Education Strategy for Africa: 2016–2025* (CESA 2016–2025). https://ecosocc.au.int/sites/default/files/files/2021-09/continental-strategy-education-africa-english.pdf

Albright, M. I., Weissberg, R. P., & Dusenbury, L. A. (2011). *School-family partnership strategies to enhance children's social, emotional, and academic growth.* National Center for Mental Health Promotion and Youth Violence Prevention, Education Development Center. https://www.cde.state.co.us/cdesped/school-familypartnershipstrategies

Amedorme, S, K., & Fiagbe, Y. A.K. (2013). Challenges facing technical and vocational education in Ghana. *International Journal of Scientific & Technology Research, 2*(6), 253–255. http://www.ijstr.org/paper-references.php?ref=IJSTR-0613-6625

Anderson, M. (2015, August). Many disabled children in poorer countries are left out of primary education, *The Guardian.* https://www.theguardian.com/global-development/2015/aug/18/disabled-children-poorer-countries-out-of-primary-education-south-africa-human-rights-watch-report

Anja, N. S. (2000). *A handbook of educational legislation: An introduction to school rules and regulations for schools and colleges of education.* Unique Printers.

Assie-Lumumba, N. D. (2005). Africana higher education: From compulsory juxtaposition to fusion by choice-forging a new philosophy of education for social progress. In Y. Waghid & B. Van Wyk (Eds.), *African(a) philosophy of education: Reconstructions and deconstructions* (pp. 19–53). Stellenbosch University.

Ball, S. J. (1994). Political interviews and the politics of interviewing. In G.

Walford (Ed.), *Researching the powerful in education* (pp. 96–115). Routledge. https://doi.org/10.4324/9781315072203

Banathy, B. H. (1992). *A systems view of education: Concepts and principles for effective practice*. Educational Technology.

Banerjee, A.V., Banerji, R., Duflo, E., Glennerster, R., & Khemani, S. (2008). *Pitfalls of participatory programs: Evidence from a randomized evaluation in education in India*. World Bank.

Bardach, E. (1984). The dissemination of policy research to policymakers. *Knowledge: Creation, Diffusion, Utilization, 6*(2), 125–144. https://eric.ed.gov/?id=EJ312744

Barrett, S., & Fudge, C. (Eds.). (1981). *Policy and action: Essays on the implementation of pubic policy*. Methuen.

Becher, T. (Ed.). (1999). *Professional Practices: Commitment and capability in a changing environment* (1st ed.). Routledge. https://doi.org/10.4324/9781351289689

Becker, G. S. (1964). *Human capital: A theoretical and empirical analysis, with special reference to education*. Columbia University Press.

Beckhard, R. & Pritchard, W. (1992). *Changing the essence: The art of creating and leading fundamental change in organizations*. Jossey Bass.

Bifuh-Ambe, E. (2020a). Harnessing the transformational potential of education to meet national and global developmental needs: Re-Thinking theory and practice in education policy of Southern Cameroons. John Hopkins University Project Muse. *Theory & Event* (Special Issue), vol. 23, no. 2. (April).

Bifuh-Ambe, E. (2020b). Educational policy for postcolonial Africa, in Oxford Research Encyclopedia of Education. Oxford University Press. (July) https://doi.org/10.1093/acrefore/9780190264093.013.1412.

Blössner, M. (2008). [Review of book *School health, nutrition and education for all: Levelling the playing field*, by M. Jukes, L. Drake, & D. Bundy]. *Bulletin of the World Health Organization, 87*(1): 75. https://www.ncbi.nlm.nih.gov/pmc/articles/PMC2649604/

Bobbitt, F. (1918). *The Curriculum*. Houghton Mifflin.

Bourne, J. (2014). Why educating girls makes economic sense. *GPE Transforming Education* (blog). https://www.globalpartnership.org/blog/why-educating-girls-makes-economic-sense

Brameld, T. (1971). *Patterns of educational philosophy: Divergence and convergence in culturological perspectives*. Holt, Rinehart and Winston.

Bregman, J., & Stallmeister, S. (2007). *Secondary education in Africa (SEIA):*

Strategies for renewal. A Regional Study of the Africa Region of the World Bank. https://eric.ed.gov/?id=ED474425

Bryman, A. (1999). Leadership in organizations. In S. R. Clegg, C. Hardy, & W. R. Nord (Eds.). *Managing organizations: Current issues* (pp. 26–42). Sage.

California. Department of Education. (2023, October 12). *Definition of a school.* https://www.cde.ca.gov/ds/si/ds/dos.asp

Cameroon Education Forum (CEF). (2016). *Reflection on the Anglophone subsystem of education in Cameroon.*

Carmela, S., & Labate, H. (2016). Report prepared for the United Nations Educational, Scientific and Cultural Organization (UNESCO), International Institute for Capacity Building in Africa (IICBA). *Teaching policies and learning outcomes in Sub-Saharan Africa: Issues and options; summary.* UNESCO IICBA. https://unesdoc.unesco.org/ark:/48223/pf0000246500

Carver-Thomas, D., & Darling-Hammond, L. (2017, August). Teacher turnover: Why it matters and what we can do about it. *Learning Policy Institute.* https://learningpolicyinstitute.org/sites/default/files/product-files/Teacher_Turnover_REPORT.pdf

Cerych, L. & Sabatier, P. (1986). *Great expectations and mixed performance: The implementation of higher education reforms in Europe.* Trentham.

Conrad, Joseph. (1899). *Heart of Darkness.* 3-part serial, 1,000 ed. *Blackwood's Magazine,* 165. Book format published in 1902.

Covey, S. R. (2004). *The 7 habits of highly effective people: Powerful Lessons in Personal Change.* Free Press.

Dei, G. J. S. (2000). *Rethinking the role of indigenous knowledges in the academy.* NALL Working Paper No. 58. https://files.eric.ed.gov/fulltext/ED479137.pdf

Derthick, M. (1972). *New towns in-town: Why a federal program failed.* Urban Institute Press.

Dewey, J. (1902). *The child and the curriculum.* University of Chicago Press.

Diem, S., Young, M. D., Welton, A. D., Mansfield, K. C., & Lee, P.-L. (2014). The intellectual landscape of critical policy analysis. *International Journal of Qualitative Studies in Education,* 27(9), 1068–1090. https://doi.org/10.1080/09518398.2014.916007

Domitrovich, C., Dusenbury, L., & Hyson, M. (2013). *Beyond academic competence: The foundations of school success.* National Governors Association. https://www.nga.org/files/live/sites/NGA/files/pdf/2013/1303EduPolicyForumNonCogniti

Downer, J., Sabol, T. J., & Hamre, B. (2010). Teacher–child interactions in the classroom: Toward a theory of within- and cross-domain links to children's developmental outcomes. *Early Education and Development*, *21*(5), 699–723. https://doi.org/10.1080/10409289.2010.497453

Downs, A. (1957). An economic theory of political action in democracy. *Journal of Political Economy*, *65*(2), 135–150. https://www.journals.uchicago.edu/doi/abs/10.1086/257897

Elmore, T, M. (1985). The era of ACES: Tradition, transformation, and the possible dream. *Journal of Counseling & Development*, *63*(7), 411–415. https://doi.org/10.1002/j.1556-6676.1985.tb02821.x

English School Handbook. (2016). *The English School's Curriculum for Basic Education*.

Fitzgerald, T. H. (1988). Can change in organizational culture really be managed? *Organizational Dynamics*, *17*(1), 5–15. https://doi.org/10.1016/0090-2616(88)90015-0

Fonkeng, G. E. (2010). *The history of education in Cameroon: 1844–2010*. Moda Publishers; Edwin Mellen Press.

Fullan, M. (2007). *The new meaning of educational change* (4th ed.). New York: Routledge.

Gay, G. (1990). Achieving educational equality through curriculum desegregation. *Phi Delta Kappan*, *72* (1). 56–62. https://eric.ed.gov/?id=EJ413176

Glass, G. V., Cahen, L. S., Smith, M. L.& Filby, N. N. (1982). *School class size: Research and policy*. Sage Publication.

Glatthorn, A. A., Boschee, F. A., Whithead, B. M., & Boschee, B. F. (2008). *Curriculum leadership: Strategies for development and implementation* (2nd ed.). Sage.

Glatthorn, A.A., Boschee, F. A., Whitehead, B. M., & Boschee, B.F. (2019). *Curriculum leadership: Strategies for development and implementation* (5th ed.). Sage.

Goggin, M., Bowman, A., Lester, J., & O'Toole, L. (1990). Implementation theory and practice: Toward a third generation. Glenview, IL: Scott Foresman.

Good, C. V. (1945). *Curriculum. Dictionary of Education*. McGraw–Hill.

Gornitzka, A., Kogan, M., & Stensaker, B. (2005). Implementation analysis in higher education. In A. Gornitzka, M. Kogan, & A. Amaral (Eds.), *Reform and change in higher education: Analyzing policy implementation*, 35–56. Springer.

Government of Cameroon. Ministry of Education. (1998). *Law No. 98/004 of 4th April 1998: The Orientation of Education in*

Cameroon. https://www.scribd.com/document/707829591/Law-No-98-004-of-4th-April-1998-on-education-in-Cameroon

Government of Cameroon, Cameroon Country Management Unit and the Education Unit, Africa Region (AFTED). (2012). *Cameroon—Governance and management in the education sector (English)*. Report No. 67201–CM. World Bank. https://documents1.worldbank.org/curated/en/874481468223463602/pdf/NonAsciiFileName0.pdf

Grumet, M. R. (1988). *Bitter milk: Women and teaching*. The University of Massachusetts, Press.

Guha, R. (Ed.). (1982). *Subaltern studies I: Writings on South Asian history and society*. Oxford University Press.

Hallak, J., & Poisson, M. (2005). Ethics and corruption in education: An overview. *Journal of Education for International Development*, *1*(1), 1–17. http://equip123.net/JEID/articles/1/1-3.pdf

Hanf, K., Hjern, B., & Porter, D. (1978). Local networks of manpower training in the Federal Republic of Germany and Sweden. In K. Hanf & F. Sharpf, (Eds.). *Interorganizational policy making: Limits to coordination and central control* (pp. 303–344). Sage.

Hannaway, J., & Carnoy, M. (1993). *Decentralization and school improvement: Can we fulfill the promise?* Jossey-Bass.

Hartnett, T., & Heneveld., W. (1993). *Statistical indicators of female participation in education in Sub-Saharan Africa (English)*. AFTHR Technical Note No. 7. Africa Technical Department. World Bank Group. http://documents1.worldbank.org/curated/en/588881468914736878/pdf/Statistical-indicators-of-female-participation-in-education-in-sub-Saharan-Africa.pdf

Higgs, P. (2003). African philosophy and transformation of educational discourse in South Africa. *Journal of Education. 30* (1).

The Himalayan Institute (HI). (2024). *Cameroon*. https://humanitarian.himalayaninstitute.org/cameroon.

Human Rights Watch Report. (2015, August). *South Africa: Education barriers for children with disabilities*. https://www.hrw.org/news/2015/08/18/south-africa-education-barriers-children-disabilities

Hutchins, M. R. (1963). *A conversation on education*. Center for the Study of Democratic Institutions.

IPAR, Buea (1977). *Institute for the reform of primary education: Report on the reform of primary education*. National Archives Buea (NAB).

Japan Internation Cooperation (2015). *Agency Annual Report 2015*. https://www.

jica.go.jp/english/about/disc/report/2015/index.html

Kanjee, A. (2009). Enhancing teacher assessment practices in South African schools: Evaluation of the assessment resource banks. *Education as Change, 13*(1), 73–89. http://doi.org/10.1080/16823200902940599

Kapambwe, W. M. (2010). The Implementation of School Based Continuous Assessment (CA) in Zambia. *Educational Research and Reviews, 5*, 99-107.

Khoza, R. (2006). *Let Africa lead: African transformational leadership for 21st-century business.* Vesubuntu Publishing.

Kindzeka Moki, E. (2018, November 7). 79 kidnapped Cameroon students freed, says church official. *AP News.* https://apnews.com/article/edd1363688524e76843e886c6ffce0aa/

Kingdon, J. W. (1984). *Agendas, alternatives, and public policies.* HarperCollins.

Kirstin koulu [Elementary School]. (2018). *Kirstin koula (English).* https://www.espoo.fi/en/units/15404

Klein, H. S., & Jacob, K. (1999). *The Atlantic slave trade.* Cambridge University Press.

Kwachou, M. (2015). Sexuality education in Cameroon: The Necessity and possibilities. *Essay Submitted in partial Fulfillment of the Requirements for Completion of the Gender, Education and Development Course.* UCL Institute of Education, London.

Lallez, R. (1974). *An experiment in the ruralization of education: IPAR and the Cameroonian reform.* UNESCO International Bureau of Education. https://unesdoc.unesco.org/ark:/48223/pf0000011325

Langtree, I. C. (2014, September 22; 2024, March 9). Defining convention on the rights of persons with disabilities (CRPD). *Disabled World.* https://www.disabled-world.com/disability/discrimination/crpd-milestone.php

Lee, Kuan Yew. (2000). *From third world to first: The Singapore story, 1965–2000.* Harper Collins.

Lengha, N. T. (2014). School health, nutrition and school performance in rural Cameroon, African Educational Research, 2(1), 43–53. https://www.netjournals.org/pdf/AERJ/2014/1/14-013.pdf

Lewin, K. L. (2001). *Knowledge matters for development.* Professional Lecture. University of Sussex Center for International Education. https://keithlewin.net/wp-content/uploads/2019/01/Keith-Lewin-Knowledge-Matters-for-Development-.pdf

Lewin, K., & Caillods, F. (2002). *Financing secondary education in developing countries: Strategies for sustainable growth.* International Institute for

Educational Planning/UNESCO.

Liliane Fonds. (2024). *See the strength in every child.* https://www.lilianefonds.org/

Lipsky, M. (1980). *Street-level bureaucracy: Dilemmas of the individual in public services.* Russell Sage Foundation.

Luhabe, W. (2002). *Defining moments: Experiences of Black executives in South Africa's workplace.* University of Natal Press.

Maclean, R. (2018, November 8). Kidnapped students in Cameroon reunited with their parents: Pupils put under "school arrest" by government after release from kidnapping allowed to go home. *Guardian.* https://www.theguardian.com/world/2018/nov/08/cameroon-kidnapped-students-reunited-with-parents-bamenda

Majgaard, K., & Mingat, A. (2012). *Education in Sub-Saharan Africa: A comparative analysis.* World Bank.

Mandela, N. (2006), Foreword. In: Khoza, R.J. (Ed.) *Let Africa lead: African transformational leadership for 21st century business* (p. 6). Vezubuntu.

Maschinot, B. (2008). *The changing face of the United States: The influence of culture on early child development.* Zero to Three. National Center for Infants and Children.

Massachusetts Department of Elementary and Secondary Education (DESE). (2015a, June). *Building supportive environments: Companion document for Massachusetts standards for preschool and kindergarten social and emotional learning, and approaches to play and learning.* https://www.doe.mass.edu/sfs/earlylearning/resources/SEL-APL-Env.docx

Massachusetts Department of Elementary and Secondary Education (DESE). (2015b, June). *Social and emotional learning, and approaches to Play and Learning.* https://www.doe.mass.edu/sfs/earlylearning/resources/sel-apl-standards.docx

Matland, R. E. (1995). Synthesizing the implementation literature: The ambiguity-conflict model of policy implementation. *Journal of Public Administration Research and Theory,* (5)2, 145–174. https://doi.org/10.1093/oxfordjournals.jpart.a037242

Meyer, H.-D., & Rowan, B. (2006). Institutional analysis and the study of education. In H.-D. Meyer & B. Rowan (Eds.), *The new institutionalism in education* (pp. 1–13). SUNY Press.

Mignolo, W. D. (2007). Delinking: The rhetoric of modernity, the logic of coloniality and the grammar of de-coloniality. *Cultural Studies,* 21(2–3),

449–514. https://doi.org/10.1080/09502380601162647

Mills, C. W. (1956). *The power elite.* Oxford University Press.

Miske, S. (2003). *Proud pioneers: Malawian teachers implement continuous assessment in primary school classrooms.* Washington, DC: American Institutes for Research.

Moloketi, G. R. (2009). Towards a common understanding of corruption in Africa. *Public Policy and Administration, 24*(3), 331–338. https://doi.org/10.1177/0952076709103814.

Mugisha. (2003). *Women and girls' education in Africa.* Springer-Palgrave.

Mukete, V. E. (2013). *My odyssey: The story of Cameroon reunification.* Eagle Publishing.

Mulkeen, A. (2010). *Teachers in anglophone Africa: Issues in teacher supply, training, and management.* Report No. 13545. World Bank.

Namiko Abe. (2018). *The Japanese education system.* ThoughtCo. https://www.thoughtco.com/the-japanese-education-system-2028111

National Association for the Education of Young Children (NAEYC). (2009). https://www.naeyc.org/.

National Education Association. (2020, September 14). *Code of ethics for Educators.* https://www.nea.org/resource-library/code-ethics-educators

National Scientific Council on the Developing Child (2004). *Children's emotional development is built into the architecture of their brains: Working Paper No. 2.* https://developingchild.harvard.edu/resources/childrens-emotional-development-is-built-into-the-architecture-of-their-brains/

Neba-Fuh, E. (2018). *The unrefined history of Southern Cameroons (1884-1984).* Miraclaire Publishing.

New World Encyclopedia. (2024). "Sub-Saharan Africa." https://www.newworldencyclopedia.org/entry/Sub-Saharan_Africa

Ngoh, V. J. (1996). *Constitutional developments in Southern Cameroons (1941-1961).* CEPER.

Oliver, E. P. (1997). *Developing the curriculum* (4th ed.). Longman.

Onsomu, E. N., Muthaka, D.I., Ngware, M. W., & Kosimbei, G. (2006). Improving access to secondary education in Kenya: What can be done? *Equal Opportunities International, 25*(7), 523–543. http://doi.org/10.1108/02610150610714367

Organization of Economic Cooperation and Development (OECD). (2002). *Teacher demand and supply: Improving teacher quality and addressing teacher shortages.* OECD Working Paper Series. Paris, France: Directorate of Education, OECD.

Organization of Economic Cooperation and Development (OECD). (2004). *Teachers matter: Attracting, developing and retaining effective teachers.* Paris, France: Education Policy and Training Division, OECD.

O'Toole, L. J., Jr. (2000). Research on policy and implementation: Assessment and prospects. Research theory: *Journal of Public Administration Research and Theory, 10*(2), 263–288, https://doi.org/10.1093/oxfordjournals.jpart.a024270

Parker, M. (2000). *Organizational culture and identity.* Sage.

Phenomenon-Based Learning [Finland]. (2017). *Wikipedia.* https://en.wikipedia.org/wiki/Phenomenon-based_learning.

Piscopo, S. (2019). Food security, nutrition and health. In P. Ferranti, E. M. Berry, & J. R. Anderson, *Encyclopedia of food security and sustainability* (vol. 2; pp. 406–413). Elsevier.

Pressman, J. L., & Wildavsky, A. (1984). *Implementation: How great expectations in Washington are dashed in Oakland; Or, Why it's amazing that federal programs work at all, this being a saga of the Economic Development Administration as told by two sympathetic observers who seek to build morals on a foundation* (3rd ed.). University of California Press.

Reimers, F. M., & O'Donnell, E. B. (Eds.). (2016). *Fifteen letters on education in Singapore: Reflections from a visit to Singapore in 2015 by a delegation of educators from Massachusetts.* Lulu Publishing Services.

Rein, M. (1983). *From policy to practice.* Routledge.

Reynolds, E. (1985). *Stand the storm: A history of the Atlantic slave trade.* Allison and Busby.

Rhodes, R. A.W. (2017). *Network governance and the differentiated polity: Selected essays, Volume I.* Oxford. https://www.google.com/books/edition/Network_Governance_and_the_Differentiate/BE4rDwAAQBAJ?

Rhodes, R. A. W., & Marsh, D. (1992). New directions in the study of policy networks. *European Journal of Political Research, 21*(1/2), 181–205.

Sabatier, P. A. (1986). Top-down and bottom-up approaches to implementation research: A critical analysis and suggested synthesis. *Journal of Public Policy, 6*(1), 21–48. https://www.jstor.org/stable/3998354

Sabatier, P., & Mazmanian, D. (1979). The conditions of effective implementation; A guide to accomplishing policy objectives. *Policy Analysis, 5*(4), 481–504. https://www.jstor.org/stable/42783358

Sabatier, P., & Mazmanian, D. (1980). The implementation of public policy: A framework of analysis. *Policy Studies Journal, 8*(4), 538–560. https://doi.org/10.1111/j.1541-0072.1980.tb01266.x

SEIA. 2007. *At the Crossroads: Choices for Secondary Education in Sub-Saharan Africa*. Washington D.C.: The World Bank.

Said, E. W. (1978). *Orientalism*. Pantheon Books.

Shu, S. N. (2000). *Landmarks in Cameroon education* (Rev. ed.). NOOREMAC Press.

Singapore. Ministry of Education. (2024). *Education system in Singapore*. https://www.scholaro.com/pro/Countries/Singapore/Education-System

Smith, R. [Walter Winchell "Red"]. (1949). Editorial. *Naugatuck Daily News*, April 6, 1949. pg. 4, col. 5. Naugatuck, CT. https://quoteinvestigator.com/2011/09/14/writing-bleed/#r+2735+1+1.

StateUniversity Education Encyclopedia. (2024). *Education-free encyclopedia search engine*. https://education.stateuniversity.com

Steiner, D. (2017). *Curriculum research: What we know and where we need to go*. StandardsWorks.

Stoecker, H. (1986). *German imperialism in Africa: From the beginnings until the Second World War*. English and German ed. Humanities Press.

Tah, P., Adebayo, B., & Busari, S. (2018, November 8). "Don't go back to school" kidnappers told freed Cameroonian students. *CNN*. https://www.cnn.com/2018/11/08/africa/cameroon-freed-students-reunion-africa/index.html.

Tambo, L. I. (2003). *Cameroon national education policy since the 1995 forum*. Design House.

Tamukong, J. A. (2004). Towards better management of public education in Cameroon: The case for decentralization. *Africa Development: A Quarterly Journal of CODESRIA, 29*(2), 134–157. https://www.africabib.org/htp.php?RID=277157811

Tierney, W. G. (1987). Facts and constructs: Defining reality in higher education organizations. *Review of Higher Education, 11*(1), 61–73. https://eric.ed.gov/?id=EJ367680

Tikly, L., Joubert, M., Barrett, A., Bainton, D., Cameron, L., & Doyle, H. (2018). *Supporting secondary school STEM education for sustainable development in Africa*. School of Education. Bristol working papers in education #05/2018. University of Bristol.

Trowler, P. (2003). *Education Policy* (2nd ed.). Routledge.

Tutu, D. (1999). *No future without forgiveness*. Rider.

Tutu, D. (2004). *God has a dream: A vision of hope for our time*. Rider.

United Nations (UN). (1960). General Assembly resolution 1541(xv) of December 15, 1960.

United Nations (UN). (1961). General Assembly Resolution 1608 (xv) of April 21, 1961.

United Nations (UNESCO). (n.d.). Institute for Statistics (UIS) Data center (database). http://data.uis.unesco.org/

United Nations (UNESCO). Institute for Statistics (UIS). (2011). *International standard classification for education (ISCED 2011)*. https://uis.unesco.org/sites/default/files/documents/international-standard-classification-of-education-isced-2011-en.pdf.

United Nations (UNESCO). Institute for Statistics (UIS). (2016–2024). *eAtlas of teachers*. https://uis.unesco.org/bdds

United Nations (UNESCO). Institute for Statistics (UIS). (2024). *Education in Africa*. http://uis.unesco.org/en/topic/education-africa

United Nations International Children's Emergency Fund (UNICEF). (2012). *The state of the world's children 2012*. https://www.unicef.org/media/89226/file/The%20State%20of%20the%20World%27s%20Children%202012.pdf

United States. Center for Disease Control and Prevention (CDC). (2005). *Summary of notifiable diseases—United States, 2005*. https://www.cdc.gov/mmwr/preview/mmwrhtml/mm5453a1.htm

United States. Center for Disease Control and Prevention (CDC). (2017, September 8). Morbidity and mortality weekly report (MMWR). *Weekly*, 66(35), 921–927. https://www.cdc.gov/mmwr/volumes/66/wr/mm6635a1.htm

United States. Centers for Disease Control and Prevention (CDC). (2020). *Characteristics of an effective health education curriculum*. https://www.cdc.gov/healthyschools/sher/characteristics/index.htm (accessed June 19, 2020).

United States. Department of Education. (2002). *Strategic Plan, 2002-2007*. https://www.govinfo.gov/content/pkg/ERIC-ED466025/pdf/ERIC-ED466025.pdf

United States. Department of Education. National Center for Education Statistics. (2003). *Trends in International Mathematics and Science Study* (TIMSS). https://nces.ed.gov/timss/

United States. Department of Education. (2010). *No Child Left Behind Act (*NCLB). https://www2.ed.gov/nclb/landing.jhtml.

United States. Department of Health and Human Services (HHS). Administration for Children and Families. Head Start ECLKC. (2010). *Interactive Head Start early learning outcomes framework: Ages birth to five*. https://eclkc.ohs.acf.hhs.gov/interactive-head-start-early-learning-outcomes-framework-ages-birth-five. (retrieved October 2018; last updated 2024).

REFERENCES

Vallance, E. (1983). Curriculum as a Field of Practice." In Fenwick W. English, (Ed.) *Fundamental Curriculum Decisions*, (pp. 154-164) . In 1983 ASCD Yearbook, Alexandria, VA. Association for Supervision and Curriculum Development , P.159.

Van Meter, D. S., & Van Horn, C. E. (1975). The policy implementation process: A conceptual framework. *Administration & Society*, 6(4), 445–488. https://doi.org/10.1177/009539977500600404

Verba, S., Lehman Schlozman, K., & Brady, H. E. (1995). *Voice and equality: Civic voluntarism in American politics.* Harvard University Press.

Verspoor, A, & Bregman, J. (2008). *At the crossroads: Choices for secondary education and training in Sub-Saharan Africa.* World Bank Publications.

Washington State. Department of Social and Health Services (DSHS). (n.d.). *Draft nutrition screening initiative policy statement:* Nutrition: Proven effective in managing chronic disease in older Americans. https://www.dshs.wa.gov/altsa/program-services/nutrition-education

Washinton. State. Department of Social and Health Services (DSHS). (2024). [Home]. *Transforming lives.* https://www.dshs.wa.gov/

Welthungerhilfe. (2023, October 3). Sustainable development goals' current status. *Reliefweb.* https://reliefweb.int/report/world/sustainable-development-goals-current-status

Westmaas, N. (2012, June 27). Forty years of how Europe underdeveloped Africa, *Pambazuka News: Voices For Freedom and Justice.* https://climateandcapitalism.com/2012/06/27/forty-years-of-how-europe-underdeveloped-africa/

White Paper of Education Reform. (1995). *Barbados educational system: Overview.* https://education.stateuniversity.com/pages/130/Barbados-EDUCATIONAL-SYSTEM-OVERVIEW.html

Willmott, H. (1993). Strength is ignorance; Slavery is freedom: Managing cultures in modern organizations. *Journal of Management Studies*, 30(4), 515–552. https://doi.org/10.1111/j.1467-6486.1993.tb00315.x

Wiredu, K. (2004) . *Prolegomena to an African philosophy of education.* Paper presented at the Faculty of Education, Stellenbosch University.

Wiredu, K. (2005). Philosophical considerations on Africanization of higher education in Africa. In Y. Waghid (Ed.), *African(a) philosophies of education: Reconstructions and deconstructions* (pp. 6–18). Oxford University Press.

Wright, H. K. (2000). Nailing Jell-O to the wall: Promoting aspects of state-of-the-art-curriculum theorizing. *Educational Researcher*, 29(5), 4–13. http://doi.org/10.3102/0013189X029005004

World Health Organization (WHO). (1946, July 22; 1948, April 7). *Constitution of the World Health Organization.* https://www.who.int/about/accountability/governance/constitution

Index

academic achievement 143, 144, 153, 194. *See also* health; *See also* poor performance
Academic Scientism 119. *See also* Traditionalism
academic standards 109, 133
accessibility 50, 99, 104
  assistive technology 138
access to education xx, xxxiii, 1, 5, 132, 205
accidents 199
Accountability Perspectivism 118, 122
accreditation 191
achievement 152, 230
adjudicator 161, 163, 176, 186, 187, 188
Adler, Mortimer 120
Administration infrastructure 219
admission arrangements 160, 161, 162, 163, 164, 169, 171, 173, 174, 175, 176, 178, 182, 183, 184, 186, 187, 188
admission authority 161, 162, 163, 165, 166, 169, 170, 171, 172, 175, 176, 178, 179, 180, 181, 182, 184, 185, 186, 187, 188
admission process xi, 160
adolescent pregnancies 146
Adult Basic Education and Training Centers 191
Advocacy Coalition approach 25
African philosophies of education 123. *See also* Ubuntu
African Union xxix, 30, 103, 183, 237
aggressive behavior 197. *See also* violence
agricultural products 68
agriculture 37, 66, 103, 168

Ahijdo, Ahmadou 12
All Anglophone Conference xxix, 226, 227
Ambazonia 12, 228, 234
American education policy 20
Anglophone problem 14
Anglo-Saxon educational sub-system 15
antisocial behavior 101
aptitude 170, 171, 178
Aquinas, Saint Thomas 119
arbitrators 160
Aristotle 119
assessment 4, 14, 42, 47, 50, 88, 89, 90, 95, 104, 116, 120, 128, 130, 148, 174, 190, 192, 194, 202, 207, 232, 242, 244
attention-deficit/hyperactivity disorder 136. *See also* learning disabilities
Australia xxxiv-267, 43-267
authentic classroom environments 37
autism 136. *See also* disabilities: developmental disabilities
automatic promotion 73, 74

Baccalauréat 108, 110
bad governance 69
Bagley, William C. 120
Baker, Eva 126
Bank Street Preschool program 59
Barbados 105, 106, 107, 248
barriers, cultural xxii, 148, 241
Belgium 9, 105
belief systems xix-267
Berlin Conference 9, 225
bilingualism 15, 38
biotechnology 103

251

INDEX

Biya, Paul 15
boarding schools 148, 165, 174
boards of education 151
Bobbitt, Franklin 125
Boko Haram. *See also* culture
Botswana 102
bottom-up approach 23, 230
Brameld, Theodore 122
Brandt, R. 126
Britain xxxiii, 6, 9, 14, 73, 108, 225
Brown, D. F. 127
budget 55, 96, 158, 195, 216, 220, 221
Budgeting 158, 220

Caesar, Gaius Julius 114
Cambridge General Certificate of Examinations 106
Cam, Diego 6
Cameroon vii, ix, xi, xv, xvii, xxiii, xxix, xxxiii, 1, 5, 6, 7, 9, 12, 13, 15, 18, 19, 20, 32, 33, 37, 40, 41, 47, 51, 68, 69, 71, 108, 109, 110, 112, 113, 129, 138, 145, 146, 151, 226, 230, 231, 234, 239, 240, 241, 242, 243, 244, 246
  Douala 6
Campbell, Doak 126
Canada 29
capitation grants 65, 66
career management 42, 51
Caswell, Hollis 125, 126
catchment area 166
Center for Disease Control and Prevention xxix, 144, 247
Central African Republic 9, 100, 230
certificates 39, 178, 191, 202
certification xxxiv–267, 115–267, 117–267, 134–267, 192–267
Chad 9, 29, 230
challenging behavior 188, 189
character development 91, 150, 151
child development research 58
childhood xviii, xxxiv, 18, 57, 58, 59, 60, 63, 64, 65, 77, 78, 131, 148
  children xxii–267

early childhood xviii–267, xxxiv–267, 18–267, 57–267, 58–267, 59–267, 60–267, 63–267, 64–267, 65–267, 71, 77–267, 78–267, 131–267
child marriages 112. *See also* barriers, cultural
Childs, John 121
China xx–267
Christianity 3–267
citizenship 17, 151, 200
City and Guilds 109
civic education 150
Civil administrators 41
  Divisional Officers 41
civil society 19, 21, 41, 47, 134, 158, 216. *See also* citizenship
civil unrest 75, 97. *See also* violence
Class repetition rates 153
class size xxxiv, 95, 134, 180, 230, 240
Code of Regulations 96
colonial educational policies xvii–267
colonial education systems 4
colonialism xix, xxiii, xxviii, 4, 8
  decolonization xxxiii, xxxiii–267, 4–267, 14–267
colonial rule 4
combined approach 24, 230
Common Application Form xxix, 177
communication xx, 25, 34, 60, 88, 103, 133, 136, 158, 190, 207, 220, 231
community 25, 40, 54, 57, 58, 59, 62, 71, 72, 75, 82, 83, 88, 89, 105, 107, 117, 123, 124, 136, 138, 140, 141, 144, 148, 149, 150, 151, 161, 163, 187, 193, 200, 205, 208, 210, 211, 212, 217, 219, 220, 232
Competencies required for teachers
  Foundational competence 191
  Practical competence 191
  Reflexive competence 191
  Standards/Ethical competence for educators 191
completion rates 99
conflict xxvii, 1, 5, 9, 17, 32, 205. *See also* violence
  civil unrest 75

conflict resolution 193
conflict-ridden environments 112
Congo, Republic of 9
Congo River 6
Conrad, Joseph 6
Continental Education Strategy for Africa xxix, 30, 231, 237
Continuing Professional Development xxix, 49, 139, 140, 231
 CPD xxix, 49, 50, 139, 140, 231
Convention on the Rights of Persons with Disabilities xxix, 137
corruption 1, 5, 32, 40, 64, 68, 74, 94, 146, 147, 151, 241, 244
Cote d'Ivoire 5
COVID-19 27
Criticalism 118, 122
Critical Policy Analysis 2–267
critical thinking xviii–267, 22–267, 104–267, 143–267, 231, 231–267
cultural heritage. *See* cultural identities
cultural identities xvii–267
culturalism 21
cultural norms 63
culture xix, xxi, 3, 5, 17, 22, 40, 62, 72, 73, 87, 88, 89, 95, 118, 120, 122, 123, 132, 232, 240, 243, 245
curriculum xxiii, 5, 37, 42, 45, 51, 57, 58, 59, 60, 62, 66, 70, 71, 72, 73, 83, 85, 86, 87, 88, 89, 90, 100, 101, 102, 103, 104, 106, 109, 114, 115, 116, 117, 118, 119, 123, 125, 126, 127, 128, 130, 131, 135, 136, 137, 141, 179, 192, 194, 195, 214, 230, 239, 240, 244, 247, 248
 curriculum development 71, 117

Dakar Education for All 29
daycare 57, 77
decentralization 12, 13, 48, 105, 168, 246
decentralization theory 13
decolonial theory 4–267
Delegation of Secondary Education 38
democracy 17, 100, 112, 121, 132, 240
democratic societies 99

Department of Elementary and Secondary Education xxix, 60, 243
Department of Health and Human Services xxx, 58, 247
Department of Health Services xxix, 58
determination year 161, 175, 176, 183, 184, 187
Dewey, John 59, 121, 125
Digital Learning Zones 203
Dinka, Fon Gorgi 226
diocese 173
Direct Government Funding 221
disabilities xxii, 27, 36, 37, 51, 132, 136, 137, 138, 139, 141, 171, 178, 208, 234, 241, 242
 developmental disabilities 136
discipline 39, 55, 115, 193, 194, 205, 206, 209
 disciplinary measures 96, 196
 disciplinary system 205
 school privileges 206
discrimination 132, 138, 169, 196, 207, 209, 233, 242
diseases 51, 101, 133, 146, 147, 247. *See also* HIV/AIDS
 communicable diseases 146
diversity 60, 89, 108, 148, 196
drinking water 146
drugs and alcohol 198
duration of training viii, 36

Early Child Development Education xxix, 65
 ECE xxix, 57, 59, 63, 64, 65, 66
early childhood xxxiv, xxxiv–267
Early Childhood Care and Development xxix, 134
Early Childhood Education viii, ix, xxix, 57, 63, 65, 217
Early HeadStart and HeadStart programs 58
early marriages 69, 112, 155. *See also* barriers, cultural
Ebong, Frederick Alobwede 227
Ecole Normale Superieure 33, 231

economic crisis 97
economic exploitation xxi–267
economic growth xix, 1, 5, 68, 99, 105, 112
educational attainment xxiii, 17, 232
educational personnel 210
Education Assessment Resource Centers xxix, 140
Education Management Information System 140, 157
 EMIS xxx, 46, 140, 157, 222
Education Management Information Systems xxx, xxxi, 46, 157, 222
education planning 156, 157
Egypt 4
elections
 secret ballot 209
electronic devices 203
electronic equipment 207
Elite theory 22
Endeley, Emmanuel M. 225
English Language Arts xv, 90, 133
environmental issues 143
Equatorial Guinea 230
equity 47, 51, 72, 97, 98, 102, 112
Eritrea 45, 99
Essentialism 118, 119
Estonia 105
Ethical competence for educators 191
ethical values 99, 151
Ethiopia 137
ethnic conflicts 1, 5, 9
ethnicity 132, 208
Eurocentric narratives 4
evaluation 52, 73, 92, 104, 118, 130, 157, 158, 194, 238
examination xvii, xxx, 2, 14, 34, 36, 45, 46, 48, 54, 71, 72, 104, 105, 106, 107, 109, 135, 147, 192, 202, 203, 204, 207, 214, 231, 232
expulsion 202

failure rate 38, 110
Fair Access Protocol 180, 188, 189
feeder school 164, 167

female education 113, 154. *See also* gender
female participation in education 152, 154, 241
female teachers 39, 54
field trips xxvi, 206, 208
financial resource management 157
Finland ix–267, xv–267, xvi–267, xxvi–267, xxxi–267, xxxiv–267, 29–267, 31–267, 43–267, 67–267, 75–267, 76–267, 77–267, 78–267, 82–267, 83–267, 85–267, 86–267, 88–267, 89–267, 94–267, 95–267, 105–267, 112–267, 245–267
 Helsinki 77
First School Leaving Certificate xxx, 109
First World War 85
Foncha, John Ngu 226
Fonds, Liliane 138
food choices 143, 147
food security 103, 245. *See also* nutrition
foreign qualifications 49, 191
foundations xxiii, xxxiv, 59, 63, 103, 216, 239
France xxi, xxxiii, 6, 9, 48, 73, 89, 108, 226, 244, 245
Francophonie 227
Franglais 34
Free Appropriate Public Education xxx, 139
Free Day Secondary Education xxx, 216
freedom of speech 209
freedom of the press 15
Free Primary Education xxx, 95, 216
Freire, Paolo 122
funding models xiv, 221

Gabon 9, 230
Gagne, Robert 126
Gambia, The 5, 45
gender viii, xi, xxx, 27, 32, 39, 49, 104, 130, 132, 133, 136, 148, 149, 152, 154, 155, 196, 207, 208, 242
 female participation in education 152
 gender gap 152, 154, 155

sex 132
gender differences 130
gender disparities 27, 104
gender equality 32, 132, 154
Gender Ratio xxx, 152
General Certificate of Education xxx, 14, 108, 109
geography 70, 120, 133
Germany xxxiv-267, 6-267, 9-267, 225-267, 241-267
Ghana xxxiv-267, 6-267, 89-267, 99-267, 100-267, 102-267, 237-267
  Ashanti 4
  Gold Coast 6
globalization xvii-267, 16-267
  cultural hegemony xx-267
  global economy 20
  global educational systems xvii-267
  imperialism xxiii-267
  migration xx-267
Golden Rule, the 150
Government Teachers' Training Colleges xxx, 36
GTTC xxx, 36, 38
graduation requirements xxxiv-267, 134-267
gross domestic product 44, 68, 98, 113, 154
  GDP 113
gross enrollment rates 68
Gross National Income xxx, 99. *See also* gross domestic product
guardians 83, 90, 205, 209, 210
Guatemala 89
Gulf of Guinea 6, 227

harmonization 69, 70, 108, 109
harmonization of the two sub-systems 70
Hass, Glen 127
health 42, 55, 59, 66, 83, 96, 99, 100, 104, 122, 133, 142, 143, 144, 145, 146, 147, 148, 149, 154, 158, 171, 174, 182, 199, 207, 238, 242, 245, 247
  health education awareness 145

medical conditions 178
mortality 112
yoga therapy 145
herbal medicines 145. *See also* health
higher education xxxiv, 20, 24, 26, 59, 97, 110, 138, 154, 232, 233, 234, 235, 237, 239, 240, 246, 248
Higher Teachers' Training College xxx, 33, 231
highly indebted poor country 68
HighScope Preschool program 58
Himalayan Institute xxx, 145, 241
Hirsch, E.D. 120
historiography 4
HIV/AIDS xxx, 1, 32, 51, 146, 158
homework 106, 198
Hong Kong 43
hooks, bell 122
Hopkins, Thomas 126
households 101, 216, 217
human capital 1, 20, 43, 99, 103, 105, 133
human capital theory 1
Humanness 124. *See also* Ubuntu
Human Resource Management xxx, 48, 232
human rights 15, 112, 124, 132, 133, 137, 138, 162
hybridity 16
hygiene 64, 133, 147, 149, 158

ICT xxx, 50, 52, 66, 70, 88, 96, 103, 104, 133, 140, 158, 159, 192. *See also* Science, Technology, Engineering, and Mathematics
  information and communication technology 103
identification card 203
inappropriate/sexual relationship 200
inclusive education 138, 139, 140, 148
India xx-267
Indiana Department of Education 126
indigenous knowledge 4, 5, 104
Indigenous Knowledge Systems xxx, 5
indigenous peoples xix-267, 3-267,

INDEX

27–267
individualism 121
individually planned and systematically monitored teaching procedures, 136
information xx, xxv, 13, 51, 67, 88, 90, 103, 121, 122, 133, 143, 145, 149, 158, 170, 174, 176, 177, 178, 179, 180, 182, 184, 185, 186, 187, 201, 204, 209, 211, 223, 231
infrastructure 42, 44, 48, 50, 55, 65, 73, 96, 103, 104, 134, 192, 217, 218, 219, 220, 221
Institutes de Pedagogiques Applique a Vocation Rurale xxx, 71
  IPAR xxx, 71, 72, 241, 242
instruction 3, 37, 42, 52, 55, 57, 73, 77, 85, 88, 89, 126, 127, 128, 131, 136, 141, 145, 192, 194, 201, 219, 235
internal efficiency 134, 223
internally displaced 75
International Institute for Capacity Building in Africa xxx, 32, 239
International Standard Classification of Education 67, 233
International Student Assessment xxxi, 43, 75, 105
Internet access 218, 219
Investing in infrastructure 220
Ireland 105
ISCED 64

Japan xx, xx–267, 43, 105, 106, 155, 241
job market 30
Johns Hopkins Institute for Education Policy 115
  Center for Research and Reform in Education 115
justice xxi, xxvii, xxviii, 72, 112, 122, 123, 132, 150

Kazakhstan 89
Kenya 89, 101, 102, 137, 244
Kilpatrick, William H. 121

kindergarten xxxiv, 18, 59, 64, 65, 77, 131, 132, 133, 168, 194, 221, 243
Kirstin Koulo Elementary School xv, 75, 76
knowledge-based economy 44

labor force 153
labor market 98, 101, 110
language policy 169
languages
  language 2, 15, 22, 34, 37, 38, 40, 55, 63, 66, 85, 86, 89, 118, 132, 169, 170, 178, 203, 213
  linguistic diversity 89
  mother tongue 83
La Republique du Cameroun xx, xxi, xxiii, xxviii, 14, 129, 221, 226, 227, 228, 229
Latin America 5
leadership 21, 32, 40, 45, 47, 105, 107, 118, 240, 242, 243
  administration 4, 39, 42, 48, 69, 116, 129, 133, 134, 158, 194, 200, 219
  school administrators 139
League of Nations 225, 234
learner rights 193
learners' behavior 194
learning achievements 223
learning disabilities 136
  cerebral palsy 136
  communication disorders 136
  dyslexia 136
  emotional and behavioral disorders 136
  intellectual disability 136
  muscular dystrophy 136
  physical disabilities 136
learning environment 47, 60, 61, 66, 87, 88, 117, 121, 130, 131, 205, 206, 230
Learning infrastructure 218
learning theories 52, 191
Lee Kuan Yew 43
Length of a School Day 212
Lesotho 45, 54

Liberalism 118, 121
Liberia 45
lifelong learning 107, 112, 231
lifestyle counseling 145
linguistic diversity 89. *See also* languages: mother tongue
literacy 5, 44, 50, 66, 67, 68, 71, 104, 106, 107, 122, 134, 149, 155, 168
literacy rates 5
literature xxv, 24, 97, 119, 120, 136, 197, 243
loss or damage 203
lost property 203
low admission standards 36
lower secondary education 44, 67
lunch break 212, 215

macroeconomic growth. *See also* economic growth
Madagascar 29
Maintenance 221
Malawi 45, 55
Mali 4
Mann, Horace 150
marginalization 14, 156
markets 99, 109
McBrien, J. L. 126
mental health 59, 122. *See also* health
mentorship 47
methodology 130, 191
Millennium Development Goals xxxi, 27, 67, 94, 233
ministerial system 48
misbehavior 193, 205
mobile and online education 50
modernization 158
monitoring and evaluation xiv, xxxi, 192, 222
monitoring and evaluation of the system 157
Montessori, Maria 58
Montessori program 58
mortality 112, 154, 247
Mozambique 29
Multiple Workstream 25

museums 88, 117

narcotic drugs 198
National Association for the Education of Young Children xxxi, 61, 244
National Education Association xxxi, 151, 244
National Examination Council 130
National Institute of Education xxxi, 44, 45
National Learning and Assessment Monitoring Mechanism 42
National Offer Day 185
national origin 132, 208
National Scientific Council on the Developing Child 63, 244
nation builders 43
nation-building 151
natural sciences 103, 104, 109, 120
neo-colonialism xxviii–267
nepotism 40, 48, 51, 146
Netherlands 105
newspapers 139
New Zealand 20, 31, 105
Niger 29
Nigeria 11, 15, 20, 75, 100, 225, 226, 228, 229, 230
Norms and Standards for Educators xiii, 190
North West Region 34, 38, 110
nursery schools 64, 211, 212
nutrition 104, 142, 143, 144, 146, 147, 149, 238, 242, 245, 248
  healthy eating choices 147
Nutrition education 142, 143
  malnourished peers 144

O

occultism 146
O'Day, Jennifer 122
oral interviews 36
organizational cultures 22. *See also* culture
Organization of Economic Cooperation and Development xxxi, 43, 101,

244, 245
OECD xxxi, 43, 75, 101, 105, 106, 244, 245
oversubscription criteria xi, xii, 162, 163, 164, 166, 169, 171, 172, 173, 174, 177, 178, 179, 180, 182, 183

Parent Co-Op Preschool program 59
parenthood 112
Parents xi, 41, 59, 70, 71, 84, 90, 94, 150, 158, 161, 162, 182, 183, 185, 209, 210, 218
Parent Teacher Associations 40, 41
Participatory Budgeting 158
partnerships 47, 62, 66, 99, 105, 216
pedagogical practices 72, 190
Perennialism 118, 119, 123
performance pay 49
personality 107
personal property 208
petroleum 68
Phenomenological approach vii–267, 23, 23–267
phenomenon-based approach 87
phenomenon-based learning 85, 86, 87, 89
philosophy of education 123, 124, 233, 237, 248
physical education 117, 170, 218
  sport 170
plagiarism
  academic dishonesty 202
Plato 119
plebiscite 11–267
policy development 4, 17, 23, 45, 75, 95, 114
policy guidelines viii, ix, 48, 65, 95
policy planning 23, 233
  policy design xxiii, 13, 18, 19, 20, 21, 22, 23, 24, 25, 26, 31, 43, 98, 107, 112, 151
policy standards 25
politicization of education 12
polytechnic 46, 106
poor performance 54

Popham, James 126
population growth 30, 113
portfolios 87, 202
postcolonial theories 4
poverty 1, 5, 27, 68, 101, 143, 146, 233, 234
Poverty Reduction Strategic Plan xxxi, 68
PRSP xxxi, 68
power xviii, xxi, 2, 14, 22, 24, 50, 113, 121, 122, 197, 218, 226, 244
practicum 36, 52, 192
pregnancy 69, 147, 155, 196
prekindergarten 168
pre-primary 64, 77
Presbyterian Secondary School Nkwen 74
primary education 28, 44, 57, 59, 63, 64, 65, 66, 67, 68, 70, 71, 73, 74, 75, 94, 95, 97, 99, 100, 137, 155, 233, 237, 241
primary school enrollment 67
problem-based learning 87
problem-solving 59, 62, 86, 104
professional development 32, 47, 55, 61, 66, 73, 96, 145
professional ethics 130
Programme for International Student Assessment xxxi, 43, 75, 105
Progressivism 118, 121
progress reports 71, 202
public education 136, 202, 246
public policy xxiii, xxvi, 17, 23, 232, 245
Public-Private Partnership 221
public theory 23
pupil premium 165, 173
Pupil-Teacher Ratio xxxi, 134

Qatar 105
qualifications 48, 49, 190, 191
quality control 50, 190
quality education 74, 94, 109, 151

radio 139

Ragan, W. B. 126
Rationalism 118, 120
Recognition of Academic Qualifications 191
Reconstructionism 118, 121
referendum 12. *See also* plebiscite
refugee settlements 75
Reggio Emilia Preschool program 58
Relative Education Qualification Values (REQV) 49
religion 2, 123, 136, 142, 165, 172, 173, 175, 176, 196, 207, 208
  Christianity 3–267
  faith 110, 121, 134, 172, 173, 179
  Islam 3–267
religious authority 164
religious denomination 165, 172, 173, 175, 176
religious organizations 216
report cards 202, 219
Required Published Admission Number xi, xxxi, 163
resource mobilization 216
Responsible User Policy 199
reunification xx–267, xxi–267, xxviii–267, 12–267, 15–267, 33–267, 69–267, 244–267
right to appeal 162, 183, 185
Rousseau 121
Rugg, Harold O. 125
rural communities 98, 220
rural schools 46

Saint Thomas Aquinas 119
Saker, Alfred 225
Sao Tome & Principe 99
SCEB x, xxi, xxvi, xxxi, 129, 130, 131, 132, 133, 134, 192, 211
scholarships 98, 106
school administrators 139
School Admissions Regulations 186
school boycotts 74
School closure xii, 185
school districts 41, 89
school dropout rate 70, 106

school libraries 202
school management committees 96
school psychology 116
Schools Adjudicator 161, 163, 176, 186, 187, 188
Science, Technology, Engineering, and Mathematics xxxii, 102
scorecard system 223
Scotland 115
Security and safety infrastructure 220
semester 36, 192
Senegal 5
Senior Discipline Masters 40
service delivery 54, 100
service learning 150
service premium 165, 173
sex 132, 146, 166, 171
sex education 146
sexual orientation 196, 208
Silva, E. 127
Singapore viii, xxxi, xxxiv, 29, 43, 44, 45, 46, 47, 48, 98, 102, 105, 106, 242, 245, 246
Sizer, Theodore 121
skilled labor 97
slave trade 6, 242, 245
Smith, Marshall 122
Smoke-Free Policy 198
Snedden, David 122
social advancement. *See also* social mobility
social-emotional learning 150
social identities 136
Social infrastructure 220
social mobility 99
Social Scientificism 118, 120
socioeconomic status 73, 132, 136, 196
Somalia 5
South Africa xxxiv–267, 30–267, 55–267, 102–267, 137–267, 241–267, 243–267
Southern Cameroons iii, vii, viii, ix, x, xi, xii, xiv, xv, xvi, xvii, xix, xx, xxi, xxii, xxiii, xxv, xxvi, xxvii, xxviii, xxxi, xxxiii, xxxiv, 11, 12, 14, 15, 16, 19, 25, 26, 33, 34, 36, 37, 38,

40, 41, 42, 43, 45, 48, 49, 50, 51, 53, 64, 65, 68, 69, 70, 73, 74, 94, 95, 107, 108, 109, 110, 112, 113, 129, 130, 131, 132, 138, 139, 143, 144, 145, 149, 151, 155, 156, 157, 160, 167, 168, 174, 181, 183, 192, 193, 208, 211, 225, 226, 227, 228, 229, 231, 234, 238, 244
Southern Cameroons Education Board xxi, xxvi, xxxi, 129, 130, 192, 211
  SCEB 131
Southern Cameroons Education Management Information System 157
Southern Cameroons Institute of Special Education 139
Southern Cameroons People's Organization 227
South Korea 43
South West Region 38
Special Education x, xxxi, xxxii, 52, 56, 133, 136, 139, 168, 234
  Aided Education 136
  Exceptional Education 136
  inclusive education 139
  special schools 137
  SPED xxxii, 136, 137, 138, 139, 140, 141
Special Needs Education xxxii, 136, 140
  Special Education 136
staffing norms 49, 95
staff supervision 194
stages of actions 22
  back-stage 22
  front-of-stage 22
  under-the-stage 22
stakeholders xxiii, 17, 18, 19, 21, 24, 25, 26, 28, 31, 33, 43, 66, 73, 107, 128, 156, 216, 217, 230
STEAM xxxii, 104, 133, 234
STEM ix, xxxii, 102, 103, 104, 105, 107, 234, 246. *See also* Science, Technology, Engineering, and Mathematics
stigma 138
Student Leadership Organization 220
subaltern 4

superstitious beliefs 147
Sustainable Development Goals xxxi, 27, 102, 234
Switzerland 105

Taba, Hilda 122
Taiwan 43
Tanner, Daniel 127
Tanner, Laurel 127
Tanzania 5, 100
teacher-child relationships 61
teacher deployment viii, 39
  teacher attrition 28, 46
teacher education 20, 32, 33, 43, 47, 48, 49, 66, 191
  teacher development 32
teacher performance 46, 54
teacher selection viii, 27
Teacher Service Commission (TSC) 49, 235
teacher shortages xxii, 15, 27, 28, 29, 31, 40, 41, 74, 100, 244
teacher-student interactions 116
Teacher Training Colleges viii, xxx, xxxii, 33, 36, 39, 72, 130, 231
Teacher Unions 55
teacher welfare 42
Teaching infrastructure 219
teaching methods 52, 58, 72, 134, 145, 192
teaching times xiv, 214
technical education 31, 32, 34, 46, 49, 102, 103, 104, 106, 107, 108, 109, 110, 112, 168, 191, 217, 237
  polytechnic 106
Technical, Vocational Education and Training xxxii, 99
technology 34, 37, 44, 50, 88, 103, 117, 133, 138, 170, 197
Telephone Game 85
tertiary education 77, 168, 235
test scores 106, 144
textbooks 37, 72, 82, 83, 104, 106, 114, 130, 135, 148, 202
Thailand 98

therapy 145
Togo 99
top-down approach vii, 22
Traditionalism 119
Transformativism 118, 122
transportation 83, 106
tribalism 40, 146
tuition 82, 99, 109
Tutu, Desmond 125
Tyler, Ralph 120, 126

Ubuntu 123, 124, 125. *See also* African philosophies of education
  Desmond Tutu 125
Uganda 45, 54, 99
UNESCO xxx, xxxii, xxxiii, 1, 28, 30, 32, 57, 67, 69, 71, 97, 118, 233, 239, 242, 243, 247
United Kingdom 225, 228
United Nations xxv–267
United Nations Development Programme xxxii, 71
United States iv, viii, xxvii, xxix, xxx, xxxiv, 28, 29, 57, 58, 59, 65, 73, 75, 77, 102, 112, 115, 118, 243, 247
Universal Primary Education xxxii, 28, 44, 67, 97, 134
Universal Secondary Education xxxii, 29
Unrepresented Nations and Peoples Organization xxxii, 228

vacancy levels 49
Vallance, Elizabeth 115
verbal warning 206
victimization 196
Vietnam 98
violence xix, 32, 155, 205
  bullying 196, 197
  sexual abuse 200
  victimization 196
visual arts 62, 88, 170
vocational education 102, 106, 110, 193, 217, 237
  apprenticeship 168
  polytechnics 168

waiting list 172, 180
Waldorf Preschool program 58
Water, Sanitation, and proper Hygiene 218
West Indies 8
Wiggins, Grant 120
work-life balance 49, 55
World Bank, The xxxi, 98, 101, 155, 238, 239, 241, 243, 244, 246, 248
World Development Report 101
World Health Organization xxxii, 142, 144, 238, 249
World History xvi, 92, 93, 94
world population 30
World War I 225

Zambia 20, 45, 53, 54, 55, 242
Zimbabwe 99

www.ingramcontent.com/pod-product-compliance
Lightning Source LLC
Chambersburg PA
CBHW061434300426
44114CB00014B/1685